LOFT LIVING

JOHNS HOPKINS STUDIES IN URBAN AFFAIRS

CENTER FOR METROPOLITAN PLANNING AND RESEARCH
THE JOHNS HOPKINS UNIVERSITY

David Harvey
Social Justice and the City

Ann L. Strong
Private Property and the Public Interest: The Brandywine Experience

Alan D. Anderson
The Origin and Resolution of an Urban Crisis: Baltimore, 1890–1930

James M. Rubenstein
The French New Towns

Malcolm Getz
The Economics of the Urban Fire Department

Ann L. Strong
Land Banking: European Reality, American Prospect

Jon C. Teaford
City and Suburb: The Political Fragmentation of Metropolitan America, 1850–1970

Norman J. Glickman, ed.
The Urban Impacts of Federal Policies

Sharon Zukin
Loft Living: Culture and Capital in Urban Change

LOFT LIVING

Culture and Capital in Urban Change

Sharon Zukin

THE JOHNS HOPKINS UNIVERSITY PRESS

Baltimore and London

The Johns Hopkins University Press, Baltimore, Maryland 21218
The Johns Hopkins Press Ltd., London

Library of Congress Cataloging in Publication Data

Zukin, Sharon.
Loft Living.

(Johns Hopkins studies in urban affairs)
Includes bibliographical references and index.
1. Lofts — Social aspects — New York (N.Y.)
2. Real estate development — New York (N.Y.)
3. Buildings — New York (N.Y.) — Remodeling for other use.
I. Title   II. Series.
HD7304.N5Z84   363.5   81-20830
ISBN 0-8018-2694-2   AACR2

The photographs in this book were taken by Richard Rosen.

FOR MY PARENTS
who have never understood why
I wanted to live in New York

CONTENTS

PREFACE: READER, BEWARE!

I first became interested in living lofts as a loft dweller. In 1975 I moved into the "raw space" of a loft in Greenwich Village that originally had served as a sweatshop in the garment industry around the turn of the century. More recently, the loft had been an artist's studio, to which the artist commuted every day from her apartment in another part of Manhattan. At that time, most of the other floors in the building were still occupied by small businessmen who were involved in "light manufacturing": a die-cutter, a silkscreen printer, a manufacturer of women's hats, two elderly men who made salesmen's sample cases, two young woodworkers. However, another floor was also used as an artist's studio, and two floors had already been converted to "mixed use" — by a photographer and a carpenter, respectively — with the use weighted toward residence rather than work.

The block as a whole, like these floors and the building, was in mixed use. Antiques dealers in the wholesale trade, who really dealt in reproductions and bric-à-brac, occupied the stores. At one corner stood a large, physically dilapidated and socially degenerate brick building, formerly a hotel, that had deteriorated into single-room occupancy by a small number of the elderly and the poor. It faced the modest quarters of a religious sect, where an off-off-Broadway theater used to present risqué plays. At the other end of the block, opposite a parking garage, there were two upper-middle-income apartment houses. The rest of the block was made up of loft buildings. Some of them remained in manufacturing use, but two had already been converted to living lofts and sold, floor by floor, as "cooperatives." During the day, men loaded and unloaded trucks in the otherwise quiet street. The antiques dealers chatted with their customers and the building superintendents in front of their stores. At lunchtime, the "supers" and workers from the businesses in the lofts above lounged on the sidewalk. At night, the street was so tranquil that I could hear the low moan of a passing subway train, half a block away.

Within two years, the character of the street had irrevocably "tipped" toward residential use. Building owners raised rents and refused to renew the leases of manufacturing tenants. The single-room-occupancy hotel was "developed" into expensive loft-apartments. On weekends the new residents sunned on their balconies. A few more loft buildings were converted from manufacturing to residential use, and from rentals to cooperatives. In 1979 my building "went co-op." I bought the loft in which I was living and bade good-bye to the manufacturers, an artist, and several residents who could not afford the market prices at which our lofts were sold. The new owners included two lawyers and an accountant. A store-owner bought one loft to live in and one to rent out. Two men bought floors purely as investments and sold them within a year. Market values on our street were high. Real estate agents referred to it as the Gold Coast of Lofts.

This experience made me approach the whole phenomenon of loft living with a certain amount of skepticism. I was particularly irritated by three unsubstantiated claims that continually appeared in the loft-living boosterism that was fostered by city officials, real estate developers, and the *New York Times:* first, that the diffusion of loft living encouraged mixed use; second, that residential conversion of manufacturing space benefited the city; and third, that the city's long-term social and economic benefits justified substantial subsidies to developers who undertook the largest conversion projects. In February 1977 I published an article on the front page of the real estate section of the Sunday *New York Times* — "In Defense of Benign Neglect and Diversity" — in which I tried to counter these claims. Then I set out to do the research that would support my arguments.

In the course of that research, I used many sources, only some of whom can be thanked by name and even fewer of whom will agree with either my framework or my analysis. Most people who heard that I was writing a book on loft living assumed that I was writing a how-to book with plenty of photographs. Those who correctly guessed that my interest was more "sociological" would have been nonplussed, nonetheless, had they known that I viewed the rise of loft living from a highly critical perspective. Basically, I am concerned with how an untested and unlikely sort of housing space — a loft — becomes a hot commodity, what social forces benefit from the rise of the loft market, and how that form of real estate development fits the general patterns of contemporary capitalism.

But this is less the study of a rather unusual real estate market in New York than an essay on a broad process of social change. Many older cities are trying to overcome their past and patch up their present by building a new identity as white-collar capitals. They seek to replace a traditional base in declining industries with wealth derived from the service sector. It is inevitable that they replace their traditional population too. The reconquest of the downtown by high-rent, high-class uses, the re-creation of an urban middle class, and the use of art and culture to further these ends — these local characteristics of deindustrialization are repeated in major cities throughout the capitalist world. So this is also a book about London and Paris, Birmingham and Lille, Philadelphia, Boston, Baltimore, San Francisco. . . .

Nonetheless, to all the cooperative real estate developers and small manufacturers in New York City who allowed me to interview them, I extend my thanks. I also want to thank the officers, district manager, staff, and members of Community Board 2 in Manhattan, where I participated in meetings from 1977 to 1979, especially Joan Swan, Ed Gold, Rachele Wall, and Rita Lee. I am grateful for information shared by August Heckscher, former national adviser on the arts; Vice-Chancellor Julius C. C. Edelstein, City University of New York; Sandy Hornick, of the New York City Planning Commission; Meg Reed, from State Senator Manfred Ohrenstein's office; Edward Potter, former research director at the Real Estate Board of New York; attorneys Paul Byard, Michael Balkin, and S. Pitkin Marshall; Charles Leslie, art gallery owner and former unofficial "Mayor of SoHo"; author Jim Stratton; Gerhardt Liebmann, former president of the SoHo Artists' Tenants' Association; Chuck Delaney, president of the Lower Manhattan Loft Tenants' Association; architect Shael Shapiro; Barbara Fisher, manager of the Greenwich Street artists' housing co-op; Lancelot Fletcher, of the Mayor's Office of Economic Development; musicians Frank Ferroucci, Rick Merrill, and Mark Morganelli; and fellow students of city ways Mel Reichler, Bill Domhoff, Carol Corden, Chester Rapkin, Bob Fitch, and Matt Edel. I am entirely responsible for the interpretation I offer of their experiences.

A large part of the research was funded by a small but indispensable faculty award from the City University of New York. This grant enabled me to hire a series of research assistants, among whom I am particularly grateful to Kevin Anderson, Philip Kasinitz, Felicia Leak, and Andrew Roth. They pursued their tasks with diligence and even, in Phil's case, ardor.

Finally, I want to share the credit for the inception of this project with Richard Rosen. His work needs made it possible for me to live in a mixed-use loft, and on his impetus I started to study a local topic. This turned out to be a crucial push in a new direction.

1

LIVING LOFTS
AS TERRAIN
AND MARKET

At the beginning of the 1970s it became fashionable, in some of the older industrial cities of the United States and Western Europe, to live in former manufacturing spaces that were converted to residential use. This new housing style emerged along the canals of Amsterdam, near the London docks, and in the old sweatshop districts of New York. Soon it spread to cities like Boston, Philadelphia, Galveston, and Portland, whose nineteenth-century factories and warehouses had fallen on hard times. It grew into a trend that influenced the redevelopment plans of smaller cities in the hinterlands whose regional manufacturing base had been eroded by suburban sprawl. Publicity-conscious towns aspired to the status of Manhattan's converted manufacturing districts. "Norwalk," for example, according to a 1979 headline in the *New York Times,* "Seeks to Be the SoHo of Connecticut." The trend to residential conversion also influenced the housing market in cities that didn't even have this sort of building stock. By 1980 building owners in Paris were advertising *les lofts*. As far away as Belgrade, an artists' association asked in 1979 for unused lofts and garrets to be rented to artists who needed space to work. But lofts really are an American phenomenon. According to the *Oxford English Dictionary, loft* refers to the relatively large, generally open space on each floor in multi-story industrial buildings and warehouses in the United States. Closer to the point, it is in America that loft living has most influenced the urban housing market, for it is American cities that have been most sensitive to the flight and return of middle-class residents and investment capital.

1

THE LOFT TERRAIN

Originally, the large amount of floor space and window area in lofts appealed to artists, who created live-in studios for both work and residence. They found that the relatively low rents in industrial areas compensated for some inconvenience (especially distance from grocery stores and other amenities) and a certain degree of noise and dirt. But around 1970, as the bare, polished wood floors, exposed red brick walls, and cast-iron façades of these "artists' quarters" gained increasing public notice, the economic and aesthetic virtues of "loft living" were transformed into bourgeois chic. In large numbers, middle-class and upper-middle-class residents began moving into lofts, too. While some of these new tenants, like the artists, fixed up their lofts themselves, others paid architects and designers to carry out extensive renovations. Unlike the artists, these residents used their lofts only for living.

While loft buildings are constructed on a comparatively small scale, their proportions are generous. Usually they have five to ten stories, with two thousand to ten thousand square feet of space on each floor. Older loft buildings have only a freight elevator, but newer ones also have passenger elevators. Ceilings are high — twelve to fifteen feet — and are supported by either vaulted arches (in smaller buildings) or columns. Architectural detail is often classical, reflecting late nineteenth-century taste for the Italian Renaissance. Columns in loft buildings are frequently fluted, and the building façades are generally cast-iron, which marks an important innovation of the time in the industrialization of construction technique. In contrast to the construction materials used in modern buildings, those used in loft buildings are more solid (brick and iron) and more valuable (often oak flooring and even copper window sills). Because loft spaces are indeed "lofty," they offer the potential for drama in everyday life. Lofts are good for exhibiting large works of art, using professional stoves and refrigerators, luxuriating in mammoth whirlpool baths, and experimenting with an avant-garde *mise en scène* or *décor*. In short, lofts present a perfect setting for gracious late-twentieth-century living.

As city governments and the press throughout the United States praised loft living as part of a general urban resurgence of the 1970s, the residential conversion of lofts began to interest sponsors of a different type. These were investors rather than owner-occupiers, or real estate developers and builders instead of tenants. Because of their priorities, the nature of the conversion process, as well as the character of the spaces that were converted, changed. Residential conversion attracted more professional types of developers. The buildings that they converted were larger than the early residential loft buildings, yet the spaces that they created were smaller, less living lofts than "loft-apartments." In New York City, the average size of an apartment in a building that has been converted from commercial use is 610 square feet, but the average size of a living loft is 2,100 square feet.[1]

Partly through the action of these real estate developers, and partly through events to which the developers responded, a real estate market in living lofts emerged and grew.

With the birth of the market in loft living, the use of the basic real estate commodity — loft space — was utterly transformed. Lofts changed from sites where production took place to items of cultural consumption. This process annihilates light manufacturing activity. Lofts that are converted to residential use can no longer be used as machine shops, printing plants, dress factories, or die-cutting operations. The residential conversion of manufacturing lofts confirms and symbolizes the death of an urban manufacturing center. In spatial terms, lofts also represent a terrain of conflict between the various social groups that compete for their use. Over time, these groups include small manufacturers, artists, middle-class tenants and potential tenants, real estate developers, the rich upper class or patrician elite of the cities, the banks that this elite usually controls, and politicians in City Hall.

It is particularly significant in this struggle that developers and city officials praise the residential loft market because it does not require direct public subsidy. This argument has two parts. First, if the conversion of manufacturing lofts to residential use does not cost cities a loss of tax revenue, or the federal government an outlay of construction funds, then loft living represents an antidote to the state's fiscal crisis. Second, if loft living generates a middle-class return to the urban center, then the city reaps a benefit — a social and financial payoff — from loft living's demographic and cultural effects. But such calculations fit the logic of capitalist cities as they have been planned and run since the early 1900s. In reality, the spread of loft living exacts a price in two senses. On the one hand, the state's benign acceptance of residential conversion indicates the final step in a long-term strategy of urban deindustrialization. On the other hand, the expansion of loft living from a peripheral social and cultural phenomenon (or "alternative urban lifestyle") to an acceptable, even a desirable, form of habitation relies not only on a change in values but also on state intervention in the housing market. This intervention creates a complicated financial and legal situation on which real estate profits are based. The development of the residential market in loft space also reflects the priorities of lending institutions like banks. To praise the spread of loft living as a result of spontaneous market forces is to accept the real estate developers' view of the world and to ignore the state's and the banks' complicity in the construction of this world.

During the early 1970s, New York City became both the harbinger and the model of loft living. One reason for New York's lead is the large number of mid- to late-nineteenth-century manufacturing buildings in downtown and midtown Manhattan and in several waterfront areas of Brooklyn. However, the mere presence of this physical infrastructure is not sufficient to explain how the residential use of these lofts developed or why it spread at that particular time. Putting it broadly, the growth of a market in living lofts, like the growth of any modern product market, requires three conditions. These are the *availability* of the product or the means of producing it, the *acceptability* of the product to the intended consumers, and the *accessibility* of a model that promotes the product's use. These are, of course, the requirements of a market in a period of mass production and mass consumption. The important point is that these factors, like the commodities created by their interaction, are socially produced. They reflect the social relations and cultural values of a particular time and place.

In the case of New York's living loft market, the existence of loft space — though not necessarily vacant — provides the minimal degree of availability. The chronic economic undervaluation of loft buildings, indicated by their low sale prices, the low rents for manufacturing lofts in them, and the difficulties that are involved in refinancing their mortgages through the banks, induces a "financial obsolescence" that enhances the apparent physical obsolescence of loft factories. Also, the manipulation of both long-term and short-term factors related to New York's deindustrialization creates a physical space — the artists' loft district of SoHo — which acts as a wedge to vacate lofts that have been continuously occupied by manufacturing tenants. In other words, the availability of lofts for residential development is shaped partly by New York's industrial ecology and partly by economic and political powers.

Nevertheless, the acceptability of lofts as an alternative to more traditional products of the urban housing market depends on the emergence of a new set of social and cultural values. Of particular importance is the changing status of art and artists during the 1960s. But the rising tide of ecological awareness, fostering an appreciation of small-scale construction and re-use, also carries the loft market forward. An expanding constituency for historic preservation and its scholarly handmaiden, industrial archeology, does its share. Finally, New York's hegemonic position (as successor to Paris) in the twentieth-century world of artistic production guarantees the accessibility of the New York model of loft living to a wide public. In addition to art dealers, museum curators, and collectors who visit New York artists in their lofts, an increasing amount of publicity has called attention to these artists' style of life and work.* Ironically, the real estate development that follows this publicity prices many artists out of the loft market. Artists who began to concentrate in SoHo lofts toward the end of the sixties are moving out by the beginning of the eighties. Rent increases drive them to Brooklyn, Jersey City, Hoboken, and even farther shores.

*For example, Gilbert Millstein, "Portrait of the Loft Generation," *New York Times Magazine,* Jan. 7, 1962; "Bohemia's Last Frontier: Artists and Galleries in SoHo," *Time,* May 25, 1970; S. Koch, "Where the Avant-gardest Work the Hardest," *Esquire,* April 1975.

In a way, loft living appears to be related to the modern "gentrification" process. Gentrification typically occurs when a higher class of people moves into a neighborhood, makes improvements to property that cause market prices and tax assessments to rise, and so drives out the previous, lower-class residents. However, in the case of lofts, the social class distinctions between old (artist) residents and new (non-artist) residents are somewhat blurred, and the real victims of gentrification through loft living are not residents at all. Before some of the artists were chased out of their lofts by rising rents, they had displaced small manufacturers, distributors, jobbers, and wholesale and retail sales operations. For the most part, these were small businesses in declining economic sectors. They were part of the competitive area of the economy that had been out-produced and out-maneuvered, historically, by the giant firms of monopoly capital. The number of employees in any of these businesses was small — perhaps fewer than ten, often fewer than fifty. Since the end of the nineteenth century, few working-class neighborhoods remained in the heart of Manhattan, so this work force no longer lived near their jobs. Instead, they commuted into Manhattan from the Outer Boroughs of Brooklyn and the Bronx, most frequently, by 1960, from ethnic and racial ghettos there. During the 1960s and 1970s, some of these workers were recruited from the large numbers of illegal immigrants — Haitians, Dominicans, Chinese — who worked "off the books" and outside labor union protection. Their employers also frequently commuted to their lofts from Brooklyn and the Bronx, and sometimes, in the more successful businesses, from the suburbs of Long Island or Westchester County.

These business owners chose to remain in Manhattan for several reasons. First, the viability of their firms depended on geographical clustering in commercial neighborhoods: the Garment Center in midtown for coats, suits, and dresses; the needle and thread trade between Twentieth Street and Thirtieth Street; the fur district around Twenty-sixth, Twenty-seventh, and Twenty-eighth streets; the printing industry on the Lower West Side; the peripheral garment and textile trade — in underwear, socks, hats, and remnants — in the middle of Lower Manhattan, on either side of Broadway; the electronics and surplus electrical parts businesses on Canal Street; the egg, butter, and cheese wholesalers between the printing neighborhood and the financial district of Wall Street. By depending on the supplies and the services of their neighbors, firms were able to save money on costs. Clustering also maximizes convenience for commercial customers. A second reason that these firms remained in Manhattan had to do with other production expenses. Until the late 1960s loft rents were cheap and stable. The urban labor supply, particularly for the less skilled jobs, was plentiful and cheap. As long as these businesses could withstand the buffets of the national economy and the decentralization of industrial production, they stayed in Manhattan.

The main victims of gentrification through loft living are these business owners, who are essentially lower middle class, and their work force. In time, many of the artists, crafts workers, performers, photographers, and carpenters who had moved into lofts in the "first generation," before 1970, also became victims of gentrification. No one knows the actual numbers of loft residents over time. At the beginning of the 1960s, estimates of the number of artists living and working in lofts ranged between three thousand and five thousand. By the end of the seventies, it is possible that over fifty thousand artists and non-artists were living in lofts that had been converted to residential use. A much larger, though still uncertain, number of people lived in fairly standard apartment houses that had been carved out of erstwhile loft buildings.

In terms of social class, there is practically no difference between residents of lofts that were converted by various means into either standardized or "alternative" housing spaces or between these residents and those who live in Manhattan's typical new apartment houses. By comparison with the rest of the New York City population, this group as a whole is highly educated, professionally trained, and well-to-do. In terms of socioeconomic status, Manhattan loft residents are in the top 20–25 percent of the New York City population.[2]

OVERVIEW OF THE LOFT MARKET

Living lofts seem to represent a typical, though rather specialized, real estate market. The loft market went through two stages, both of which, according to conventional wisdom, bear witness to the interplay of supply and demand. First, the decline of small businesses that had occupied lofts continuously through most of this century, in addition to the expansion to more modern industrial plants of those firms that had survived into the 1960s, caused vacancies in loft buildings. This created the factor of supply. As these vacancies increased, new tenants — primarily artists seeking large living and working spaces at a cheap rent — appeared to claim the empty spaces for their own use. This suggests that supply created demand. As usual, the new residential rents were higher than existing manufacturing rents, and the growing demand for lofts by residential tenants encouraged further rent increases. In the absence of new manufacturing tenants, landlords began to advertise "lofts for artists." A minor market was born. The second stage of the loft market developed when the demand for living lofts expanded to middle-class people who had no connection with the arts. Their demand encouraged landlords to increase supply as though they were operating in a conventional housing market based on new construction.

By 1975 loft rents had become competitive with apartment rents. As

Partial view of a Greenwich Village loft before and after renovation. *Above,* the first residents confront the agony and the ecstasy of renovating "raw space." *Below,* after renovation, the space assumes a form compatible with "loft lifestyle."

The developer's objective is to fit as many loft-apartments as possible into the available space. Here is a typical floor plan of a converted loft building with approximately 13,000 square feet on each floor, aimed at the upper-middle-income housing market.

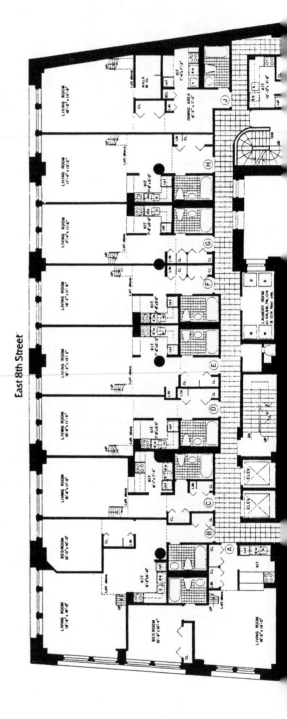

East 8th Street

9

individual units, lofts were no longer necessarily cheaper than conventional apartments. At that time an acceptable market rent for a one- to three-room apartment — for a middle-class Manhattanite — was $350–$450. The average rent for a living loft in 1977 was just under $400.[3] But lofts also require an additional investment to make them habitable. They have to have hot water pipes and water heaters, gas pipes and space heaters, bathrooms and kitchens. Those fine wooden floors have to be refinished and repaired. The wide expanse of walls, ceilings, and columns has to be replastered and repainted. Of course, the investment required for renovation varies enormously. An average expenditure toward the end of the seventies was about $7,000 a loft, although living lofts that have been featured in glossy magazines like *New York* or the *New York Times Magazine* may have cost $50,000 to $100,000 to renovate. The time spent in making a loft barely habitable, on the one hand, or comfortable and even elegant, on the other, also varies. Two to six months represents a reasonable time for making renovations. Obviously, both time and money depend on individual budgets. Lower-income loft dwellers either do their own renovations or hire moonlighting or non-union labor. More affluent residents who hire professional designers and builders may be able to finish their renovations sooner. Alternatively, it is possible to rent or buy a loft that has already been renovated by a first-generation residential tenant. In that case, the previous tenant usually demands a "fixture fee" to recoup his or her investment. This fee also varies enormously. Newspaper advertisements in the mid-1970s mentioned fees from $1,500 to $100,000.

Despite these expenditures, loft rents in the seventies still offered a good deal because of the space involved. An apartment in a newly constructed building with as much space as a loft — which might be a five-, six-, or seven-room apartment — rented for at least $600 or $800 a month. In more exclusive neighborhoods, rent for this much space would be $800 to $1,000 a month. In real estate measurements, this means that the resident of a conventional Manhattan apartment paid at least seven dollars per square foot a year. In contrast to the real loft dweller, tenants in converted loft-apartments also paid more of a "market" rent. A private study of loft buildings in 1977 found that the average rent per square foot in living lofts was $2.28 a year, but the tenant in the average converted loft-apartment paid $7.68.[4]

Until 1975 or so, living lofts in New York City suffered from a murky legal status. Statutes that mitigated against loft living — essentially the local building codes and zoning restrictions — were not enforced but nonetheless remained on the books. This inhibited the banks, which were not notoriously adventurous, anyway, about venturing into untested real estate markets, from making loans to buy lofts or to repair them. So loft building owners often lacked funds to make the structural improvements for a legal residence. The low level of institutional financing created a peculiar twist to the loft market. Though the residential use on which the market was based remained predominantly "illegal," * market prices for lofts and loft buildings rose higher and higher.

But the entry of professional developers into the market demanded an end to this situation. Loft living had to be institutionalized. On the one hand, the developers' dependence on bank financing for both acquisition and construction costs required that the legal status of loft conversions be regularized. On the other hand, the larger investment and consequently larger risk that these developers took mandated that the city administration make a concurrent commitment to this sort of development. No market could be firmly established if tenants ran the risk of being evicted from their loft-apartments. Nor would professional developers become heavily involved in residential conversion if the city government were to backtrack from its support for middle-class housing to support for manufacturing. Similarly, developers did not want to give up the possibility of more lucrative new construction for rehabilitating old buildings unless the city could guarantee that it would not return to the slash-and-burn policy of wholesale urban renewal that had been practiced until the early 1960s. Finally, accustomed as they had become, by 1970, to state subsidies for *any* sort of real estate activity, developers did not want to enter the loft market at solely their own financial risk.[5]

New York City's government was not oblivious to these needs. The close alliance between the Democratic party organization — both "regulars" and "reformers" — and the real estate tycoons who have always contributed heavily to local political campaigns assured City Hall's attentiveness to real estate interests. This was true regardless of which politician sat in the mayor's chair.[6] Moreover, the leading Establishment newspaper, the *New York Times,* featured extremely favorable coverage of the loft market. This position was thoroughly understandable in light of the personal commitment since the early 1900s of the Sulzberger family, who owned the *Times,* to clear Manhattan of industrial uses. Between 1975 and 1977 the Sunday *Times* real estate section and the Real Estate Board of New York, a trade association for the real estate industry, issued a barrage of publicity in favor of loft development.

The Real Estate Board's 1975 report on loft buildings dramatically made the point that in manufacturing use such buildings were no longer viable. They suffered from vacancies, tax delinquencies, and foreclosures. The sickness of loft buildings documented "the drastic effect of manufacturing's decline upon real property" in general. While the disease was diagnosed as chronic — "The area's manufacturing activity shows no signs of recovery, and its tax base is eroding" — the board nonetheless found a

---

* A 1977 study by the New York City Planning Commission found that 91.5 percent of all loft conversions in Manhattan were illegal and only 8.5 percent were legal.

favorable prognosis in residential conversion: "Demand for apartments, exceedingly strong for buildings already converted . . ., could be expected to support a considerable residential expansion." Indeed, the following year the *Times* was quite sanguine about redevelopment possibilities. A 1976 article quoted a partner in a prestigious law firm, who had served as an assistant New York State attorney general in charge of cooperatives and condominiums, as predicting: "By 1985, the fashionable and artistic projects and complexes that will emerge will make this area [of Lower Manhattan] some of the most valuable real estate in New York City."

Likewise, the director of the Mayor's Downtown Action Office, who some years earlier had worked with artists living in lofts on the Lower East Side, spoke glowingly of developing an arts-and-crafts base in midtown. "There are 100,000 crafts people here," he said, "but the city has no epicenter for them. It could be a natural extension of the garment center, which attracts 50,000 department store buyers a year. Those stores are increasingly opening boutiques offering weaving, wall hangings, woodwork, leather work, jewelry and other handcrafts. We could create a brand new industry in the city." Furthermore, the benefits of this redevelopment were shared by the city and new residents. Loft dwellers got "the biggest bargains in the city," according to a vice-president of the biggest real estate firm in New York. "Where in America," he asked, "can you get such space, which is two to three times the size of the average home or three-bedroom apartment?"

Through the mid-1970s, articles continued to appear praising residential conversion and the "revitalization" of old manufacturing neighborhoods into new art centers. SoHo by this point had become outrageously successful, but there remained to be described the chic *manqué* of lofts on the Bowery and the residential conversions of a convent in Brooklyn Heights, a nursing home on the Upper West Side, and numerous other factory and office buildings. At length, one of the *Times*'s two architecture critics concluded, "The 'recycling' of older buildings is the keystone of a new urban movement that may be for the late 1970s what the brownstone revival was for the early part of the decade — a method of channeling investment back into the center city and propping up what had been until recently an altogether depressed real estate market in many cities." [7]

So loft living started as a trend, turned into a "movement," and finally transformed the market. In short, the urban revitalization that the *Times* and the Real Estate Board were pushing *required* that loft buildings be converted from manufacturing to residential use. Industry was dead; long live loft living — in its space. Throughout the 1970s the real estate industry used the pages of the *Times* to curry public attention for proposals to expand and subsidize loft development. These proposals began in some confusion in 1970 and 1971, when plans to tear down the loft buildings of Lower Manhattan and replace them with new high-rise apartment projects and even a sports center competed with plans to make SoHo a coherent artists' zone and a landmark historic district. In 1974 and 1975 the developers proposed eliminating all legal restrictions on the neighborhoods, floor size, and buildings that could be converted to residential use. They also suggested removing the legal barriers against loft living by non-artists. Most significant, perhaps, they proposed the extension of a tax subsidy popularly called "J-51" to cover large residential conversions.

In 1975, section J-51-2.5 of the Administrative Code of the City of New York was amended by the City Council to offer a combination of long-term tax abatement and tax exemption to developers or owners who undertake the residential conversion of large commercial and manufacturing buildings. It is this law that, ultimately, makes the living loft market secure for professional real estate developers. With J-51 on the books, these developers assure bank financing for both acquisition and construction costs. With J-51 subsidies, these developers charge rents that they call "lower than market prices." Although most residential conversions of loft buildings continue to be "illegal" and thus ineligible for the J-51 tax subsidy, a steadily increasing number of living lofts — and *all* loft conversions for the rental market that are undertaken by large professional developers — have qualified for these abatements and exemptions.[8] Even more significant than the relatively small number of loft conversions that qualify for the benefits, the existence of J-51 has exerted a "demonstration effect" on the loft market. With J-51, the city administration showed its irrevocable commitment to destroying New York's old manufacturing lofts.

THE QUERY OF SUPPLY AND DEMAND

This overview of the loft market raises questions about almost all the major assumptions that commonly explain the rise of loft living. First is the basic factor of *supply*. Common sense as well as common knowledge suggest that the loft market began with the search for alternative uses for empty or under-utilized lofts. The unprivileged position of small business in modern economies, the increasing dispersal of manufacturing activities from established urban centers, the flight of investment capital from the northeastern United States that accelerated after 1965, and the downturn in the nation's industrial economy through the 1973–74 recession obviously contributed to an increase in the supply of lofts. Despite the removal of loft buildings in some areas for the construction of new offices, most loft neighborhoods remained intact. Indeed, the lack of modernized lofts drove many successful manufacturing firms to seek space for expansion and rationalization outside Manhattan — in Long Island City, Brooklyn, the Bronx, and even New Jersey and Connecticut.

Yet French sociologists who studied the urban renewal of Paris in the

1960s and 1970s had found that apparent use patterns of buildings and land may be falsified and manipulated. Even land that has remained in heavy use can be "liberated" — or forcibly vacated — to change its use to a more profitable one. What appears to be an unused or an underused space may have been used, until quite recently, with no lack of demand and no excess supply. But at some point, real estate developers may find that this land or the buildings on it represent a likely spot for a new office complex, an apartment house, or even a park. They mobilize the zeal of city officials, who find the site admirably suited for satisfying collective needs. The land is acquired, with or without public approval, help, and subsidy. The existing buildings are torn down, and the erstwhile tenants are dispersed and replaced with higher-rent uses. If the historic working-class *quartiers* of Paris could be destroyed in this way, then the loft districts of New York may also have been vacated by design.[9]

Then there is the factor of *demand*. Why did people in the 1970s rush to rent lofts as housing? Originally, it seemed that loft living attracted two types of residents: suburban parents whose children had grown up and fled the nest and those grown-up children who were setting up their first apartments. In either case, two assumptions were involved. First, people assumed that loft living, as unconventional housing, attracted unconventional people, or at least people in search of the unconventional: "closet hippies" looking for "marginal chic." Second, people assumed that lofts succeeded where regular apartments failed, drawing back to the city center suburban denizens who otherwise had no desire to move in. But these assumptions were wrong. Most studies show that a tiny percentage of middle-class people move back to the city from the suburbs, whether the city is New York, Philadelphia, Chicago, or San Francisco. And as we have already seen, loft residents' occupations and incomes are middle class rather than "marginal." Those people who move into converted loft-apartments are even more thoroughly "conventional." Besides, the investment of time and money that is required for moving into a loft, as well as the absence of many conventional amenities in the building and in the neighborhood, probably discourage some middle-class people from moving into lofts. Of course, the converted apartment houses have those amenities, so they attract the people who would live in new apartments — if they could afford the rent.

But perhaps there is an aesthetic component to the demand factor — a *Zeitgeist* that finds expression in the inhabiting of old factory spaces and thus identifying in some existential way with an archaic past or an artistic style of life. If this is true, then the question of timing becomes crucial. Sweatshops existed for many years, and no one had ever suggested that moving into a sweatshop was chic. Also, artists had lived in lofts at least since the 1930s, and no one but their inamoratas or inamoratos had ever found these impoverished spaces romantic. So if people found lofts attractive in the 1970s, some changes in values must have "come together" in the 1960s. There must have been an "aesthetic conjuncture." On the one hand, artists' living habits became a cultural model for the middle class. On the other hand, old factories became a means of expression for a "post-industrial" civilization. A heightened sense of art and history, space and time, was dramatized by the taste-setting mass media. This suggests that the supply of lofts did *not* create demand for loft living. Instead, demand was a conjunctural response to other social and cultural changes.

Just as supply and demand were affected by factors external to loft space, so the market in living lofts was also shaped by the needs of *investment capital*. These needs influence the trends of capital flight or capital disinvestment, when money flows from one region or sector to another because the chances for profit are greater there. The process occurs in several steps. As profits decline on investment in a region, land and building values fall. Liquid assets are pulled out and reinvested elsewhere. This pull-out of actual and potential investment capital creates a shaky feeling about the future of the area and a gradually dilapidated or outmoded physical infrastructure. This in turn causes values and prices in the "declining" region to fall further and, correspondingly, values and prices in a new region to "boom." Thus after capital flight, property in an old region or neighborhood is "devalorized." Its market value is depressed in relation both to its past or future uses and to comparable property elsewhere. So an investor could buy it cheaply. The immediate returns would not be astronomical. But capital that is invested in the "built environment" never completely dissipates. Certain substantial buildings remain for years in the urban infrastructure. Transportation and communication lines can be regenerated or remodeled. Central city land that lies close to financial centers retains some perennial value. When the investment climate changes, this property is available for redevelopment. As building stock it can be rehabilitated. Its use can be changed. The capital that it represents can be *re*valorized as market values around it rise again. In many cases, the low price of devalorized property attracts investors who can not afford, or can no longer afford, to put their money in other regions or other activities. At that point, investment capital returns, in new forms, to the old area.[10]

In addition to the secular devalorization of property in Lower Manhattan, short-term economic cycles also cause investment capital to move from one New York real estate market to another. Between 1960 and 1965, housing benefited from an influx of investment, especially the new construction of upper-class and upper-middle-class apartment houses in midtown Manhattan. From 1965 to 1970, investment was channeled into new office construction, again mostly in midtown. By the beginning of the seventies these patterns had created an oversupply of office space and an undersupply of housing. There was also a concentration of new investment in midtown. In contrast to that hub of redevelopment activity, Lower Manhattan presented a startlingly clean slate for capital investment. This potential was obvious to the financial community, whose headquarters in Wall Street straddled the southern tip of the area.

From 1956 to 1972 the financial community and the patrician elite that was still based in corporate offices there floated several different plans for redeveloping Lower Manhattan. The long gestation period indicates how important a redevelopment strategy was and how committed these powerful people were to it. Nevertheless, by the late sixties the strategy had encountered its nemesis. Constituencies emerged to provide articulate opposition to the two key principles on which redevelopment was based: public financing and wholesale clearance of existing neighborhoods. Financing was supposed to be arranged in large measure through the sale of state-backed bonds. This procedure had already aroused suspicion because of the state's unlimited responsibility for repaying the bonds and because the sale did not have to be approved by the voters. Instead, the management of both financing and construction was undertaken by a special New York State agency, the Urban Development Corporation, which was accountable to neither the voters nor the legislature. By the end of the 1960s the UDC's unchecked authority, as well as the close relation between its creator, Governor Nelson Rockefeller, and the major proponent of Lower Manhattan redevelopment, Chase Manhattan Bank president David Rockefeller, did not inspire public confidence. This was also the period of middle-class backlash, often on the part of owner-residents of four- and five-story "brownstone" townhouses, against the eviction-destruction–new construction methods of urban renewal. These middle-class homeowners' interest lay in "neighborhood preservation" rather than in new construction.[11]

During this entire time an aura of uncertainty hung over the destiny of Lower Manhattan's loft areas. The cloudy investment climate for redevelopment had a dual effect on the loft market. In the short run, uncertainty kept the prices of Lower Manhattan real estate down. Loft rents were so low that anyone — artists, say — could afford to move in, in ever greater numbers. Meanwhile, viable firms that planned to stay in business looked for more secure, though not necessarily more "modern" or cheaper, space. But investors realized that in the long run, property in this area could only increase in value. That realization introduced the motivation to speculate in loft properties. The resulting financial climate created the most remarkable conjuncture of the loft market: the birth, between 1968 and 1971, of the "neighborhood" of SoHo. Far from being either an indigenous or a spontaneous artists' community, SoHo was really a creation of the investment climate.[12]

A final major factor in the rise of the loft market was *state intervention.* The common explanation of the loft market makes a critical assumption that this market was created without such intervention. It assumes that the initiators of the loft market were the "first generation" of loft dwellers — primarily artists and other adventurous souls — who staked their claim to residentially virgin territory at their own risk and their own expense. "Urban homesteaders," they are called, or "pioneers in the urban wilderness." [13] This characterization goes along with the standard assumption that the loft market was created by autonomous forces of supply and demand. As the discussion so far suggests, however, these concepts camouflage the real factors behind real estate development. Similarly, the concept of loftsteading conceals the fact that state intervention in the housing market operates under many guises. The development of the loft market in the 1960s and 1970s was thoroughly intertwined with such forms of state intervention in the economy as the federal tax structure, local tax incentives like J-51, urban redevelopment plans, the expansion of state employment for artists, the quantum leap in state support for the arts through grants, local laws like zoning resolutions and building codes, and local political initiatives to "preserve" neighborhoods through increased residential use. By this late point in capitalist economies probably no real estate market develops without state intervention. [14]

LARGER CONCERNS BEHIND THE LOFT MARKET

No matter how specialized the market or how idiosyncratic the developers and planners, real estate development on the local level fulfills the needs of nationally ranked capitalists and politicians. Although investors and builders, as well as officials, in any city are generally local people, they are connected both personally and organizationally to their business and political associates all across the country. They are also highly dependent on decisions that are made in government agencies in Washington, D.C., and in corporate board rooms around the world. Because of the varied sources of their capital, their responsibility to state agencies, and the shifting rates of profit on their diverse investments, they are tied into a national and an international network. Relations within this network and the calculations of its individual members determine what gets built, how it is built, where it is built, and the timing of development. [15]

As real estate activity in financial capitals draws in more investment and bigger investors, it becomes permeated by national and international influences. Foreign investment in local real estate, notably in cities like Manhattan and Los Angeles, as well as in farmland, represents only one form of such penetration. The expansion of successful local real estate firms into construction, management, and development in other localities represents another form of "nationalization" of the real estate market. But more strategically, national penetration of local real estate markets takes the form of concerted capital investment and disinvestment. It is the flight of investment capital, through the deindustrialization of older manufacturing centers like New York City, that creates preconditions for the residential redevelopment of loft space.

There is, as yet, no succinct discussion of the process of deindustrialization in modern economies, and even less that could be considered an analysis of its role in contemporary social change. While there are plenty of historical conjectures about the earlier disappearance of traditional crafts industries in countries like Poland and India, few people can imagine what deindustrialization might mean today in an industrial power such as the United States. Certainly we already recognize ills, problems, and changes. But we don't readily know whether they are symptoms or symbols, causes or consequences. In any event, deindustrialization is a long-term process that is connected with change in production, movement of capital, and the rates of return on investment that cause planners to think up new investment strategies on a global level. Thus deindustrialization is part of the "long waves" of economic activity — long-lasting alternations between prosperity and decline — that mark all kinds of local, national, and international cycles. The deindustrialization that we see in the loss of manufacturing jobs — and the accompanying unemployment of men and women, the shutdown of productive facilities, and the disuse of certain types of skilled work in which they specialized — may be only a partial phenomenon. It affects some regions, especially older manufacturing centers, strongly. It underlines the decline in the contribution of particular industrial sectors, such as steel, textiles, and automobiles, to the nation's economy. However, it may not cause a decline in a country's total industrial output or even reduce the production level in a declining sector. Moreover, the loss of manufacturing activity may coexist with an expansion of the service sector. Some of that expansion may occur in other regions, like the Sun Belt, but some of it, notably the high-level business of international banking and finance, may remain concentrated in the old metropolitan core.

It is important to ask what occurs in particular places as deindustrialization unfolds. On the one hand, industrial jobs may simply disappear as the production process to which they refer is eliminated or relocated. On the other hand, these jobs may be replaced by different sorts of jobs — or they may not. In the short run, this creates the possibility of enlarging a socially dependent population, or forcing the emigration of skilled workers outside the old industrial core. But there is no way of knowing, in the long run, whether these processes will lead to an absolute economic and social decline. Cities and regions hope for a regenesis in the form of a more advanced — some say "post-industrial" — society. What we see now in cities that pursue this dream is painful dislocations in the work force, the expansion of offices and middle-class housing into former working-class and manufacturing milieux, and political realignments that are based on which social classes, and which economic activities, have the right to use the city's space.

Within this general context, the creation of a local real estate market in converted factory space relates to three major processes. First, as an investment and as housing, the use of real estate plays a role in assuring new patterns of reproduction for both capital and labor. Second, the marketing of real estate affects relations between social classes and between subclasses that compete for property and neighborhoods. Third, the rise of a real estate market establishes new means for accumulating capital, or where investment money goes in search of profit. Let us briefly flesh these out.

As my critical overview of the loft market has already suggested, the residential conversion of manufacturing space sets the stage for the definitive end of traditional industrial activity. Factory space that is subdivided into apartments, with kitchens and bathrooms, is dead as far as productive activity is concerned. Thus the most fundamental part of a mode of production — the space where products are actually produced — is shifted to another use. This new use refers to a purpose quite different from the reproduction of capital in industry. As housing, the former factory space provides for the reproduction of the labor force. Significantly, the workers who are housed here are professionals, academics, executives in private industry, government bureaucrats, other service-sector employees, and self-employed artists. These social strata differ from the classical industrial proletariat, who by this point are reduced in numbers and housed much farther away from the urban center. The new "means of production" — in modern offices — are now surrounded by their own "working-class districts" of high-rise apartment houses, brownstones, and converted loft buildings. Insofar as the converted loft space remains in mixed productive and residential use, it provides facilities for an "artistic mode of production," that is, for a craft industry that follows rather than precedes industrial production. Similarly, the expansion of the work force in this "cottage industry" permits the enlargement of the sphere of nonproductive labor. Meanwhile, the share of productive labor in the urban economy steadily diminishes. In short, the residential conversion of manufacturing space provides a substantial part of the infrastructure for a supposedly post-industrial urban economy.

Just as this infrastructure fulfills the physical needs of the service-sector and white-collar employees, so it deprives small manufacturers and their relatively unskilled work force of the space that they need to work. Marginal businesses and firms that rely on low overhead are pushed out of their low-rent spaces by middle-class competition. Given the age and lower-middle-class background of many of these business owners, they respond by closing up shop. Frequently, they retire early and move away to other regions. Because their children are probably either professionals or service-sector employees, they don't want to take over the family business. Their workers undoubtedly lack the capital for buying the firm, and there is no government program to keep these firms operating or to subsidize worker ownership. The workers may also lack the expertise to run the firm. Besides, they may be unwilling to take the risk of low-profit entrepreneurship in a declining industrial sector. They may well realize that the constriction of loft space is related to city policies that emphasize commitment to the middle class rather than the working class, to housing instead of manufacturing, and to investment in Manhattan rather than the Outer Boroughs where they live.*

Yet at the same time, middle-class constituencies rise and fall in defense of their housing interests. The elusive ideal of neighborhood stability inspires a quest for compatible uses and suitable tenants. Ever sensitive to changes in property values, middle-class homeowners sometimes become aggressive opponents of real estate development. They don't want their homes to entice speculation. But one of the more interesting types of real estate speculation in the city plays on the urban middle class's desire to be near cultural advantages. In particular, the presence of an "arts infrastructure" has already demonstrated its worth in attracting middle-class users and enhancing property values. The example of SoHo — a "Disneyland for the aesthete," as a New York writer calls it [16] — springs readily to mind. However, this sort of development does not necessarily depend on arts activity that is indigenous to the area. Instead, developers utilize cultural institutions and even implant them as a stratagem for their redevelopment plans. Cities with smaller concentrations of artists and craftspersons than New York have used them, nonetheless, to attract development, and the many people who have recently taken up crafts work can be encouraged to rent work or display space as the first step of a redevelopment process.

The hopes for redevelopment that are thus engaged set out a lure for real estate investors. It is difficult to try to unravel the priorities that underlie an investment strategy, and nearly impossible to trace the hidden moves of capital that joins many sources. But it is apparent that the investment that goes into a real estate market is interconnected with investment opportunities elsewhere. The loft market, for example, keeps capital invested in real estate when it would otherwise be used for other purposes. This has two interesting effects on the economy. First, it prevents money from being used "productively," that is, to create new products and new jobs. Even though investments in real estate produce profits, they remain,

---

* This policy orientation, particularly during the Koch administration, which came to office in 1977, can be documented through critical press coverage — not in the *New York Times* but in the *Village Voice* — and the "Performance Audit of the Industrial and Commercial Incentive Board," issued by the New York City Comptroller's Office in March 1979.

in a sense, "fictitious" capital. Yet investments in a growing loft market generate more investment opportunities. In fact, they provide an opportunity to invest in a no-growth situation. In the short run of an interim between real estate booms, when no new construction can get financed, the recycling of an old building fills an investment niche. In the long run of a limited-growth economy, an established market in recycled buildings remains a viable investment opportunity. So the means of accumulation that the loft market represents is both like and unlike that of other real estate markets.

Although this analytic framework relies on the work that is being done in the new field of urban political economy and the urban sociology that it has influenced, I have deliberately ignored an idea that is popular there, the idea of "urban struggles." Social critics like to think that out there in the world that they describe, some heroic social group is synthesizing into practice — either intuitively or consciously — the critics' theses and antitheses. But theory is rarely put into practice in this way. The urban struggles that we see are generally not the historic contests of which manifestos are made. The groups that have been directly involved in the loft market are not social "enemies." Indeed, the most dramatic struggles that have been fought over the loft terrain camouflage the real interests that are at stake. Like the place of social classes in contemporary capitalist society, the role of social classes in the rise of the loft market is a complicated story.

This chapter has made only a preliminary exploration of the loft terrain. Although New York City is the undisputed capital of loft living, the same processes are at work in many cities. Even if other cities don't have an expanding high-class service sector and a loft market like New York's, they have intimations and illusions about economic survival that point them in that direction. So they have movements for historic preservation and arts-and-crafts centers that serve as centerpieces for an intended scenario of real estate development. So far, I have explained the common assumptions about the rise of the loft market in New York between 1965 and 1975. The New York market has had a crucial effect on the creation of similar markets in recycled buildings in other cities.

The factors on which any contemporary real estate market depends — supply, demand, investment capital, and state intervention — must be examined more carefully. Vital to the creation of this particular market, the political context of deindustrialization must be scrutinized. The links between investment and politics in deindustrialization must be shown. Also, the aesthetic conjuncture of the 1960s that made lofts a viable commodity — the changing tastes and styles of life — has to be described. Because state support for the arts, especially in the form of housing for artists, facilitated the development of the loft market, the relation between art and power must be explored. Similarly, the motivations of different types of loft developers and loft landlords, and the various development scenarios that they followed, should be explained. Finally, since state intervention made loft living profitable for professional real estate developers, it is crucial to confront the various roles of the state as it provokes both development and speculation.

In this richness of subject, the facts alone are complicated. A mere chronological account of the rise of the loft market would confuse because of the peculiar distinctions (such as "legal" and "illegal" loft living) and the lengthy descriptions (like "J-51") that are necessary to understand the unfolding of events. So the chapters that follow tell a Rashomon-like story about the market in lofts, and the city and the people that determined it. The story basically runs according to a plan that is suggested by the factors I have mentioned: the preparation of a downtown terrain through long-term changes in production and investment strategies; the establishment of a particular demand for loft space on this terrain among certain segments of the middle class; the rise of a market in old buildings by the integration of a subjective demand for art and history with an objective demand for housing on the part of consumers and for placement on the part of investors; the response of real estate developers to these demands; and the inventiveness of the state as local government adapts to a more intensive use of urban space. Each chapter gives a somewhat different perspective on the underlying competition that is involved in a new use of space and necessarily introduces more characters into the story. The patrician elite, city politicians, and small manufacturers are followed by artists, landlords, tenants, developers, and community groups. Fortunately, real estate development is most frequently an anonymous venture, so I have been able to keep the mention of names to a minimum. I have also tried to keep numbers simple and vocabulary straightforward. A familiarity with the neighborhoods of Manhattan is not essential. After all, for all modern city dwellers, real estate is familiar territory.

2

INVESTMENT AND POLITICS

In a sense, the deindustrialization of New York can be viewed as a qualified disaster. Loss of jobs for the manufacturing workers who can be neither reschooled nor retooled to fit into a service economy is disastrous — for them. Loss of value in industrial plant, including small loft buildings that were constructed in the late nineteenth and early twentieth centuries, is disastrous — for the building owners. But for those who have capital to invest in the physical infrastructure of an expanding service economy — in office buildings, housing, and retail facilities — deindustrialization is a prerequisite to profit. Of course, long-term trends in industrial development on both the national and international levels greatly affect local growth. However, local elites also play a role in facilitating capital shifts. The deindustrialization of New York in general and investment in loft buildings in Manhattan in particular do not proceed in isolation from the rest of the world economy. Secular industrial decline, the special vulnerability of small businesses, and changing investment patterns of financial institutions set the context in which loft buildings lose their value as industrial space. Their subsequent regeneration in the form of living lofts reflects an alliance between investment and politics. So the "liberation" of a supply of lofts in Lower Manhattan during the 1960s was preceded by reduction in the number of manufacturing jobs, removal of financing for industrial properties, and legal discouragement of industrial uses.

GENESIS

Economic Decline, 1950–70

The deindustrialization of America really began much earlier than we suspect. If we look for an indicator in the number of manufacturing jobs, we find that the classical industrial era ended in the decade following

23

Table 1
Employment of the Labor Force in Selected Industries in New York City,
1950, 1960, 1970

Industry	Labor Force		
	1950	1960	1970
Total employed	3,276,415	3,307,548	3,191,370
All manufacturing	966,448	870,354	657,054
(Percentage of total employed)	(29.5%)	(26.3%)	(20.5%)
Machinery industries, except electrical	39,329	34,482	26,769
Garment industry	324,753	269,199	177,198
Printing industry	98,319	104,856	91,501

Source: U.S. Census Bureau, 1950, 1960, 1970

World War II. In the United States, the number of people employed in manufacturing was largest in 1956. But in New York City, the size of the industrial work force peaked in 1947. To some degree, the subsequent decrease in the number of manufacturing jobs was compensated for by increases in labor productivity or the use of more efficient machines. Partly, too, the decline in industrial employment was offset by a corresponding expansion of service-sector work. From 1950 on, less than a third of New York City's work force was employed in manufacturing, and by 1970 this proportion had declined to one fifth. Annual job loss in manufacturing reached about 16,000 between 1960 and 1965, subsided to 400 a year between 1965 and 1969, and rose again to 15,900 at the end of the decade. Generally, the job opportunities that New York City lost were gained by other regions. Even before the end of the nineteenth century, factories spread to the New York suburbs. Later, new factories opened up in southern states that had not previously developed an industrial base. After 1960, companies with headquarters in the Northeast increasingly diffused their industrial production over the southeastern and southwestern United States, as well as to places like Hong Kong, South Korea, the Philippines, Mexico, and Guatemala. Nevertheless, in 1970, New York still had a greater concentration of manufacturing, wholesale, and trucking jobs than any other city in the United States (see table 1).[1]

The garment industry, traditionally a mainstay of this industrial concentration, showed particular sensitivity to rising labor costs. Between 1950 and 1960, jobs in the garment industry decreased by 17 percent. Over the next ten years the rate of loss doubled, to 34 percent. The second major pillar of New York's manufacturing economy, the printing and publishing industry, enlarged its work force somewhat between 1950 and 1960, perhaps as part of the general service-sector expansion. But it, too, showed job loss by 1970, largely because of automation. A less significant, though typical, industrial sector, the machinery industry, experienced a slow and steady decrease in employment during the whole 1950–70 period. Many of the people who lost their jobs in this secular decline were marginal workers and often members of minority groups. Sixty percent of New York's manufacturing, wholesale, and trucking jobs in 1970 were at the semi-skilled or unskilled level of operatives and laborers. However, job loss in the printing industry, which has always recruited from a more "aristocratic" stratum of the working class, affected more highly skilled, more highly paid, and more white male workers.

Historically, the heart of New York City's manufacturing activity has been the loft buildings of Lower Manhattan. As late as the early 1970s, more than half the city's manufacturing jobs were located in Manhattan. And over 55 percent of the city's industrial floor space was in those buildings. Many of the lofts were used for the "light manufacturing" typical of the city's two biggest industries, apparel and printing. As recently as ten years ago the garment industry still provided a large proportion, 28 percent, of Manhattan's jobs.[2]

Surprisingly, through most of this century the loft space in which these industries are concentrated has been under constant attack. Before the Depression, hostility toward manufacturers inspired efforts by the patrician elite — New York's bankers, lawyers, and civic-minded industrialists — to restrict manufacturing to circumscribed areas or zones. Their success in creating a special zone for the garment industry, in the area known since that time as the Garment Center, enabled them to prevent further manufacturing expansion to choice midtown real estate. It also inhibited social contact, even at minimal eyeball level, with a group of manufacturers and their workers whose social class and ethnicity annoyed the local upper class. Because the elite wanted to stay in Manhattan, it developed its own plans for the land on which loft buildings stood. The "best" use for this space, according to their property-based logic, was in high-rent housing and even higher-rent offices.[3] In the long run, the elite succeeded in imposing their logic of spatial organization through zoning. In the short run, during the deindustrialization that followed World War II, this logic remade the map of Manhattan. During the urban building boom that lasted from the mid-1950s to the mid-1960s, new office and housing construction reduced Manhattan's loft space by more than 9 million square feet. While this left over 373 million square feet of loft space as late as 1969, it nonetheless represented a threatening inroad into the manufacturers' territory.[4]

Though New York manufacturers seem feisty, they have no real political strength. Certainly since the 1970s they have had no way of competing for loft space against a "better" use. Though an individual manufacturer may be able to pay a higher rent for his factory, the very presence of factories impedes redevelopment for white-collar uses. Moreover, the structural position of these firms in the national economy is weak. The tenacity of small business as a form of economic activity camouflages the enormous vulnerability of each small business firm. Generally, small businesses rise like the phoenix from commercial disasters. In recent years, however, at least in New York, their deaths have outnumbered their births. As long as manufacturing still takes place in Manhattan, it is done in small manufacturing firms, but the number of such firms has steadily decreased. So this type of deindustrialization has an immediate impact on the relative strength of demand for industrial space. Labor and materials costs keep the total dollar volume of manufacturing high. Yet manufacturers employ fewer production workers, and they seem to require, in the aggregate, less production space. Between 1958 and 1972 in Manhattan, the number of firms in the garment industry shrank by almost half. The fur business was cut back to half its size, the number of printing firms decreased slightly, and machine shops were decimated (see table 2).

The disappearance of these firms remade the map of Manhattan. The character and pattern of Manhattan's specialized commercial neighborhoods was steadily eroded between 1950 and 1980. Some little streets disappeared in order to make superblocks and super-corporate headquarters. The clusters of manufacturers, jobbers, suppliers, wholesalers, and distributers were "busted." Traditional centers of the garment and printing industries such as the Broadway Corridor, on lower Broadway between Canal and Eighth streets, Lower Fifth Avenue, between Seventeenth and Twenty-second streets, and the Flower Market district, which was also the furriers' center, between Twenty-sixth and Twenty-eighth streets around Sixth Avenue, were broken up slowly from 1958 to 1968 and faster from 1968 to 1978 (see maps and table 3). If we look only at the number of machine shops in different neighborhoods of Manhattan, we see graphically what happens to the whole pattern when small industrial spaces disappear (see figure 1).

According to the conventional wisdom of supply and demand, these losses should have had a devastating impact on the real estate market in manufacturing lofts. City planners and urban economists had long assumed that the more successful manufacturers move out of lofts in search of more modern physical plants (preferably in one-story buildings) in less congested areas, where taxes and wages are probably also lower. In a period of secular economic decline as well as a sharp, sudden downturn in business activity, vacancy rates in loft buildings should rise as small manufacturing tenants have to close up shop. The resulting loss in rental income should spur defaults on mortgage and property-tax payments. Eventually, the owners of loft buildings may lose their property through a new wave of foreclosures.

This logic is compelling. Yet even in the face of competition over loft space with high-rent users, monopoly capital's overwhelming advantages, inflation and recession in the national economy, changes in world markets, and steadily increasing credit restrictions, small business usually shows an

Table 2
Decline of Manufacturing Activity in Manhattan, 1958–77

	1958	1963	1967	1972	1977
Establishments					
Total	22,854	20,714	17,841	14,929	13,289
With 20 or more employees	(6,155)	(5,658)	(5,216)	(4,360)	(3,800)
Garment industry	10,329	9,079	7,517	5,716	5,096
Women's and misses' outerwear	(3,533)	(3,105)	(2,696)	(2,326)	(2,552)
Fur goods	(1,424)	(1,382)	(1,153)	(694)	(516)
Printing industry	3,972	3,950	3,563	3,350	3,242
Machinery, except electrical	486	391	335	290	220
Production Workers					
Total	335,369	293,906	278,300	225,600	191,300
Garment industry	167,261	149,034	138,300	114,900	104,100
Women's and misses' outerwear	(68,241)	(62,125)	(58,300)	(51,800)	(53,600)
Fur goods	(7,093)	(6,866)	(6,500)	(3,300)	(2,600)
Printing industry	55,348	55,261	52,600	42,200	31,800
Machinery, except electrical	4,071	3,351	2,800	2,300	1,400
Value Added by Manufacture					
Total	$4.2 billion	$4.7 billion	$5.7 billion	$6.4 billion	$8.9 billion
Garment industry	$1.6 billion	$1.7 billion	$2.0 billion	$2.2 billion	$2.8 billion
Women's and misses' outerwear	($735 million)	($807 million)	($982 million)	($1.0 billion)	($1.5 billion)
Fur goods	($86 million)	($101 million)	($108 million)	($76 million)	($101 million)
Printing industry	$1.4 billion	$1.8 billion	$2.4 billion	$2.8 billion	$4.3 billion
Machinery, except electrical	$49 million	$50 million	$48 million	$55 million	$44 million

Source: U.S. Census Bureau, *Census of Manufactures,* Geographic Area Series, 1958, 1963, 1967, 1972, 1977

impressive tenacity. When a U.S. congressional committee studied the problems of businesses in the ten largest cities in the United States, it found that the smallest firms (with fewer than twenty-five employees) generally planned to keep their operations stable. Fewer small businesses planned to expand, but in contrast to the largest companies, fewer planned to shrink their size.[5] Another study found that most new jobs tend to be generated by small firms — a tendency which the banks may call "volatility" and the economists "dynamism." Nevertheless, the independent entrepreneur seems to be the generator of employment, particularly in cities of the old industrial North.[6]

But the big investors who control the implantation of industrial activity — corporate headquarters and banks — seem convinced that small man-

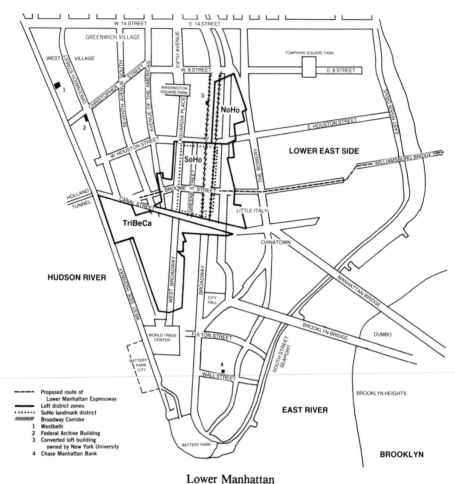

Lower Manhattan

ufacturers are an archaic breed. So they don't need any space. Better to invest in a new urban infrastructure, where lofts are irrelevant and rents are high. They see no logic to Jane Jacobs's old idea that an urban economy grows by a kind of cell division, and that the best way to encourage entrepreneurial mitosis is to supply small spaces, perhaps somewhat dilapidated, at modest rents.[7] Indeed, for those who believe that the urban economy depends on the development of a "post-industrial" or service-sector infrastructure, there is no logic to Jacobs's idea. Those things aren't being built anymore.

Economic Crisis, 1972–76

By the time the New York City government got around to studying the decline of employment, in the 1970s, the archaism of small manufacturing

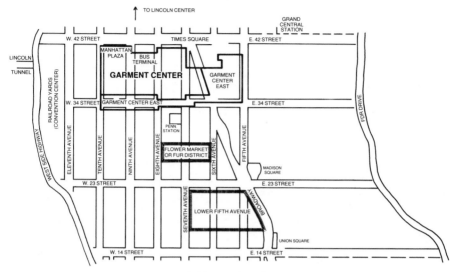

Midtown South

was a foregone conclusion. Ignoring the high proportion of existing small businesses, particularly in manufacturing, city officials concentrated their attention on the potential loss of large firms and corporate headquarters.[8] They more or less gave up on big industry, that is, on the relatively big industry that was located in New York. They reasoned that these firms found New York's loft buildings physically obsolete. So they focused on the symbolically strategic jobs in more modern spaces, by wooing large companies to keep their headquarters in Manhattan. Not only was corporate business bigger and more elegant than small manufacturing, but it was also white-collar rather than blue, and white, of course, rather than Hispanic, Chinese, or black. It was also more consistent with the patrician elite's image of New York as a world capital.

But because they waited until the 1970s to study the use of industrial infrastructure, city planners had a much better case against the small manufacturers and the loft buildings that they occupied. The national recession of 1973–74, as well as a steep decline in the position of competitive capital in general and in the New York region in particular from 1969 to 1976, accelerated job loss in these areas. Between 1970 and 1974 New York City employment decreased by 300,000 jobs, and between spring 1974 and spring 1975, by another 80,000 jobs. The city and the metropolitan region suffered greater economic decline than other areas in the United States, even more than the rest of the generally fading Northeast.[9] The New York region's share of the Gross National Product dipped from 12.3 percent in 1972 to 11.3 percent in 1975. Small businesses lost 310,000 jobs, or 6 percent of their labor force, two thirds of this decrease

Table 3

Decline in the Number of Businesses in Three Areas of Lower Manhattan, 1958–78

Area	1958	1968	1978
Broadway Corridor			
Garment industry	165	240	149
Miscellaneous manufacturing	93	78	54
Underwear	81	70	31
Trading and merchandising	67	31	24
Textiles	60	33	32
Printing industry	60	50	24
Novelties	55	36	14
Buttons, stitching, threads, and fabrics	51	41	30
Hats and caps manufacturers	50	45	42
Miscellaneous services (including doctors and lawyers)	47	35	48
Housewares	40	17	19
Bags, handbags, and leather goods	36	38	32
Miscellaneous suppliers	35	12	18
Machines	27	9	17
Possible residences	16	53	236
Curtains and drapes	13	3	2
Fasteners, binders, and molding	13	6	5
Miscellaneous businesses	13	14	19
Photographers and color labs	10	0	3
Trucking and construction	5	1	4
Flower Market and florists' goods	4	1	0
Precision tools	2	1	1
Fur goods	0	1	0
Lower Fifth Avenue			
Garment industry	205	225	103
Miscellaneous manufacturing	93	42	42
Underwear	8	13	6
Trading and merchandising	25	13	13
Textiles	13	16	11
Printing industry	84	84	121
Novelties	50	24	12
Buttons, stitching, threads, and fabrics	42	20	14
Hats and caps manufacturers	5	11	9
Miscellaneous services (including doctors and lawyers)	35	51	57
Housewares	15	26	21
Bags, handbags, and leather goods	26	21	33
Miscellaneous suppliers	20	11	25
Machines	30	14	13
Possible residences	483	388	913
Curtains and drapes	7	4	4
Fasteners, binders, and molding	13	11	9
Miscellaneous businesses	30	11	30
Photographers and color labs	28	39	96
Trucking and construction	15	16	2

Table 3 *continued*

Area	1958	1968	1978
Flower Market and florists' goods	3	4	0
Precision tools	0	0	2
Fur goods	0	0	3
Flower Market District			
Garment industry	160	108	29
Miscellaneous manufacturing	103	75	150
Underwear	14	12	4
Trading and merchandising	67	32	87
Textiles	11	9	176
Printing industry	134	165	37
Novelties	75	56	11
Buttons, stitching, threads, and fabrics	21	26	21
Hats and caps manufacturers	32	6	5
Miscellaneous services (including doctors and lawyers)	24	36	50
Housewares	16	9	9
Bags, handbags, and leather goods	30	77	33
Miscellaneous suppliers	12	12	16
Machines	18	26	17
Possible residences	78	64	461
Curtains and drapes	10	9	22
Fasteners, binders, and molding	6	11	3
Miscellaneous businesses	6	7	9
Photographers and color labs	16	48	22
Trucking and construction	13	1	1
Flower Market and florists' goods	24	33	29
Precision tools	0	0	0
Fur goods	273	265	177

Source: Reverse Telephone Books, Manhattan, 1958, 1963, 1968, 1973, 1978. These directories list subscribers in reverse of the usual order, i.e., by address rather than by name. Access courtesy of New York Telephone.

in manufacturing. Nor was the slack in employment taken up by investment in new machinery. Net investment dropped from an amount that had already lagged about a third behind national levels to a figure that barely covered depreciation costs. The extent of disinvestment by the region's businesses hurt New York terribly.[10]

Capital disaccumulation had an obvious effect on the viability of loft buildings. A study carried out in 1975 by the Real Estate Board of New York presents a dismal picture of tax delinquencies, foreclosures, and vacancies. The total dollar amount of tax delinquencies on loft buildings doubled from 1973/74 to 1974/75 (from $3.5 million to $7.9 million), and the number of foreclosure suits that were brought against loft building owners increased from nine in 1970 to twenty-five in the first half of 1975.

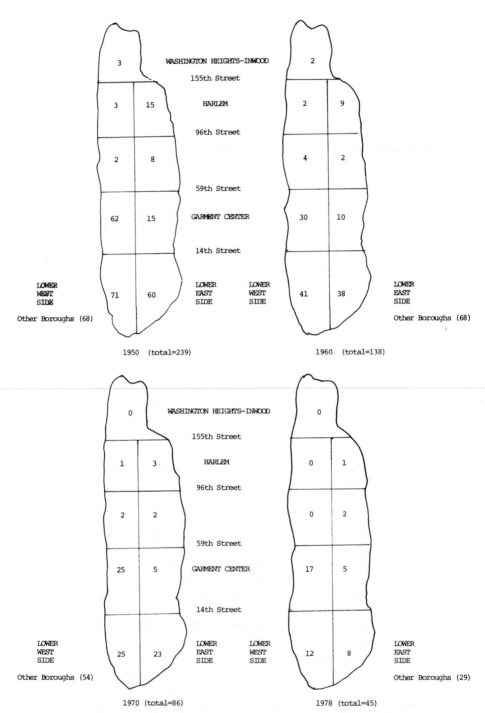

Figure 1. Number and location of individually owned machine shops in Manhattan, 1950–78. Data are from *Manhattan Yellow Pages,* 1950, 1960, 1970, 1978-79. Maps researched by Kevin Anderson.

32

As for vacancies, six Manhattan real estate agencies had 4.1 million square feet available for immediate rental in manufacturing lofts (in unspecified neighborhoods). This represented a disastrously high vacancy rate of 31 percent. Two years later, a similar study of 1,586 buildings in downtown and midtown Manhattan's commercial zones by the City Planning Commission (CPC) found a vacancy rate of only 1.6 million square feet, or 5.5 percent. Like the 1975 study, this report also found that most of the vacancies occurred in smaller lofts: 30.4 percent of the vacancies were in lofts of less than 2,500 square feet, and 39.8 percent in lofts between 2,501 and 5,000 square feet. This represented a disproportionately high vacancy rate. There were no vacancies in larger lofts (between 5,001 and 7,500 square feet) and few in the largest lofts (over 10,000 square feet). This study also shows that 10.5 percent of the real estate lots in the sample (or eight out of a total of seventy-six) were delinquent in their tax payments for 1976/77. The amount of these arrears totaled $83,880.[11]

How reliable are these reports? Despite the job loss that we already recognize, several points about the 1975 and 1977 studies are questionable. First, the data about vacancies are unsystematic, probably because vacancy rates are usually kept secret by building owners. Second, the Real Estate Board's 1975 sample is not strictly comparable with the City Planning Commission's sample. Nor is it defined methodically. Third, the far more dismal picture of vacant, impoverished loft buildings that the Real Estate Board presents may have been influenced by the recommendation that the board used this report to support: that the city should encourage residential conversion.

The vacancy data are suspect, finally, because by 1975 residential conversion had already made a sizable impact on the viability of manufacturing space. In 1977, CPC estimated that a thousand industrial loft buildings in Manhattan were in residential use on at least three floors. The higher rents that landlords got from residential tenants made the buildings' market value rise. In turn, this influenced higher tax assessments ("assessed value"). Furthermore, between 1970 and 1975 real-estate tax rates rose 33 percent — to compensate, in part, for the city's budget deficits. This means that higher tax rates and higher assessed values may have accelerated tax delinquencies and accumulated indebtedness so as to affect a higher rate of foreclosures. Moreover, by the middle of the 1970s, manufacturing tenants started to complain vociferously — to CPC, to the mayor, to anyone who would hear them — that their landlords deliberately created and maintained vacancies in order to facilitate residential conversion. So the sequence of deindustrialization, on the one hand, and vacancies, arrears, and foreclosures, on the other hand, may have been somewhat skewed by the conversion process itself.

Some data that I collected in 1978 suggest that residential conversion may have had a pernicious effect on the manufacturing tenants of loft buildings during this period. I did a "tracer study" of manufacturers who occupied lofts in the three neighborhoods already mentioned — the Broadway Corridor, Lower Fifth Avenue, and the Flower Market district — between 1963 and 1978. I divided this fifteen-year period into three five-year periods: 1963–68, 1968–73, and 1973–78. Then I picked a random sample of thirty-four loft buildings in these three areas that had undergone at least some residential conversion, according to the 1977 CPC report, and compiled lists of the tenants who occupied these buildings in each of the five-year periods. Many of the former tenants could not be located in 1978, and most of those who could be found at new locations in the metropolitan area were not very responsive to my inquiries. Probably a majority of the firms that disappeared had gone out of business, and those that remained feared that I was somehow connected with a city tax agency. So I was able to study only a tiny sample: forty-six firms that had moved out of loft buildings in the three neighborhoods between 1963 and 1968, before the market in living lofts developed, and thirty-nine firms that had moved between 1973 and 1978, when the loft market hit its stride. A somewhat higher percentage of tenants reported moving out on their own volition in the *later* period — reflecting, perhaps, the greater viability of firms that were left intact after the shake-out of the 1973–74 recession — but significantly, an extraordinarily high percentage of moves between 1973 and 1978 that were forced by the landlords — 81 percent — were initiated *because of residential conversion* (see table 4).

In 1978 the *New York Times* reported a case that confirms to a bizarre degree the point that my small sample makes. Between 1973 and 1978 a cap and hat manufacturer was forced to move twice: first from the Broadway Corridor to Lower Fifth Avenue, then from there to the Flower Market district. Each move was initiated by the landlord's decision to convert the building to residential use.[12] Certainly, the reasons for the sample's moves also show the influence of a downturn in the business cycle. After 1973, fewer firms move out because of expansion, and more firms move out because they rationalize production. But the moves suggest that as the tenants' position weakened, from 1968 to 1978, so the landlords' position was strengthened. During this time, the landlords' efforts to derive greater profitability from loft buildings came down to a choice between two stratagems: either raise the rent or convert the buildings to residential use.

Economic Viability of Loft Buildings

Manhattan loft buildings, like most urban property, belong in the realm of competitive capital. Ownership of loft buildings is diffuse rather than concentrated, so that loft building owners tend to be small property owners. They are individuals or partnerships rather than institutions such as banks or real estate holding corporations. As a group and a generation, many loft building owners were formed by the same economic conditions

Table 4
Reason for Manufacturing Tenants' Moving out of Loft Buildings,
1963–68 and 1973–78

Reason for Move	1963–68		1973–78	
	Number	Percentage	Number	Percentage
Landlord's choice	22	*48*	16	*41*
Residential conversion	10	45[a]	13	81[b]
Renovate building	3	14		
Raised rent	2	9	3	19
Empty / sell / raze building	2	9		
Co-op building	1	4		
Decreased services	1	4		
Unspecified	3	14		
Tenant's choice	24	*52*	23	*59*
Expansion	20	83[c]	13	57[d]
Rationalization	2	8	7	30
Contraction			1	4
Out of business	1	4	1	4
Started new business			1	4
Crime in neighborhood	1	4		

Note: Figures are only for those firms still in business in the area in 1978.
[a] This figure represents 22 percent of all moves.
[b] This figure represents 33 percent of all moves.
[c] This figure represents 44 percent of all moves.
[d] This figure represents 33 percent of all moves.

as were their small manufacturing tenants. In fact, many loft building owners were small manufacturers. Influenced by the Depression, they bought the buildings in which their lofts were located as a hedge against possible crisis and eviction. Often, both building owners and manufacturers are immigrants from Eastern or Southern Europe whose original source of investment capital was a small amount of savings from an even smaller business. In most cases, through the 1960s, loft building owners owned their buildings for twenty or thirty years. This means that by the 1970s many of these owners have died or retired. As property owners, they have pursued the financial and tax advantages of periodically refinancing their purchase costs by taking out second or third mortgages. Typically, the stability of loft building ownership is reflected in a pattern of "trading" mortgage commitments back and forth between the owners and a number of local savings banks.

When I looked at the mortgage histories of my sample of thirty-four loft buildings in the Broadway Corridor, Lower Fifth Avenue, and the Flower Market district, I found that this pattern of trading mortgages back and forth held true until the mid-1960s.[13] The records also show that until the early 1970s purchase prices for loft buildings remained stable and fairly low. Indeed, the sale prices were generally the same as, or even below, the assessed values (including the value of both the land and the buildings on it). While the prices varied between $100,000 and $200,000, according to building size, the timing of refinancing the mortgage(s) for each building varied in apparent, regular synchronization with the waxing and waning of the tax advantages for interest on debt payments.* During this time, the amount of mortgage debt outstanding on each building seems to have held steady at around 80 percent of the purchase price. Relative to the capital involved in other kinds of commercial real estate, these debts were very low. They averaged around $100,000. The sample seems to present a valid picture of loft building ownership. It fits with what we know anecdotally about loft landlords and also with an earlier systematic survey of 255 loft buildings in SoHo by urban planning expert Chester Rapkin. From information collected in 1962, when SoHo was still used solely for manufacturing, Rapkin found that the majority of buildings were held by small owners, almost half of whom had bought the buildings before 1945. There was a very low turnover rate in ownership. Assessed value at that time, too, approximated the buildings' market value.[14]

The stability of ownership and of sale prices of loft buildings through the 1960s is reflected in the stability of their tenancy and their rents. Of the 650 manufacturing firms in SoHo that Rapkin studied in 1962, 24 percent had been in the same area of the city since before 1942, 25 percent had moved into the area between 1942 and 1952, 16 percent had been there for between five and ten years, and 35 percent had moved in during the preceding five years. The overwhelming majority of these firms (74 percent) had always been located in SoHo.[15] Similarly, in 1977, when I did a survey of twenty small manufacturers who were located in a block of loft buildings in the Broadway Corridor that were slated for residential conversion, I found that half the firms had occupied their lofts for more than fifteen years, and nineteen had been in those buildings for more than five years. Almost half of them, or nine of the firms, had been there throughout their entire business history.

A major reason for the stability of these manufacturing tenants was the low rent that they paid for their lofts. The 1977 sample, most of whose lofts faced Broadway, paid an annual rent of between $1.00 and $1.50 per square foot. Most of the 1962 SoHo sample, with lofts both on Broadway and in the smaller side and cross streets, paid an annual rent of between

---

* A "crossover phenomenon" occurs when increased payments on the principal of a mortgage loan begin to exceed decreasing depreciation charges. "From this point on, cash flow is not sufficient to meet taxable income, and the property should be sold or refinanced," according to John MacMahan's authoritative real estate textbook, *Property Development: Effective Decision Making in Uncertain Times* (New York: McGraw-Hill, 1976), p. 257.

$0.75 and $1.00.* These loft rents had changed remarkably little over the preceding half-century. A study of the garment industry in New York in 1923 found very similar rents in the same areas: lofts on Broadway between Canal and Fourteenth streets rented for $0.75 to $1.00 per square foot, and lofts in the adjacent side and cross streets were somewhat cheaper ($0.50 to $0.75 per square foot). Then as now, rents for lofts closer to the midtown business district ran twice as high.[16]

So ownership and tenancy patterns suggest that the market in manufacturing lofts and loft buildings held stable through the 1960s. These patterns do not show the drastic erosion by vacancy that long-term data on economic decline and the 1970s studies of loft buildings imply. Indeed, the 1962 SoHo study emphasizes that at that time the vacancy rate in decent loft buildings throughout Manhattan was low (less than 2.0 percent). New construction, mostly of office buildings, meant that the supply of loft space was gradually contracting, and new waves of small manufacturing tenants continued to keep demand high.[17] During the slow economic decline of the 1960s, this market was somehow destabilized and destroyed. Job loss data indicate that the destabilizing factor was inside the market relation, on the side of demand, in the decline of small manufacturing activity. But far more significant in initiating destabilization of the loft market was the deindustrialization that was envisioned by lending institutions and urban renewal plans.

EXODUS

Banks and the state have a long historical relationship with the deindustrialization of New York. At least as early as 1910 the local patrician elite, whose old wealth was based on urban real estate, whose new wealth came from industry and railroads, and whose members predominated at the apex of the banking and legal communities, developed the first American urban plan. They planned to "upgrade" the center of the city, Manhattan, by moving manufacturing activity and working-class housing to the Outer Boroughs (especially Brooklyn, the Bronx, and Queens). This project eventually took shape in the first regional plan of 1929. The upper class was motivated socially and culturally as well as economically. They had a serious aversion to the presence of workers, primarily immigrants from

---

* This calculation of annual rent, which is commonly used in commercial, though not residential, real estate in the United States, is based on a standardization of rent in terms of dollars per square foot per year. Thus it controls for the size of the rented space. For example, a 5,000-square-foot loft that rents for $1.00 per square foot has a gross annual rent of $5,000, while a 10,000-square-foot loft that rents at the same rate pays a gross annual rent of $10,000.

Southern and Eastern Europe, so close to the heart of Manhattan's elite locale, Fifth Avenue. Both the workers and their employers came largely from the same, non-Anglo-Saxon ethnic background. Besides the cultural shock of running into these people on or near Fifth Avenue, the physical expansion of the garment industry threatened an incursion of low-rent loft buildings into prime real estate territory. The patrician elite also recognized an opportunity to profit from upgrading Manhattan. They could profit, first, as the group with the capital and the political connections that were necessary to engage in large-scale real estate development or redevelopment. In Manhattan, the upper class would be able to buy out the small owners of factories and tenements and to replace these buildings with more profitable, "better" uses: office buildings, exclusive stores, upper-class and upper-middle-class apartment houses. But the upper class would also be able to profit from speculation in land in the Outer Boroughs. There they could develop farmland for manufacturing and working-class housing.[18]

Although planning in capitalist societies lacks the direct legal force that it has in socialist states, and must therefore rely on indirect inducements through such means as zoning resolutions, the Regional Plan of 1929 worked remarkably well. Yet it could not work quickly. Not until the late 1950s was the city irreversibly committed to the deindustrialization of Manhattan. There were economic and political reasons for this delay. In the country as a whole, the Great Depression and World War II forced a long period of inactivity on the construction industry. In New York City, where the small factories and small businesses of the early industrial era continued to provide the majority of blue-collar and many white-collar jobs, the building and business owners made up an important constituency in the dominant Tammany Hall wing of the Democratic party, which ruled City Hall. As long as Tammany ruled, it was impossible to destroy completely the real estate infrastructure that supported competitive capital.

Nevertheless, even during the Depression, and often with the help of federal government funds, local elites laid the groundwork for a new post-industrial infrastructure. Investors in this infrastructure included national corporations, large commercial banks, and big real estate developers. During the 1930s and 1940s a series of highways, housing projects, and a major tunnel construction created an important perimeter around the financial capital of Wall Street in Lower Manhattan.[19] Between the late forties and the late fifties, banks made available an increased amount of investment capital in the form of mortgages and construction loans. In general, this mortgage money was responsible for the postwar boom in housing construction in the suburbs. However, it also financed urban renewal in the central cities. Despite some pressure to use this money to rebuild slum housing, funds were monopolized by business interests. The

Table 5
Mortgage Transactions on Thirty-four Loft Buildings in Lower Manhattan

| | Mortgagee or Assignee | | | |
Year	Banks	Individuals	Real estate companies, etc.	Unknown
Before 1945	8M	2M	1M	1M
1945–49		1M		
		1A		
1950–54	1M			
1955–59	2M	1A	2M	
1960–64	5M	2M		1M
		1A		
1965–69	8M	2M	7M	1M
	5A	4A	5A	
1970–74	4M	7M	10M	
	6A	5A	7A	
After 1974	4M	3M	17M	
	10A		11A	

Source: Department of Finance, New York City, 1978

Note: M indicates the number of new or multiple mortgages initiated; *A* refers to the number of mortgage assignments.

net effect of this reinvestment in the cities benefited the service sector and the patrician elite and their allies at the expense of small manufacturers.

Disinvestment and Politics

Rapkin's data on SoHo show that during the post–World War II building boom institutional investment was consistently withdrawn from industrial infrastructure. The institutions that had generated 75 percent of all the funds in first mortgages on SoHo's loft buildings before 1945 decreased their financial commitment to 51 percent in 1945–49, 36 percent in 1950–54, 17 percent in 1955–59, and 11 percent in 1960–62. These institutions included savings banks, savings and loan associations, commercial banks, trust companies, and insurance companies.[20] In my 1978 sample of thirty-four loft buildings, the mortgage histories show practically no new financing between 1945 and 1959, some pickup in activity, mostly by banks, between 1960 and 1964, and a stampede of new mortgages and mortgage assignments after 1965 (see table 5). Disinvestment in the loft buildings where small manufacturing firms were located was paralleled by disinvestment in the transportation network on which they depended. Rail freight service, in particular, could not attract the financing that was vital for modernization. When both private railroads and government agencies refused to invest in this kind of service, existing conditions rapidly deteriorated. Between 1950 and 1975, as the *New York Times* reported in

1980, rail freight shipments to the New York City region declined from 40 percent of the nation's total to 10 percent. Though about half of this loss occurred after the 1973 recession, the pattern was set much earlier. To some degree, the decline of rail freight service to Manhattan was part of a larger regional shift (to the suburbs and to the southwestern United States) and a sectoral shift (from railroads to trucking). But the net effect of disinvestment in the transportation part of the old manufacturing infrastructure was felt most keenly by New York's garment and printing industries, which rely on rail freight to distribute their products.

Certainly, banks prefer to invest capital in big loans at high interest rates, such as loans for new construction, rather than in relatively small mortgage loans on old industrial buildings. Loans on industrial buildings bear the low interest rates that are consistent with low risk. Also, mortgages are sometimes subject to state-imposed ceilings on "usurious" interest rates. Between 1953 and 1966, while mortgage money for Manhattan's loft buildings was drying up, developers had no difficulty in getting banks to finance new office construction. This was a growth period even greater than the first major "boom" in office building, which lasted from 1925 to 1933. In contrast to the earlier period, when 30,400,000 square feet of office space was constructed, the 1953–66 boom added 50,895,000 square feet to Manhattan's stock of office space.[21]

The banks' disinvestment came earlier and quicker than the city government's disengagement from a commitment to manufacturing. In 1950 a plan for revising New York City's zoning rules still gave top priority to preserving space in the center city for existing and future light manufacturing use. The reason for this consideration was jobs. The plan did acknowledge New York's preeminent role as a service-sector capital. As in most postwar American cities, more workers in New York were already employed in service jobs than in manual work. By 1948 the ratio was 1.41 white-collar workers to every blue-collar worker. But the 1950 plan envisaged that this ratio would remain constant, that is, that manufacturing jobs would hold their own. Moreover, the planners thought that the expansion of New York's major service industries — banking, wholesale trade, entertainment, and communications — had either peaked or would peak shortly. So it became more important to protect jobs by protecting the space where, realistically, more jobs could be generated: "Factory production which will give much of the basic employment needed to sustain the City's economy can be fostered, particularly in the durable lines, if sound planning and zoning supply protected sites for these purposes." The plan projected a slight increase in manufacturing space even in Manhattan's small loft buildings.[22]

By 1958, when the next plan for rezoning New York City appeared, the vocabulary, the tone, and the priorities had shifted. The 1958 Voorhees Plan focused on "blight" rather than jobs. The major perpetrators of blight were manufacturers: heavy industries that encroached upon light manufacturing areas and any industries whose mere presence constituted a nuisance in residential and commercial neighborhoods. Chiding planners and politicians for their failure to drive incompatible, or "nonconforming," uses from zones in which they did not belong, the Voorhees Plan urged, essentially, the swift enactment of the 1929 Regional Plan. With this goal in mind, zoning should be used energetically, methodically, and "scientifically" to remap New York into definitive residential, manufacturing, and commercial districts of various levels of activity. Thus zoning would also buffer residential neighborhoods from other uses. In addition, the Voorhees Plan suggested the relocation of "modern industrial plants" in vacant or other areas in the Outer Boroughs. The plan's most specific set of suggestions mandated a limited number of years for phasing nonconforming uses out of the zones where they had been permitted to locate — which indicates, perhaps, how high a priority the deindustrialization of Manhattan had assumed. "It is time for New York City to stop living in zoning's past," wrote James Felt, president of his own large real estate company, chairman of the City Planning Commission, and an ally of master planner and power broker Robert Moses, in the preface to the Voorhees Plan. "The price is too high in terms of overbuilding and congestion in some parts of the city while others are vacant and blighted." [23]

Whatever the price in the past or the future, these proposals were incorporated in the real rezoning of 1961. According to the new resolutions, heavy industry was supposed to relocate to the Outer Boroughs, and light manufacturing was shunted to the western and eastern waterfronts of Manhattan. The entire center of the island was cleared of potential industrial use by rezoning from manufacturing to various commercial designations. This meant that building owners (or developers) were given the go-ahead to convert manufacturing space in these zones to residential use. Such conversion would take place "as of right." Moreover, the rezoning actively discouraged the continued use of this space for manufacturing. If the zoning regulations were enforced, then in most areas of Lower Manhattan an expired lease on a manufacturing loft could not legally be followed by a new lease to another industrial tenant.

The 1961 rezoning is significant because it signaled the city's definitive acceptance of the elite's old plan to deindustrialize Manhattan. Yet these intentions were not immediately perceived, for at least two reasons. First, the city continued to express its commitment to maintaining the strength of the blue-collar work force. However, this commitment existed only in the realm of public statements by city officials and public reports by city agencies, such as the City Planning Commission's 1971 report, "Planning for Jobs." On this level, the rationale behind the 1961 rezoning appeared to be a desire to protect manufacturing space against an incursion by nonindustrial uses, that is, office buildings and public housing projects.[24] But in the real world where subsidies and building permits are granted, the city consistently favored new office and housing construction. The second reason that no one perceived the goal of deindustrialization behind the 1961 rezoning was related to the lack of immediate demand for land for redevelopment in Lower Manhattan's loft districts. During the 1960s, new construction in midtown Manhattan was booming. Not until the slow-down of 1970 did Lower Manhattan seem attractive to large numbers of developers. It is interesting that when I interviewed the owners of twenty small manufacturing firms in a commercial zone in the Broadway Corridor in 1977 – sixteen years after the passage of the zoning resolutions – they were not aware that theirs was *not* a manufacturing zone. Indeed, they found it hard to believe that their landlord could do an as-of-right conversion of their buildings. Although the zoning resolutions had been on the books for twenty years, the city had no reason to enforce them until real estate interests – developers and landlords – wanted that space.

The link between banking and zoning, between the withdrawal of mort-gage money from loft buildings and the outlawing of industrial activity in that space, is politics. During the 1950s the redevelopment of New York and many other urban centers in the United States was financed by an informal partnership between the federal government and local real estate developers.[25] A series of programs passed by Congress under the rubric of urban renewal channeled state subsidies to local business elites, who cleared "blighted" downtown areas of existing uses and replaced those buildings with new construction. In part, these subsidies consisted of direct grants to private builders and developers for acquiring center-city land and tearing down the buildings that stood on that land. In fact, from 1949 to 1960 *more than half* of all federal funds for urban renewal were subsidies for *buying land*. The federal government also guaranteed loans which were both generated and absorbed in the private sector. When banks showed reluctance to invest in certain high-risk projects, the federal government offered low-interest loans directly to the developers. The deals and alliances that emerged in each city's urban renewal plan were brokered by the politicians who controlled the municipal government. Although there was pressure from sources in Washington – conservative members of Con-gress and housing agencies – to create new housing, the redevelopment of downtown areas generally decimated working-class neighborhoods and the small businesses that had thrived in them.

In this context of urban renewal on a national scale and its brokerage by local political elites, a very significant shift occurred in New York City's ruling Democratic party. Between 1958 and 1961, the Reform wing of the Democratic party overthrew the machine of Tammany Hall. The Reform triumph was celebrated publicly in 1961, with the electoral victory of Mayor Robert F. Wagner. But this election did not signify the Reformers' taking control of City Hall so much as it did City Hall's taking control of the Reform movement. Since Wagner's first election as mayor in 1953 he had been allied with Carmine DeSapio, the Tammany boss. Wagner broke with DeSapio in the late fifties because of a series of disagreements over which candidates for local office the party should support. He then ran for reelection on an anti-machine platform. So the Reform movement's arrival at City Hall in 1961 was due to a personal dispute "over politics," as a couple of knowledgeable observers put it, "not principle or issues or ethics." [26]

Wagner's switch from Tammany to Reform Democratic politics had a decisive impact on the plans to deindustrialize Manhattan. Cut off from his previous base of support, he was driven to seek new political allies. While Tammany had always coexisted, albeit uneasily, with patricians — and Wagner personally symbolized this symbiosis — the elimination of formal Tammany control over the city government permitted the patrician elite to run its own candidates. It could also proceed to the final stages of its 1929 Regional Plan.

To some degree, economic conditions had inhibited the plan's realization. From the Depression through the postwar boom period, the private sector could take only incremental steps toward destabilizing the real estate infrastructure that favored small manufacturing activity. The banks did withdraw mortgage money from Lower Manhattan loft buildings and invest in new office construction. But when Wagner broke with Tammany and sought new political allies, the patrician elite got direct control of the local state power, which was crucial to redevelopment. First, they could push through the zoning revisions that widespread redevelopment required. Second, with the mayor's active brokerage, they could finance their projects with urban renewal funds. And they would no longer have to compete with Tammany clients and Tammany patrons for a share of these funds.

Redeveloping Lower Manhattan

From the late 1950s to the early 1970s the patrician elite floated several schemes to reconstruct Lower Manhattan from Wall Street up to the midtown commercial district. The wide swath down the center of Lower Manhattan was bounded by wholesale food markets and increasingly inactive piers. On the East River was the Fulton Fish Market; on the Hudson River were the egg and dairy market, Washington Market for fruits and vegetables, and the wholesale meat district. To David Rockefeller, of Wall Street's Chase Manhattan Bank, the whole was an area "largely occupied by commercial slums, right next to the greatest concentration of real estate value in the city." [27] Part of this dense network included the classic ghetto — ethnic working-class neighborhoods like Little Italy and Chinatown — that existed brick cheek by concrete jowl with solid blocks of industrial loft buildings. The only exception to this pattern was the bourgeois area of Greenwich Village, whose brownstone and brick houses had attracted middle-class residents and real-estate developers as early as the 1920s. [28]

The relatively cheap, stable prices of loft buildings and working-class housing represented an open invitation to real estate developers who were anxious to keep acquisition costs low. Long before the acceleration of job loss in Lower Manhattan's manufacturing districts implied the sale of vacant buildings, Rockefeller said, "I don't know of any other area in the city where there's as good an opportunity to expand inexpensively." [29] Rockefeller envisioned an expansion that would defend his bank's Wall Street bailiwick. In contrast to midtown, the old financial district had not benefited from the boom in new office construction. Many prestigious corporate tenants (including both company headquarters and law firms) had moved uptown, causing property values to fall and vacancies to rise in the Wall Street area. Because the Rockefellers owned a considerable amount of property in Wall Street, they stood to lose by these developments. They also lost prestige because they refused to leave the area — especially after their rival, Citibank, moved uptown.

To promote a redevelopment scheme that would bolster these interests, David Rockefeller formed a typically American civic group of big businessmen with patrician and political connections. This group, the Downtown-Lower Manhattan Association, was established in 1956. Over the next fifteen years, under Rockefeller's chairmanship, the DLMA initiated and lobbied for a series of development projects that together comprised a Lower Manhattan Plan. The plan that the DLMA presented in 1965 offered a "new town," in effect, for members of a financial and professional elite who would both work and live in the Wall Street area. At its most ambitious, the Lower Manhattan Plan called for the destruction of the "commercial slums" that David Rockefeller disliked and their replacement with new office buildings and new upper-class and upper-middle-class apartment houses. A great new demand for this type of housing would be met by grandiose technology — involving the building of high-rise apartment houses, joined by plazas and walkways above street level, on landfill in the East and Hudson rivers. "Manhattan Landing" would be built to the east, "Battery Park City" to the west. A giant office building complex (the World Trade Center) would provide places of work for the new residents, while commuters could drive right in on a new Lower Manhattan expressway that would link directly to the northern suburbs (through the East River Drive) and the western suburbs (through the West Side Highway). This expressway, which would be built across Manhattan, from river to river, along a widened Broome Street, would seal off the enclave of Lower Manhattan from the rest of the island. Just north of the expressway, on the site of the manufacturing district of SoHo, a large, middle-income housing project would provide further insulation. An additional use for the land that could be cleared by tearing down loft buildings in SoHo would be offered by a sports stadium. As the *pièce de résistance* of the plan, at least in its earliest form, the housing project north of Broome Street would be financed by Title I urban renewal funds from the federal government.[30]

The Lower Manhattan Plan really represented an accretion of projects that were presented to the public bit by bit over a period of years. Although few of these projects were built during Wagner's remaining term in office, plans for redevelopment accelerated under the leadership of Wagner's successor, Reform mayor and patrician attorney John V. Lindsay. The core of the plan — the office construction, which was apparently closest to David Rockefeller's heart — was joined with the luxury housing that Robert Moses and others favored. Together, the new offices and housing comprised the plan that was accepted by Lindsay's new City Planning Commission in the mid-1960s. But the Lower Manhattan Expressway dated back to a project of Moses's from 1940. Brooklyn Bridge South, a middle-income housing project in the general eastern area, was announced by Moses in 1959. The World Trade Center, which was not built until the mid-1970s, was proposed in 1960. The Title I housing project that was to be built on the site of SoHo died a slow death between 1963 and 1965, and the plans for a sports stadium and a Lower Manhattan expressway rose and fell from 1961 to 1971. "Battery Park City," which was announced in 1969, will be built during the 1980s. "Manhattan Landing," a joint project of David Rockefeller and Mayor Lindsay, was unveiled with much publicity in 1972 but never won acceptance. By 1980 it was replaced with plans for a South Street Seaport marketplace and tourist center.

It proved impossible to realize the Lower Manhattan Plan as a whole. Difficulties of financing its various elements, as well as competition for the direct federal funds on which it relied, took their toll. Political opposition to the construction plans of the Rockefellers — including, by the mid-1960s, David's brother Nelson as governor of New York State — also had some effect. This opposition was intensified by Governor Rockefeller's creation and utilization of supra-legislative institutions, such as the financing structure of the Urban Development Corporation and the administration of the New York-New Jersey Port Authority, to support redevelopment plans. Though both Rockefellers, Mayor Lindsay, Robert Moses, and the building trades unions tried to circumvent political opposition to the plan, they were finally defeated by a variety of other constituencies and other interests.

First, ghetto unrest in the mid-1960s called attention to a constituency of the urban poor that competed with middle- and upper-income projects for each city's quota of federal funds. As Rapkin had calculated in 1962, building a middle-income housing project on the site of SoHo would use up all the Title I funds that were allocated to New York City for a whole year.[31] This would leave no money for low-income housing. Even more than other mayors, Lindsay was highly sensitive to votes — as well as violence — in the ghettos. Second, a group of opponents to the Lower Manhattan Plan arose among Lindsay's Reform constituents. Middle-class homeowners in the Greenwich Village area adjacent to SoHo — who were, in many cases, also active in the Village's Reform Democratic organization — expressed vociferous opposition to the slash-and-burn school of urban clearance and redevelopment. These activists mobilized behind the Jane Jacobs credo of neighborhood and building preservation.

A third source of opposition to the Lower Manhattan Plan came from the Tammany officials who had maintained their places in the city administration, together with some traditionally influential blue-collar labor unions. They proposed an alternative East River Development Plan. This plan, which was formally put forward by the city's Department of Marine and Aviation and supported by the International Longshoremen's Association, involved filling in part of the Hudson River. In addition, the printing industry, which had superseded the port in the city's economy, pressed for commercial renovation of its facilities along the Lower West Side. That suggestion garnered some support from Mayor Wagner, who opposed the longshoremen's plan. However, Wagner's successor, Mayor Lindsay, supported office construction over renovation of the printing plants. A final constituency in the political struggles over the Lower Manhattan Plan emerged gradually during the 1960s, and partially through the state's patronage. This was a constituency devoted to the arts and to historic preservation. Uniting artists, patricians, and an educated part of the middle class, the group opposed large-scale redevelopment, urban expressways, and tearing down of old buildings.

But during the 1960s no one could have foreseen that such politicking would halt the Lower Manhattan Plan. Understandably, the commitment to these projects on the part of both the state and the private sector — with all the fanfare and clout attendant on two Reform mayors, Wagner and Lindsay, and two Rockefellers, David and Nelson — caused great uncertainty among the owners and tenants of Lower Manhattan loft buildings. For years mortgage money had been tight. If the Lower Manhattan Plan were realized, then the city administration would seize the land and the buildings on the land, and sell the development rights to real estate developers at a low price. Tenants would be dislocated; owners would be displaced. The immediate result was a drastic destabilization of the loft market in terms of both tenancy and ownership.

After years of inactivity, loft building owners started to try to get out of the market and speculators or investors tried to get in. Mortgage transactions in my sample of thirty-four loft buildings show an abrupt increase in the middle of the 1960s, just when the Lower Manhattan Plan was announced (see table 5). Between 1960 and 1964 mortgage activity on these

Table 6
Turnover of Manufacturing Tenants in Lower Manhattan Loft Buildings, 1963–78

	1963–68	1968–73	1973–78
A. Sample as a whole			
Number of buildings	33	33	38
Number of shifts out	254	241	288
Average shifts out	44.4%	49.0%	58.0%
	Percentage of manufacturing tenants' shifts out		
B. By size (Lower Fifth Avenue and Flower Market areas only)			
Over 8,000 sq. ft. ($n=4$)	42.5%	47.0%	56.0%
4,000–5,000 sq. ft. ($n=10$)	41.2	42.5	67.1
2,000–3,000 sq. ft. ($n=8$)	47.0	64.0	47.0
	Percentage of manufacturing tenants' shifts out		
C. By location			
Lower Fifth Avenue ($n=13$)	44.0%	44.3%	63.1%
Flower Market ($n=9$)	42.6	60.1	50.0
SoHo ($n=5$ in 1963–68 and 1968–73, $n=7$ in 1973–78)	30.2	48.6	72.7
NoHo and Greenwich Village ($n=6$ in 1963–68 and 1968–73, $n=9$ in 1973–78)	43.2	42.0	46.7
Total Broadway Corridor, i.e., SoHo, NoHo, and Greenwich Village ($n=11$ in 1963–68 and 1968–73, $n=16$ in 1973–78)	36.7	45.3	59.7

Source: Reverse Telephone Books, Manhattan, 1963, 1968, 1973, 1978

buildings began to pick up to pre-1945 levels. Between 1965 and 1969 the number of new mortgages and mortgage assignments rose dramatically. The activity continued into the 1970s, with some decline in the role of banks, probably due to a general slowdown in the real estate sector, and an increasing development on the part of individual investors.

Although vacancies did not necessarily increase in the same proportions as mortgage activity, the turnover of tenants did. Shifts of manufacturing tenants out of the buildings in this sample increased in the 1968–73 period, particularly in SoHo, the sample area most immediately affected by the Lower Manhattan Plan. The average rate of shifts by manufacturing tenants out of these buildings between 1963 and 1968 was 44.4 percent (see table 6). In 1968–73 this rate increased to 49.0 percent. By 1973–78, when the residential market for these lofts was firmly established, the shift rate of *manufacturers out* was up to 58.0 percent.

Possibly some of the increase in turnover was due to the accelerated job loss in manufacturing after 1973. However, SoHo was destabilized first and fastest of the three manufacturing neighborhoods in the sample. If we consider that the occupancy of smaller lofts is problematic because their occupants are smaller, and therefore less viable, manufacturers, then we do indeed find that the market in the smallest loft buildings (between 2,000 and 3,000 square feet per floor) was destabilized first. But even the relative stability of tenancy in the larger lofts was destroyed during the 1973–78 period. This suggests that in addition to the economic troubles of small manufacturers, real estate speculation in the loft market accelerated the destabilization.

Two points about the destabilization of the loft market are significant: the rapidity of destabilization, once it began, and the fact that changes in ownership (1965–69) preceded fluctuations in tenancy (1968–73). The sequence and timing of these changes imply the denouement of a long-term process rather than the onset of a sudden crisis. Although job loss in manufacturing accelerated *after 1973,* the loft market had *already* been destabilized. It was destabilized by the historical devalorization of New York's industrial infrastructure — the capital the loft buildings represent — and the repeated onslaught on this infrastructure by members of the patrician elite and their allies in early Progressive and modern Reform city administrations.

The particularly early and rapid destabilization of the loft market in SoHo, as distinct from other industrial areas, bears witness to three different developments of the 1960s. First, the devalorized area's proximity to Wall Street and to Greenwich Village made it susceptible to "colonization" by both the formal projects of financiers and developers and the informal moves of artists. While David Rockefeller and the DLMA were drawing up plans for SoHo, artists were establishing a beachhead there by moving into lofts. Second, by the latter half of the 1960s new cultural and aesthetic values forced a revision of public attitudes toward SoHo's loft buildings. Previously considered "Hell's Hundred Acres" — because of several large fires there — or "the Wastelands of New York City" — in a 1962 planning study that recommended urban renewal — by 1970 the five hundred loft buildings of the *South Ho*uston Industrial area emerged as SoHo, "one of the few concentrated, homogeneous groups of a particularly important and handsome development of protomodern buildings — the cast-iron fronted commercial construction of the nineteenth century." [32]

In this emanation, the district attracted the attention of some patrician types whose civic duties included patronage of urban beautification schemes. The historic link between the typical upper-class civic association and urban renewal now took the form of an interest in "historic preservation" of architecturally worthy old buildings. Interestingly enough, the cast-iron buildings that were supposed to be preserved stood where upper-class businessmen's plans aimed at destruction. The incongruity between pet projects of basically the same patrician group suggested, as usual among the upper class, an eventual marriage of convenience. In this case, philanthropic aesthetics would be wed to real estate economics.* Preserving cast-iron buildings was fine. In a world of finite resources and increasingly perishable materials, a historic monument can only increase in value. But in the meantime, the patricians' sensibility to the arts fed into a third development of the 1960s: the discovery of the social power of New York artists.

To some degree, this power was self-generated. The artistic success of the New York School of Abstract Expressionism in the 1940s and 1950s, followed by the even greater commercial success of artists like Frank Stella, Claes Oldenburg, and eventually Robert Rauschenberg, as well as the market-oriented pop artists of the early 1960s, drew world attention to New York as a center of artistic creation. Publicity in turn stimulated expectations of public support for the arts. In the social context of the early 1960s, artists joined other groups in pressing their demands for public support on the state. The Artists' Tenants' Association (ATA), which was formed by five hundred petition-signers, "most of them vanguard artists," in 1960–61, became the vocal representative of a growing and increasingly self-conscious arts community. Significantly, ATA's charter-petition originated in a dispute over the right of artists to live in lofts, that is, to use as their studio-residences lofts in buildings that were not zoned for residential use.

The dispute began in a wave of evictions (more than a hundred, according to an ATA representative at the time) which were related to fire hazards rather than zoning violations. Apparently, a series of fires in loft buildings had aroused the anxiety of the Fire Department (and elected officials) that in the event of a serious conflagration, fire fighters would be unable either to find or to save artists who might live in a burning building. This worry led the Fire Department to press their colleagues in the Buildings Department, which bore responsibility for enforcing both zoning resolutions and building codes, to start eviction proceedings against artist-residents. Contemporary accounts estimated that from five thousand to seven thousand artists were living and working in lofts that from the outside were indistinguishable from ordinary manufacturing lofts. So there was no way for fire fighters, especially at night, to locate artist-residents. In this context, ATA organized to protect the artists' right *as artists* to violate the zoning regulations. During the summer of 1961 ATA threatened to boycott all art exhibitions in the city, from the beginning of

---

* In terms of individual unions, it is interesting that at the end of the 1960s David Rockefeller was chairman of both the DLMA and the board of trustees of the Museum of Modern Art.

the important fall season, unless the city administration canceled its eviction policy.

Media coverage was sympathetic to the artists. Moreover, the timing of their action was politically opportune. It was in the fall of 1961 that Mayor Wagner ran for reelection as a Reform candidate. In his search for new allies and responsive constituencies to replace the lower-middle-class and working-class Tammany Democrats, Wagner discovered the artists. Although they were not a numerous constituency, artists were important symbols of Wagner's switch to Reform. They also offered a means of reaching and pacifying two larger, politically significant constituencies: the patrician reformers like Mrs. Eleanor Roosevelt and Senator Herbert Lehman whose backing was still essential in New York State politics, and the middle-class citizens who became active in local Reform clubs (notably, the Village Independent Democrats) in the late fifties and early sixties. Meeting with ATA representatives over the loft-eviction dispute, Wagner said, "The artist working in New York is assured of the city's continuing interest in his welfare and his work." Furthermore, the city administration and ATA negotiated an agreement that legitimized the artists' use of lofts as studio-residences. Use of the lofts for living only (rather than living and working) was not permitted. In return for compliance with certain safety and registration regulations,* artists now had the right — as artists — to compete with small manufacturers for loft space at relatively cheap rents.

Three years later, artists claimed that the city administration was harassing them again. They resented the "bureaucratic" restrictions of the certification procedure by which artists were granted individual entitlement to live in lofts. They complained about a shortage in loft space because the city administration would not allow them to live in lofts in areas outside Lower Manhattan. There was also some question about the continued eviction of artists from their lofts.

Nevertheless, the legitimization, through an exercise of state power, of the artists' right to live in manufacturing lofts set an important precedent. For the artists themselves this legitimization represented the right to protected space. Though dispersed from block to block, their lofts provided a basis for common identification and a community of interests, and thus also for further political mobilization. ATA was an obvious forerunner, for example, of Artists Against the Expressway, a group formed in 1969, and the SoHo Artists' Tenants' Association. The indirect support of the arts which the state offered through protected access to loft space presaged the direct support of arts production in the mid- to late 1960s.

---

* Artists had to meet certain building specifications, register their residence with the Buildings Department, and alert the Fire Department to their presence by posting a special sign on the building's exterior — "Artist in Residence" (A.I.R.).

But from the perspective of long-term deindustrialization, the artists' protected entry into manufacturing zones signified an incursion, with the state's blessing, into space that had previously been reserved for manufacturers. At the time, people thought that the battle lines were drawn between, on the one side, artists, humanists, and "the people," and, on the other side, the power structure – the city government, Wall Street tycoons, and big real-estate developers – that wanted to tear down Lower Manhattan. Little did they realize that in this struggle artists represented both a constituency and a surrogate. Eventually, the loft buildings themselves, rather than the land they stood on, emerged as a contested terrain.

LEVITICUS

Literally, state intervention in struggles over urban terrain involves making laws about the proper use of space. Zoning is perhaps the best-known type of such legislation. It mandates which uses can and cannot take place in particular areas of the city. Speaking simply, there are zones for residence, commerce (retail stores and offices), light manufacturing, and heavy manufacturing and some zones where specific mixed uses are permitted. The criteria for dividing zones may be quite complex and sometimes even contradictory. The apparent irrationality of these criteria shows, for example, in Manhattan's Lower Fifth Avenue area (between Fourteenth and Twenty-third streets), where the dividing line between various subcategories of manufacturing and commercial zones runs between and around buildings rather than between whole blocks or districts. Nevertheless, on a more basic level, the rationale of zoning practices conforms to the logic of capital accumulation. The advantage of zoning over unregulated land use is that it minimizes the risk that real estate investment will be threatened by the proximity of value-decreasing uses.[33]

In addition to zoning, building codes specify the proper use of space according to characteristics of the building or of the occupants. Building codes categorize apartment houses (or "multiple dwellings"), single- and two-family houses, and various types of commercial and industrial facilities. They also dictate the standards for fire protection, general safety, hygiene, and public order to which builders, landlords, and occupants must adhere. Besides zoning and building codes, which directly regulate the use of space, other types of legislation influence decisions over how space is used by affecting the financial benefits that can be derived from various possible uses. Rent controls are a common example of how laws can affect the rate of return on investment in real estate. The existence of rent controls on particular types of buildings influences the owner's or the builder's decision about what sort of use will be most profitable. Also influential on such decisions are tax code regulations that make it advantageous to invest capital in one kind of real estate or another – because of depreciation rates, tax deductions, and preferential treatment for home-ownership, for example. Since the 1970s changes in the federal tax code have favored historic landmarks, national parks, and wildlife sanctuaries.

Between 1961 and 1976 changes in zoning resolutions, building codes, and other laws on the local level, in New York City and New York State, enhanced the embryonic market in converted lofts (see table 7).[34] We have already seen how the rezoning process of the late fifties and early sixties aimed at the elimination of manufacturing use in the central swath of Lower Manhattan and how that process fit the long-range calculations of the patrician elite, the banks, and big real estate developers. We have noted the synchronization of rezoning with the restructuring of political alliances. But the state's abandonment of small manufacturers was final-ized with changes in the building codes and other laws. Such legislation was enacted even as job loss in the urban center proliferated.

Rents and Codes

Least noticed but indicative of these changes was the expiration, rather than the enactment, of a law. In 1962 two rent-control-type laws, dating from the post–World War II inflation period, which had established a "fair rental" price on all nonresidential space in New York City expired. This marked the end of an attempt at commercial rent stabilization. Although these laws had always been considered temporary expedients, there seems to have been no political struggle over the possibility of renew-ing them in 1962. The Reform Democrats and Mayor Wagner certainly did not regard this as an issue. Since vacancy rates in Manhattan loft buildings were low at the time, the lapsing of commercial rent-control-type laws indicates how little state support small manufacturers could command.*

In 1964, with the destabilization of the market in manufacturing lofts and the political mobilization of New York artists, the New York State Legislature passed an amendment to the Multiple Dwelling Law known as Article 7-B. This amendment entitled artists – primarily painters and sculptors – and their families to rent manufacturing lofts and commercial spaces for combined living and studio use. In the law itself, the reason for legitimizing this zoning violation referred to the high cost of urban land (that is, rents) and the low means of artists, the artists' need for large work-ing spaces, and the social value that big cities derive from concentrations of artistic production: "The cultural life of cities of more than one million persons within this state and of the state as a whole is enhanced by the residence in such cities of large numbers of persons regularly engaged in the visual fine arts." To qualify for this entitlement, artists had to be cer-tified as "regularly engaged in the visual fine arts, such as painting and

---

* This contrasts with the anachronistic but historically based politics of a city such as Paris, where the *petits commerçants* do enjoy rent control and relocation rights.

Table 7
Local Laws Affecting the Formation of the Loft Market, 1961–76

Zoning resolutions	Building codes	Other laws
1961 Rezoning of New York City		
		1962 End of rent stabilization on commercial property in New York City
	1964 Article 7-B (New York State): legalization of visual artists' residential use of lofts	
		1965 Landmarks Preservation Law passed (New York City Administrative Code)
	1968 Amendment to Article 7-B: expansion of artists' category to include performing and creative artists	
1971 Creation of artists' district within SoHo manufacturing zone	1971 Amendment to Article 7-B: eased building restrictions for lofts in converted buildings; simplified artists' certification procedure	
		1973 Designation of SoHo as historic district (Landmarks Preservation Law)
		1975 Revision of J-51 program to provide tax benefits for large-scale residential conversion (New York City Administrative Code)
1976 Expansion of artists' district in SoHo; legalization of artists' residential conversions in NoHo		
Creation of TriBeCa, legalizing residential conversion for artists and non-artists		

sculpture, on a professional fine arts basis and so certified by an art academy, association or society." The law was supposed to expire in 1968, but any artist's living and working in a loft — or the mere application for a living loft — under Article 7-B would constitute an important precedent. Once any loft in a building was "converted" in this way, the building as a whole could be kept in residential use, probably at somewhat higher rents, rather than reverting to manufacturing use. Obviously, this had a further destabilizing effect on the loft market.

Instead of expiring in 1968, Article 7-B was amended to increase the categories of artist who could apply. Persons who were "regularly engaged . . . in the performing or creative arts, including choreography and filmmaking, or in the composition of music on a professional basis" were now entitled to the same protected access to manufacturing loft space as were painters and sculptors. As in the original Article 7-B, the same grounds justified their competitive advantage. On the one hand, artists had no money; on the other hand, they brought value to the city and the state.

Three years later, another amendment facilitated the artists' and building owners' compliance with the provisions of the law. For owners, first, and artist-tenants, second, the revised Article 7-B lowered the standards by which loft buildings could be occupied for residential use below those of ordinary apartment houses. Also, the 1971 amendment made certification as a bona fide artist more subjective and more easily available. The New York City Department of Cultural Affairs took over the major responsibility for certification, and the criteria now included only need for space and commitment to art, and not professional competence or occupational definition.

New Zones

At the same time, the New York City Board of Estimate passed a zoning resolution that legalized artists' joint living and working lofts in the manufacturing zone of SoHo. Artists could legally convert lofts in buildings smaller than 3,600 square feet. (This figure refers to lot size; the actual interior dimensions would be somewhat smaller.) This limitation was intended to protect access to loft space for the larger, supposedly financially more viable manufacturers. Similarly, living lofts smaller than 1,200 square feet would not be considered legal. This provision was intended to outlaw real estate developers' subdividing lofts into studio apartments for non-artists. Artists who had already converted larger lofts or smaller parts of lofts in SoHo were graced by a "grandfather clause" that permitted them to consider such spaces legal. Even before this resolution was passed, some artists and small real estate developers had bought buildings and converted them entirely to living lofts. The 1971 zoning resolution legalized these buildings for residential use.*

In 1976 the Board of Estimate approved two new zoning resolutions

---

* An additional complication in this zoning resolution distinguishes between three different types of light manufacturing districts within SoHo, with some difference regarding exceptions to the upper and lower size limits for legal living lofts.

that increased artists' protected access to manufacturing loft space in SoHo and in the area immediately *N*orth of *Ho*uston Street, between SoHo and Greenwich Village, which took on the acronym NoHo. The lot size of buildings where loft living was now legal was extended to 5,000 square feet. This extension probably legalized artists' residence in a quarter to a half of all the buildings in SoHo. Protected access to loft space for manufacturers was limited to the Broadway Corridor, whose frontage was considered most attractive to manufacturing tenants. Protected space for manufacturing and commercial tenants was also retained on the ground floor of loft buildings, which was considered most convenient for loading and unloading shipments. In these two places the space could not be converted to residential use. However, the law did provide for possible exceptions. The building owners could apply for a waiver from this provision, the best grounds for such a waiver being "financial hardship." In practice, these applications were granted if the owner (who by this time was either a landlord or a cooperative of resident owner-occupiers) demonstrated that he/she/it had sought a manufacturing or commercial tenant but could not find one who would pay the rent that was necessary for "carrying" that floor according to the building's financial obligations.

Also in 1976, the Board of Estimate approved the creation of yet another acronymic district for loft living — TriBeCa — a *tri*angular area *be*low *Ca*nal Street, just north of the Wall Street financial center. The provisions that legalized certain types and sizes of buildings for loft living in TriBeCa are more complicated than those for SoHo and NoHo, but the point of the law is simpler and more dramatic. Anyone, artist or non-artist, can legally convert a loft to residential use in this district. Now called "loft dwellings," living lofts in TriBeCa must be clearly distinguishable from ordinary apartments. They cannot be smaller than 1,000 square feet, and they must feature relatively open, that is, unenclosed space. Nevertheless, the legitimization of living lofts through progressive zoning resolutions and changes in the building code, as well as the standardization of converted loft space on the model of typical dwelling units, suggests that by the mid-1970s the real estate market in residential lofts was firmly established.

Two additional laws had an effect on the new loft market by increasing the financial benefits of real estate investment in loft conversions. The first law had to do with historic preservation, and the second with tax abatements for residential conversion. First, the city administration declared SoHo a historic landmark district in 1973. The law that enabled the city to do this was fairly recent. Passed in 1965, under pressure from historic preservationists, the law set up a public Landmarks Preservation Commission, which had the power to bar exterior renovations on buildings in whole districts that were designated as having "special character or special historical or aesthetic interest or value." From 1965 on, the Cast Iron district in the middle of SoHo was recognized as having such a character, at least by cognoscenti though not by real estate developers. When a developer's plan to build the sports stadium fell through in 1971, pressure mounted to declare SoHo a landmark district. Once the designation passed, in 1973, it created a monopoly effect on rents. But it also had a "spillover" effect on the market value of living lofts in other neighborhoods. Soon after SoHo's architecture was recognized as "historic," the rents and sale prices of lofts in less distinguished buildings and neighborhoods also rose.*

Tax Incentives

When J-51 was amended after lobbying by developers in 1975, its meaning was changed to benefit professional developers rather than owner-occupiers. As it was first passed in 1954, the law was intended to correct the worst abuses of cold-water flats. By extending tax benefits to small property-owners who upgraded the apartments that they rented out in their own homes, the city government hoped to encourage them to bring their property up to "Class A" housing standards. In the 1975 revision, the benefits reflected a new market situation. Though they were still geared to the production of rental housing, they were directed at conversions rather than upgrading, and big buildings instead of small ones. According to a city housing administrator who drafted the new law, the purpose of rewriting it was to systematize the various uses of the rehabilitation program that had developed over the previous twenty years. But this reason obscures the change in the law's orientation and the resulting new uses to which the law was put. Because J-51 now covered the "gut rehabilitation" that residential conversion of old factories required, the major beneficiaries, in terms of dollar amounts, were large developers. They covered the costs of creating the standard apartments (with enclosed bedrooms, bathrooms, and kitchens) that J-51 mandated with bank loans. However, getting a bank loan to cover improvements on rental property was not so easy for an owner-occupier. Indeed, in terms of the money that they have to lay out in costs in order to qualify for an eventual tax abatement and exemption, small owners pay much more, proportionately, than large developers. Moreover, J-51 gave the developers who could generate the capital for a complete residential conversion and gut "rehab" an advantage over the small investors who could not. The general effects of J-51 on the loft market were, first, to insert a new category of loft-apartments at typical upper-middle-income rents beside the more marginal submarket of convert-it-yourself loft space and, second, to spread residential conversion into neighborhoods where the zoning resolutions of 1971 and 1976 did not permit loft living.

---

* The whole topic of the social and economic costs and benefits of historic preservation is now recognized as problematic.

Despite some political struggles in 1978 and 1981 over the renewal of J-51 by the City Council, state power on the local level remained firmly committed to residential conversion. In some ways, this commitment was presented to the public as support for housing opportunities, and thus for middle-class housing consumers. But in reality, the city government's commitment to housing represented the reverse of its support for deindustrialization. This type of housing carried with it support for real estate developers and the remaking of Lower Manhattan as a white-collar enclave. At the same time, in the midst of the city's fiscal crisis, local elected officials continued to express pious concern about job loss. This concern did not stimulate any attempt to make new political alliances with the small manufacturers who still remained in business. By the early 1980s, when a partial rezoning of Manhattan's loft districts gave the city government an opportunity to defend both manufacturing and development, many factories and small businesses had already been displaced by residential conversions. The mechanisms that were established to aid the remaining industrial and commercial tenants — primarily financial and spatial compensation — did not make up for the years when small manufacturers complained of being mistreated by city administrators who worked in offices concerned with economic development. Furthermore, under no pressure from the state, banks ignored the possibility of granting federally guaranteed, small-business loans.[35]

The history of state intervention in the loft market from 1961 to 1976 does not encourage the illusion that state power will be used, in our time, to aid competitive capital over monopoly capital, or manufacturers rather than financiers and developers. Such state laws as are enacted still tend to support capital mobility — with the hope that labor will follow the flight of jobs. Though the job losses that are connected with regional deindustrialization are generated independently of real estate development, the decisions of manufacturers, big investors, and politicians are interconnected. Thus any analysis of deindustrialization and reindustrialization must take account of the social class whose fortunes are founded on real property, as well as industrial and financial capitalists and the state. Similarly, the interaction of various social classes over particular parts of the urban terrain cannot be considered superficially as class struggles between obvious antagonists. Such struggles have unanticipated consequences. They also set precedents by which seemingly uninvolved contestants can profit. In the destabilization and re-creation of the loft market, as in the world of work, these struggles goad into competition groups that are powerless against the larger forces of society. They also activate the cultural and aesthetic values that shape these groups' demands. Without the changes in values of the 1960s, living lofts could have become neither a real estate market nor a terrain of urban conflict.

3

THE CREATION OF A "LOFT LIFESTYLE"

Until the 1970s, living in a loft was considered neither chic nor comfortable – if the possibility was considered at all. Making a home in a factory district clearly contradicted the dominant middle-class ideas of "home" and "factory," as well as the separate environments of family and work on which these ideas were based. Since the 1950s, suburbia had so dominated popular images of the American home that it was almost impossible to imagine how anyone could conceive the desire to move downtown into a former sweatshop or printing plant. Yet the real estate market in living lofts that has developed over the past ten years could not have begun without such a desire, at least on the part of a few people. The market could not have grown so fast – in the process, transforming lofts from old factory spaces into hot commodities – if this peculiar desire had not also struck the imagination of more people in cities all over the country. Whether they actually bedded down among the printing presses or merely accepted loft living as a possible residential style, people began to find the notion of living in a loft attractive. This happened because of two changes that occurred in the 1960s: a change in lofts and a change in middle-class patterns of consumption.

On the one hand, the movement of industry and investment out of old manufacturing centers made larger, more impressive lofts available for alternate uses. Until that point, lofts that had been used for living – mostly by artists who were "living poor" – were fairly small, often unheated upper floors of two- and three-story storefronts, and distinctly uncomfortable. On the other hand, an increasing number of middle-class people moved into certain cultural patterns, particularly an active appreciation of "the arts" and historic preservation, which had previously been upper-class domains. Their growing identification with fine arts production and fine old buildings led them first to try to protect space for artists and historic preservation and then to appropriate this space — which was often in loft buildings — for themselves. In this process, art and historic preservation took on a broader meaning. They became both more commercial and less elitist.

The changing appreciation of old loft buildings also reflects a deeper preoccupation with space and time. A sense that the great industrial age has ended creates melancholy over the machines and the factories of the past. Certainly such sentiments are aroused only at the end of an era, or with a loss of function. As a perceptive observer of "eccentric spaces" points out, "We visit the docks in London but not in Rotterdam because commerce is romantic only when it has vanished." [1] Only people who do not know the steam and sweat of a real factory can find industrial space romantic or interesting. But in many ways industrial spaces are more interesting than "post-industrial" offices, apartment houses, and shopping centers. Their structure has both a solidity and a gracefulness that suggest a time when form still identified "place" rather than "function." Their façades are often adorned with archaic emblems and sculpture, apparently showing the equally archaic skills of masons and carvers. Yet this ornamentation is a conceit of nineteenth-century technology. The façades of many loft buildings that were constructed between 1820 and 1880 were cast in standardized iron parts that could be ordered from a catalogue, mounted, and taken apart at will. Ironically, the mass production of an earlier industrial era looks to our eyes like individuality.

During the 1960s a consensus slowly grew that such buildings should not be torn down to make room for new, high-rise construction that bore little relation to the area or the people around it. Though far from the majority view, this line of thought spread from Jane Jacobs's somewhat subversive ideas about neighborhood preservation and urban vitality — which have sold more than a quarter-million copies of her 1961 book — to highly commercial renovations like San Francisco's Ghirardelli Square, Boston's Faneuil Hall, and the New York artists' district of SoHo. An appreciation of "small" and "old," instead of "large" and "new," also appealed to the sixties' liberal social conscience. In America's inner cities, the wholesale destruction of tenements for the sake of urban renewal during the fifties and early sixties gave rise to protest and backlash. Some people blamed the destabilization of low-rent ghetto communities, in part, for the riots of the mid- to late sixties. Several years before, sociologists had called attention to the good social relations between people who live in such communities, in articles like "Some Sources of Satisfaction in a Residential Slum" and Herbert Gans's elegy on Boston's Italian West End, *The Urban Villagers.* Preserving rather than destroying city neighborhoods took on a broader meaning in the 1970s because of the growing concern with the earth's ecology. Even in the early sixties the impending or real demolition of distinguished old buildings — like Pennsylvania Station in

New York City — threatened people with a sense of irreparable loss. Like the recyling of scarce resources, the adaptive re-use of such buildings eventually attracted greater public support.[2]

In this context, loft living is more significant than the relatively small number of SoHos or loft dwellers implies. It marks a different perception of space and time and a new relation between art and industry. In a narrower sense, the market in living lofts that developed after 1970 also sells the social and cultural values of the 1960s to middle-class consumers of the seventies and eighties. But are living lofts really such a radical departure from conventional housing? Although loft living seems to reject suburbia and all it represents, living lofts have some of the same spatial values as a typical suburban home, particularly a preference for lots of air, light, and open space. Certainly lofts are located on busy city streets rather than grassy plots, but inside, a loft has an air of detachment from the city.

This suggests that loft living is appealing, in part, because it is paradoxical. The incongruity of living in a factory does not cease to surprise us. From the outside, of course, a loft building looks like a factory, but inside, we find a home. Although homes are considered private space, the openness of a loft makes it a public space. Lofts are also predominantly homes for non-child-centered households — for single persons and couples without children. Yet the association between loft living and a home-oriented interest in stylish cuisine and décor promotes a new cult of domesticity. Because it represents both home and work, hedonism and domesticity, and public and private space, loft living is paradoxical. Its success in the urban housing market demonstrates that at this time paradox sells.

Discussing the lure of any market is a tricky matter. Consumers' desires are so shaped by the commodities that are available, as well as by image-making and status-seeking, that considering them may be almost irrelevant. The shrinking size of typical new apartments and the mass media's privileged treatment of loft living certainly influenced the market in living lofts. Yet it is a fact that this market did not exist in any significant measure before 1971. Since that time, "living lofts" has become a household word in cities of the United States and Western Europe, and loft living has been elevated to a fashionable residential style. To some degree, deciding to live in a loft may reflect a fairly narrow economic choice. Particularly for artists who want a large space at a cheap rent, renting a loft amid the flotsam and jetsam of urban commerce may be just a question of marginal utility. But many people choose to live in a loft because the space itself appeals to them. On the one hand, they like the giant scale or the "raw," unfinished quality of a loft. On the other hand, they identify with the sense of adventure or the artists' ambiance which still clings to living in a loft neighborhood. To determine why these people want to live in lofts involves more subtle issues than mere supply and demand. Not only have lofts changed over the past thirty years but so have cultural and aesthetic standards.

FROM "LIVING POOR" TO LUXURY

In 1953, New York artist Robert Rauschenberg returned from a trip to Europe and, practically penniless, looked for a place to live. "With his customary good luck," art writer Calvin Tompkins says, Rauschenberg "found a loft on Fulton Street, near the fish market, a big attic space with twenty-foot ceilings but no heat or running water; the rent was fifteen dollars a month, but he talked the landlord into letting him have it for ten. A hose and bucket in the back yard served as his basin, and he bathed at friends' apartments, sometimes surreptitiously, asking to use the bathroom and taking a lightning shower at the same time." Ten years later, when the Jewish Museum on Fifth Avenue organized the first major retrospective exhibition of his work, Rauschenberg was living and working in another loft farther uptown, on the edge of Greenwich Village. Tompkins reports that when he visited Rauschenberg there,

> the doors of the freight elevator opened directly into Rauschenberg's loft. . . . Sam, the taciturn black superintendent who operated the lift during the day, had agreed to let Rauschenberg have the key after 6 P.M., so he could get up and down. . . . The loft was about a hundred feet long by thirty wide. A row of supporting columns ran down the middle, but otherwise it was clear, unobstructed space. Tall, grimy windows let in the distinctively white light of downtown New York — also the roar of trucks on Broadway. Near the windows was a big, ramshackle wire cage containing a pair of kinkajous. . . . Beyond the cage stood a group of large objects — a car door, a window frame, a roof ventilator mounted on wheels — components of an unfinished five-part sculpture. . . . Paintings, combines, and sculptures from the recently concluded Jewish Museum retrospective were stacked against the wall farther along. There was a big table in the middle of the room, its surface cluttered with magazines, pictures clipped from magazines, felt pens and pencils, and tubes of paint and other materials. Toward the back of the room, a counter projecting from the end wall formed an alcove for the refrigerator, the electric stove, and the bed — a mattress laid on the floor. All the rest of the loft was work space.[3]

In 1960, Rauschenberg's slightly younger contemporary, artist James Rosenquist, rented a studio for fifty dollars a month. It was not far from Rauschenberg's first loft on the Lower Manhattan waterfront, "in a beautiful area around Coenties Slip. It used to be [abstract painter] Agnes Martin's studio and it was all cracked plaster . . . no decoration . . . very stark." After inventing his new Pop Art style in that studio, Rosenquist was discovered by two art gallery owners. In 1963 he moved to a loft farther uptown, in the area that eventually became known as SoHo.[4]

During the same period, three prominent artists whose standard of living was very different from that of the unknown Rosenquist and the relatively unknown Rauschenberg invited eight hundred members of New York's art community to a social gathering that also "took place in a loft." But this 1961 party amazed art writer Dore Ashton because it was held in "a loft with parquet floors, spotless walls and a majestic colonnade running its length. . . . Pinkerton men were stationed at the door." For Ashton, this loft party symbolized a change from "the comfortable old group" of artists to "the new Artbusiness community." "It was a far cry," she says, "from the days of penniless bohemianism when the lean and hungry artists had themselves resembled thieves."[5]

By the end of the decade, when photographs and descriptions of artists' lofts began to reach a wider public of magazine readers, the journalists declared that loft living had panache. A 1970 article in *Life* magazine, "Living Big in a Loft," could easily inspire either envy or repugnance, and it is impossible to decide which *Life* intended when it wrote about the artists living in SoHo's loft buildings, "Behind these grubby façades lurks an artists' colony. . . . Sixteen-foot ceilings, 45-foot rooms, and community spirit." The large interior photographs show as much air, space, and light as any suburban home could claim. Although the trapeze that one artist had installed in his loft, or the eight-by-twenty-four-foot painting on which another was working, exceeded the scale of most American houses, the Oriental rug, track lighting, polished wood floors, comfortable sofa and chairs, and bicycle in the background of the most prominent photograph looked reassuring. Indeed, upper-middle-class *Life* readers could probably identify with artists "Bill and Yvonne Tarr [who] still live in Scarsdale, but plan to join Bill's assortment of welded steel and bronze sculptures in the Tarrs' 90-foot-long studio later this year. The kitchen, bath and family rooms will be at ground level, with a living-dining-bedroom combination perched on the elevated platform halfway between the loft's ancient wooden floor and a curved skylight reaching to the 16-foot-high ceiling."[6]

Several months later, the glossy *New York* magazine — the first and most widely copied chronicle of urban "lifestyle" — also focused on SoHo's artists. Although they had come to an industrial area in search of cheap space, these artists evidently knew how to live — which mainly involved combining living and working. "They set up modern kitchens, living rooms, bedrooms and bathrooms along with their studios. When night came they did not go home like everyone else in SoHo, because they *were* home." Home for artist Gerhardt Liebmann, for example, is divided between a studio in the front half of his loft and a fifty-foot length of living space in back, with a rock garden, a skylight, and slate floors.[7]

Over the next few years, magazines praised the versatility and the creativity of loft design. In many lofts, the integration of work space, living areas, and art objects was paralleled by a fluid adaptation to structural features (primarily light, floor, and volume) and "incidental" arrangements. Photographed in the professional journal *Progressive Architecture,* for example, "the loft of artist Lowell Nesbitt is divided by eight-foot-high partitions used to display his own work. Various living areas are defined by the semi-open hexagonal spaces created by the partitions, by groupings of plants, and by painted circles on the wooden flooring." Mixed uses and high ceilings continued to invite multilevel design. In a loft that was featured in the Sunday *New York Times Magazine* in 1974, architect Hanford Yang built a three-level living area to display his art collection. Artist Gerhardt Liebmann, whose loft had been photographed by *New York* magazine in 1970, turned up again in 1974 with one of "the great bathrooms of New York." By now he "has a flourishing greenhouse in the bathroom of his SoHo loft. 'The bathroom is an ideal place to raise plants if you have the light,'" he says. And SoHo, according to *New York* magazine, was now the ideal place to live if you wanted excitement.[8]

A 1976 *New York* magazine article on extravagant house plants — "Six City Jungle Habitats" — shows large trees growing in a designer's SoHo loft. Another article, on an architect's elegant 140-foot-long loft, lauds the design detail as "a short course in neoclassical art *trompe l'oeil*" that evokes "an Italian palazzo." The design of a passage between the loft's columns, or "colonnade," is said to be "loosely derived from a Vicenza building façade by the sixteenth-century architect Andrea Palladio."[9]

By 1978, women's sportwear designer Adri Stecking (known professionally as Adri) was saying to a *New York Times* reporter, "I fell in love with SoHo and walked the pavements for months, but I couldn't find the loft I wanted." So she rented a loft — purely for living — near midtown, south of the Flower Market district. "Each floor contained about 4,000 square feet," says the *Times;* "'a quarter of an acre [*sic*]!'" says Adri. "There were big windows facing each point of the compass," and Adri's loft "was high enough to see the roof-tops of buildings on each side and New Jersey to the west, separated by a blue strip of Hudson River. The sun streamed in at all hours." But the focal point of Adri Stecking's spacious new home is even more remarkable. "It's an eight-foot square Jacuzzi whirlpool bath that accommodates ten people, is set into a white tile platform reached by eight steps, and is equipped with a cat board should any [*sic*] of the two resident felines fall into the pool." The *Times* devoted a full page to photos of Adri in her Jacuzzi and her kitchen, the floor plan of the loft, and an interview with Adri and her interior designer.[10]*

---

*This article caused some dismay because it appeared at a time when the city government's concern over job loss had directed criticism against the residential conversion of loft buildings. The reporter made clear that Adri had bought a co-operative loft that was occupied by an economically viable manufacturer who "was in no hurry to leave." Nonetheless, a commercial tenant has no "statutory right," as some residential tenants in New York do, to remain beyond the expiration of their lease, and Adri "moved in as soon as she was able to."

Although American living lofts generally convey a sense of modern elegance through a spareness of design that is enhanced by the opulence of larger-than-life decoration and industrial appliances, as another *Times* article, also in 1978, showed, the loft style was easily adaptable to an eclectic juxtaposition of seventeenth-century, Art Deco, and "High Tech" design. This time the loft was in Paris, but the language is familiar: "Once upon a time, thermos bottles were manufactured in the lofty space shown above. Then interior designer Andrée Putnam moved in on it, connected it to her seventeenth-century Paris apartment and transformed it into elegant quarters for working and entertaining." [11]

By 1980, readers of the *Times* had become so familiar with living lofts that a home furnishings reporter considered a twenty-foot ceiling in the living room matter of factly, as one of several "common design problems." "'The scale was enormous and quite a problem,'" says the designer of a model loft-apartment in a converted factory. "The bare walls . . . were 'too high, too overpowering.'" The reporter recommends his solution as inexpensive and ingenious: "Using nine separate pieces of canvas, the designer created an enormous 12-foot-square hanging that is delineated with adhesive tape into two-foot-square grids. . . . The upper left square sports a black triangle. 'That's the same effect as the . . . window,' he noted, pointing to the skylight on the adjacent wall." [12] Indeed, the high ceilings, exposed brick walls, hanging plants, and open spaces of the loft style have become so well known that they inspire parody. An issue of the satirical *Not the New York Times* that was published during the 1978 New York City newspaper strike featured a bogus interview with Cary Grant and Andy Warhol, who had converted their Upper East side apartments to the "loft look."

With no intention of irony, the overstatement of real estate advertisements reveals what loft living now represents to a sophisticated, affluent public. Directed to "the discriminating buyer" — or at least to someone who can afford the $54,000 to $120,000 purchase price and a monthly maintenance charge between $300 and $600 — an ad from the *New York Times* in May 1980 promises "THE ULTIMATE in Loft Living":

> Looking for the ultimate loft apartment? Our large duplexes give you everything that makes loft living so great . . . the expansiveness of OPEN SPACE . . . the spectacularly HIGH CEILINGS (up to 16 ft.) . . . the FREEDOM to create your own living environment . . . PLUS spectacular SKYLINE & RIVER VIEWS!
> We've added an elegance you wouldn't expect of the loft lifestyle . . . magnificent lobby, intercom . . . carpeted hallways . . . deluxe appointments & amenities . . . luxurious large new kitchen areas & stylish Oak stripped floors, etc.

An advertisement that was posted, placard style, on a Manhattan lamppost at about the same time plays to both a sense of style and a sense of history.

> These spectacular lofts are for artists, photographers, performing artists and urban pioneers with creative minds. At the corner of Prince Street in the SOHO HISTORIC DISTRICT.
> CO-OP LOFTS:
> — Magnificent gallery spaces
> — Only one loft per floor — 5000 sq. ft. . . . .
> — Fantastic gallery and performing arts spaces. . . .

Beneath a reproduced drawing of the building as it looked in 1860, the advertisement reads, "The finest business structure and most famous shop of its time . . . the first fireproof building in New York . . . constructed of white marble . . . specially inspected by the Prince of Wales on his visit to the United States. . . ." *

A third ad that ran in the *Times,* in March 1980, appeals to both luxury and practicality. It represents a real estate developer selling co-operative loft-apartments of approximately the same size but "in three neighborhoods, in three distinct price ranges." The first and least expensive loft-apartments are in a converted factory near but not in a gentrifying, brick townhouse neighborhood of Brooklyn. They provide "up to 1400 square feet of open space, enhanced by high ceilings, oversize windows, and beautiful parquet floors." The second option, in a converted office building in TriBeCa, promises "up to 1185 square feet, the space is open, and the feeling is larger than life. . . ." The third and most expensive offering, in a converted warehouse on the fringe of Greenwich Village, marks "the return of The Great New York Apartment. From 1370 to 2850 square feet of the most beautifully laid-out open space in the city. With breathtaking views, terraces, gardens, Manhattan's only glass-walled elevator, and impeccable workmanship." By this point and this price level, lofts have moved "uptown." There is little left to distinguish loft living from luxury housing.

Nevertheless, the advertisements imply that loft living still retains several distinctive characteristics: open space, a relation between art and industry, a sense of history, and a fascination of the middle-class imagination with the artist's studio.

---

* In light of New York City's 1976 zoning resolution on SoHo and NoHo, the adjacent artists' loft districts *S*outh and *N*orth of *H*ouston Street, respectively, these living lofts seem to have a doubtful legal status. That resolution permits residential conversion of loft buildings in these areas *for artists only,* according to an established certification procedure. Buildings that front on Broadway, as this one does, cannot be converted to joint living and working use *even by artists* if the floor size exceeds *3,600 square feet.* Probably the developers who were selling the floors in this building had applied for a Buildings Department permit for studios with accessory living space, which New York City law did not consider a residential category until recently.

Residents' garbage, deposited in front of a loft building, vies with an art gallery for the attention of passers-by.

SPACE AND SELF

A home, as French philosopher Gaston Bachelard says in *The Poetics of Space,* can mean many contradictory things to its inhabitants. It evokes an image of both stability and expansiveness, a primal "hut dream" that inspires calm rooms that seethe with inner turbulence. "The house even more than the landscape," Bachelard notes, "is a psychic state." [13] In different periods and different cultures, the size of a house, the layout of the rooms, the passage from one room to another, indicate not only a sense of "home" but also a sense of the self that is "at home" there. In sixteenth-century Europe, for example, people thought that self-expression was possible only in small rooms, yet by the eighteenth century, their descendants preferred large, airy rooms. In the late nineteenth century, tastes changed once again. Mid-Victorian homes were warrens of small, specialized rooms separated by walls, passageways, and closets that "associated each space with a function or activity that assumed cultural, indeed ceremonial meaning." [14]

Needless to say, tastes in housing, like all architectural styles, are constrained by available technology, materials, and costs. Tastes must also change over time. The sixteenth-century preference for small rooms indicates a withdrawal in spatial terms from the corporate identities and large gatherings of medieval society to what we think of as Renaissance individ-

Strolling through the wholesale dairy distributors' neighborhood, an explorer can easily envision loft living in Lower Manhattan.

ualism. The eighteenth-century room parallels a new conception of the public self, which demanded a more public space even in the privacy of the home. The late-nineteenth-century "specialization of space," as historian Burton Bledstein calls it, symbolizes a retreat into private space to protect the individual from undefined, and therefore dangerous, encounters. All these examples project a middle-class, or even an upper-middle-class, understanding of the relation between space, self, and society. Because the middle class generally neither inherits baronial ancestral halls nor can afford to reconstruct such palaces, the housing that the middle class builds or buys necessarily reflects new ideas about space, and what it represents, in each time period. In that sense, loft living is part of a larger modern quest for authenticity. Old buildings and old neighborhoods are "authen-

tic" in a way that new construction and new communities are not. They
have an identity that comes from years of continuous use, and an individuality that creates a sense of "place" instead of "space." They are "New
York" rather than "California," or "San Francisco" rather than "Los
Angeles." Such places grow organically, not spasmodically. Because they
are here today *and* tomorrow, they provide landmarks for the mind as well
as the senses. In a world that changes moment by moment, anchoring the
self to old places is a way of coping with the "continuous past." So loft living rejects functionalism, Le Corbusier, and the severe idealism of form
that modern architecture represents. As a style, it is respectful of social
context. Thus living lofts are a logical continuation of the middle-class
movement back to brownstone townhouses that began in the late fifties.
Ironically, loft living turns to factories in search of a more human habitat.
Living in a loft is an attempt to replace modernism's mass production of
the individual with an individualization of mass production.[15]

Living lofts, especially in an on-going manufacturing area, re-create the
"mixed use" of earlier urban neighborhoods. To some degree the attraction
to artists' living and working lofts — mixed use in the loft itself — represents
an attempt to overcome the separation of home and work that some social
psychologists find so alienating.[16] If the isolation of middle-class residential suburbs breeds despair, then the mixed use of loft neighborhoods
should foster affirmation in the middle-class psyche. Of course, a middle-
class preference for strictly residential neighborhoods pre-dates the
suburbs by many years. Since the rise of separate middle-class and
working-class housing markets in the 1840s, urban houses and neighborhoods have been predominantly either residential or commercial. Most
people still prefer purely residential housing and neighborhoods — for
either escape or exclusivity. But symbolically, the mixed use in loft living
reconciles home and work and recaptures some of the former urban vitality.

In another way, too, living lofts represent an effort to supersede the
intense privacy of the detached suburban house with a more public space.
The sheer physical layout of most lofts, interrupted by few doors or walls,
opens every area and every social function to all comers. This eliminates
most rituals *de passage* and creates an impression of informality and
equality. In a loft's vastness no single object or person can dominate.
Similarly, the absence of architectural barriers between "service" and
"entertainment" areas eliminates the hierarchy of functions that is typical
of most household arrangements, as well as the hierarchy of persons —
either male or female — who perform those functions. Nor does the architectural plan of a loft readily permit the hierarchy of specialized rooms
that was so popular in middle-class Victorian homes. Lofts don't have
drawing rooms, morning rooms, or dressing rooms. Because loft areas are
divided only according to general uses — "living" and "working," for exam-

ple — they imply an easy transition from one activity to another, a sense of proportion and a purposefulness that may really exceed the loft dweller's. The appropriation of large space in a loft also reverses the sixteenth-century association between small rooms and self-expression. Loft living reflects a self that continually demands "more space" to prove its individuality.

Living in a loft is a little like living in a showcase. Because of the structure of many small industrial buildings, most lofts are entered directly from the elevator. So guests penetrate immediately into the living area. This contrasts with the gradual transition between "outside" and "inside," and public and private space, in a typical home. Even in the modest lofts that do have an entrance hall, both guests and hosts feel a mutual obligation to "see" and "show" the whole loft. Of course, the uniqueness of each loft arrangement — due to the absence of standard floor plans and the unexpectedness of architectural detail — makes living lofts a kind of tourist attraction that most houses or apartments cannot be.

But it would be wrong to imagine that lofts use space in a totally new way. Strong elements of continuity connect today's living lofts and older American housing types, beginning with the brick walls, plane surfaces, and exposed structural elements (wooden beams) in early New England houses. Indeed, architectural historian Siegfried Giedion characterized the typical American floor plan that developed between 1850 and 1890 as the most open, the most flexible, and the least subdivided that was possible. Because of both a lack of skilled labor and a colonial dependence on the British Georgian style, American construction throughout the nineteenth century stressed a lack of pretentiousness, a direct approach to building materials, and an attention to comfort. Even the ideal house that Henry David Thoreau imagined before 1850 seems remarkably like a living loft. It would have "only one room . . . where some may live in the fireplace, some in the recess of a window, and some on settees, some at one end of the hall, some at another, and some aloft in the rafters with the sparrows, if they choose." [17]

Thoreau's central image reappears in master-craftsman Gustav Stickley's description of the prototype house that he designed around 1900:

> We have from the first planned houses that are based on the big fundamental principles of honesty, simplicity, and usefulness. . . . We have put into practical effect our conviction that a house, whatever its dimensions, should have plenty of free space unencumbered by unnecessary partitions or over-much furniture. . . . It seems to us much more friendly, homelike and comfortable to have one big living room into which one steps directly from the entrance door . . . and to have this living room the place where all the business and pleasure of the common family life may be carried on. And we like it to have pleasant nooks and corners which give a comfortable sense of semi-privacy and yet are not in any way shut off from the larger life of the room. . . .

> Equally symbolic is our purpose in making the dining room either almost or
> wholly a part of the living room. . . . Such an arrangement is a strong and
> subtle influence in the direction of simpler living because entertainment
> under such conditions naturally grows less elaborate and more
> friendly. . . .[18]

Another reason for the decline of formal entertaining, as Stickley also
notes, was the increasing number of middle-class households without servants. Unlike the rigid domestic division between "upstairs" and "down-
stairs," the housewife who did her own cooking did not readily accept an
enforced isolation in the kitchen, away from the rest of the family. Early-
twentieth-century feminists had demanded that the kitchen be eliminated
entirely from individual homes and replaced with nearby communal dining
halls. But in the thirties and forties, this radical demand was subdued by
the rapidly expanding production of labor-saving, mechanical devices for
doing kitchen work and by changes in the physical layout of kitchens.
Frank Lloyd Wright's innovative houses opened up the kitchen to the dining room so that the "work-space," as Wright called it, flowed into the living area. Wright also adapted to home kitchens the principle of "streamlin-
ing" that had been developed in nineteenth-century railroad travel with the
creation of the Pullman dining car. Wright's preference for the open floor
plan, along with the home-buying public's desire for ever more open and
more flexible living areas, influenced the design of the suburban tract
houses that were built in great numbers after World War II. Suburban
ranch homes had large efficient kitchens that flowed into multi-purpose
"dens" or "family rooms." The open space of this suburban style, as well as
the 1960s revival of Early American rural homes and barns, prepared the
way for the acceptance of living lofts.[19]

ART AND INDUSTRY

While Frank Lloyd Wright and several other innovative, early-
twentieth-century architects freely incorporated elements of industrial
design into residential and institutional structures, they transformed these
elements to harmonize with the structure as a whole instead of merely
transplanting them from one context to another. The architects' sense of
proportion and a kind of propriety maintained the distinctiveness of
residential, as opposed to industrial, style. No one could mistake their
homes for factories. Even architectural reformers like Walter Gropius and
the Werkbund group in Germany wanted to impose painterly and sculp-
tural standards on industrial design rather than elevate industrial buildings
and products as they were into art forms. There were good reasons at that
time for both a symbiosis and a separation of art and industry. On the one

hand, the increasing mechanization of all aspects of life inspired a very rational borrowing of industrial techniques for domestic uses, and the rigorous standards of industrial construction imposed an austere beauty on factory spaces that contrasted with the elaborate fussiness of Victorian homes. When Gropius, on a visit to the United States in 1913, admired American factory design, he compared the grain elevators to the Pharaohs' tombs.[20] On the other hand, the separation between work and living space that increased with industrialization created two totally distinct markets for industrial and residential products. Although industrial products were more effective, products for the home were "prettier." In large part, of course, residential products were designed for female consumers.

During the 1970s, industrial design began to permeate nonindustrial markets. In some cases, as when someone buys an industrial vacuum cleaner for home use, this reflects a demand for a more efficient product. However, when it involves a conscious aesthetic choice, it implies stripping away the artifice of décor and finding beauty in unadorned functionality. Using Cor-Ten steel, which rusts in contact with the air, on the outside of a new building or exposing the steam pipes and vents of a loft building and painting them red can look both simple and elegant. But other examples, such as the mass of exposed structural and nonstructural elements in the Beaubourg art center in Paris, can be overblown and garish. What is interesting is that this appropriation of industrial design — finding art in industry — has been so thoroughly accepted in a mass market.

Loft living has played an important role in "domesticating" the industrial aesthetic. The factory origins and the present mixed use of many lofts suggest, in the interest of authenticity, the adoption of an industrial style. Also, the spaciousness of a loft permits the use of some industrial and commercial products that are too large to fit into a standard middle-class apartment. The exaggerated scale of a loft provides a natural setting for the new cult of domesticity that worships restaurant and supermarket equipment, industrial carpeting, and Pirelli rubber tiles. In the loft with the whirlpool bath, for example, the owner "loves to cook. [She] is enamored of her Garland range, her stainless-steel Sub-Zero refrigerator and what she calls her 'garage.' This is a storage area that will hold, in addition to her pots, two metal carts with chopping block surfaces that extend the kitchen work areas and are convenient for service at parties. She is planning to have four small tables, like restaurant tables, in the dining area next to the kitchen and the steps to the Jacuzzi." In this loft, the work space of the kitchen not only extends into the living area but it dominates the living area. Surely it is no historical accident that the spread of loft living roughly coincides with the successful introduction of the electric "food processor" into the American mass market. The Cuisinart, or rather its heavy-duty predecessor, the Robot-Coupe, had been used in French restaurant kitchens for years. But not until 1971 did a smaller version, the Magi-Mix, spread to the home market in France, and two years later the arrival of the Cuisinart created a stir on the American market.

Of course, the serious devotion to cuisine, or at least to reproducing in the home techniques of food preparation and appreciation that used to be restricted to restaurants, is part of a larger professionalization of leisure activities. The middle-class jogger who reads *The Book of Running* and the unemployed middle-class wife in the movie *An Unmarried Woman* who starts working in an art gallery are closely related to the home cook who tries to cook up some fresh duck livers in a *vinaigrette* sauce or to whip his own *crème fraîche* into a *blanquette de homard*. After all, the *nouvelle cuisine* is neither less fattening nor less studied that its culinary predecessors.

The professionalization of home cooking and the introduction of industrial products for home use are also related to the decline of gender-related household chores, especially the association between kitchens and "the little woman." In this sense, the feminism and gay activism of many visible loft dwellers in the early years provide another reason why the loft lifestyle became linked with an industrial aesthetic. Quite a few of the first-generation SoHo residents who took part in the movement to legalize artists' living lofts there (1969–71) or whose lofts were pictured in magazines were men or women who lived alone or gay (primarily male) couples. Photographed in their lofts, discoursing knowledgeably about the merits of the Cuisinart or metal wall studs and plasterboard, these people became both part of the mainstream, home-oriented public and arbiters of home style. In a similar gender-free sense, a survey of Manhattan loft residents found that an extraordinarily high proportion of couples refused to identify a man or a woman as head of the household. Or consider the household arrangements of Carl Sontheimer, the engineer who introduced the Cuisinart into the American home market in 1973: "Sixty-five-year old Sontheimer is also a passionate amateur chef. He does all the cooking at home, according to Shirley, his wife and business associate, 'because he likes to.' Naturally, he uses the Cuisinart." [21]

In his introduction to a hip guidebook to SoHo and environs, writer Stephen Koch combines the themes of sexual liberation, suburban alienation, and the social image of artists in a passage so portentous that it might almost be a parody of loft living and the new cult of domesticity:

> The inevitable and unnatural sexual resonances of having been raised in mom's town (where life is lived), remote from work in dad's town (the unseen, meaningless uninhabitable city) is resolutely eliminated. Suburbia and its wall-to-wall alienations have led to a new image for the ancient one of the artist and androgyne, and after the misadventures of the sixties, it finds itself taking a social rather than specifically sexual expression. True enough an industrial look has been important to the modern artist's virility. But the

style's stronger aim is to resolve the sexually laden contradictions of recent American childhood. In SoHo, working and living are at last reunited and work becomes *real.*[22]

However, the reason that people develop a sentimental — or a sensual — attachment to the industrial aesthetic is that it is *not* real. To be precise, it is *no longer* real. When people discover art in industrial design and bring that "art" into their homes, they are making the same existential choice that attracted them (or others) to loft living. They are choosing to return to a more manageable past. As each generation of machines becomes more complicated, we withdraw "into dreams of obsolete machines and see ourselves among windmills, clipper ships, even trolley cars." In essayist Robert Harbison's view, "there is no nostalgia like the nostalgia for simpler machines, which are now imbued with the warm glow of a smaller past."[23]

Curiously, as each generation of mechanical devices has become *smaller,* people have brought *larger* machines into their homes. New devices like minicams and microfiches are not yet as familiar as the large machines of the past. Yes, people do buy microwave ovens, but they buy them because they are efficient rather than aesthetically pleasing. The microwave oven is relegated to the working mother who has no time to cook a roast; the serious cook buys a restaurant stove and a reliable set of thermometers.

Though we live in a transistorized age, we seek a human scale in big, solid objects. This is the sentimental and sensual side of "High Tech" style. To some extent, the taste for industrial trash baskets, reinforced steel shelving, and hospital faucets is also a flight from the throwaway mentality of our plastic culture. Dreaming of durables, we associate the old industrial materials with even older natural ones. The juxtaposition of industrial and natural is successfully exploited by an increasing number of new shops, including a very fine food store in a SoHo loft described by the Italian magazine for architects *Abitare:* "In line with the general reassessment of things genuine and hand-made, a place like this could not be anything but successful. Amid refined white pipes and pillars, they sell milk pans, wooden spoons, naive graters and above all every possible type of excellent food — lots of Italian things — all adding up to the opposite of anonymous."[24] Inevitably, the result of using an industrial aesthetic as "the opposite of anonymous" is that, over time, as the style is established, more and more shops — and lofts — look the same.

Probably the most significant aspect of the domestication of the industrial aesthetic is time. People find art in industrial forms when their industrial use appears to become obsolete. Like Gothic ruins in the nineteenth century, artifacts of the Industrial Age now inspire nostalgia for the past. This sentiment grows as the pace of change speeds up. Of course, artists have always been attracted to industrial design when it is new and dynamic. At the beginning of this century, Gropius admired American factories and Le Corbusier studied the clean lines of industrial machines. Duchamp, Léger, Picabia, and the Constructivists incorporated industrial parts and images in their paintings, and Duchamp even dared to exhibit an industrial product — a urinal, in fact — as "his" art work. But theirs was an elitist appreciation of the industrial aesthetic. They found art in industry because industrial forms matched what they were trying to create in "real" works of art like paintings or buildings. Except for collages, a form that precedes the industrial era, artwork whose physical quality most resembles industrial machines — sculpture, for example — did not imitate industrial design. Until the post–World War II period, industry's influence on art was primarily visual.

Beginning in the late forties, however, artists developed a more visceral feeling about industrial forms. The increasing automation of industrial production and the "accelerated depreciation" of industrial machines that this caused inspired an artistic appreciation of older mechanical devices. The degradation of manual labor that automation also implies may imbue the older machines that require human labor with a sense of humanity. In any case, artists soon scavenged the industrial aesthetic as though they were hunting for souvenirs. They constructed their own machines, using obsolete industrial parts — junk — and set them in motion with electric motors. During the 1960s, Jean Tinguely in Paris and Rauschenberg in New York played with the industrial aesthetic. They took it apart and re-used it in objects that had no function other than to entertain. Pop Art like Andy Warhol's Campbell's soup cans exaggerated the standardization of industrial forms. The reproduction of Warhol's lithographs and silk-screens, and the mass-produced knock-offs that they inspired, brought the image of industrial art into thousands of homes.

If artists spread a trail of cultural clues before the wider public, then the contrast between the 1934 "Machine Art" show at the Museum of Modern Art in New York and the 1968 exhibition that Pontus Hulten organized, "The Machine As Seen at the End of the Mechanical Age," is extremely important. The 1934 exhibit, influenced by the Bauhaus gospel, showed great enthusiasm. In contrast, the 1968 show, as its name implies, offered a visual eulogy. The emblem of the 1968 exhibit was Jean Tinguely's complicated mechanical contraption, *Hommage à New York*. At the opening, Nelson Rockefeller had the honor of pulling the string that activated it. Within several minutes, in a puff of smoke, Tinguely's piece demonstrated its ironic point: it destroyed itself. As Hulten, then director of the Moderna Museet in Stockholm and later director of the Beaubourg, tried to describe the artists' sense of this period, "We are surrounded by the outward manifestations of the culmination of the mechanical age. Yet, at the same time, the mechanical machine — which can most easily be defined as an imitation of our muscles — is losing its dominating position among the tools of mankind; while electronic and chemical devices — which imitate the processes of the brain and the nervous system – are becoming increasingly important." [25]

The artists' conclusion followed that of the business leaders and the sociologists, who had been propounding their idea of progress – a cybernetic vision of a fully automated figure – since the late forties. However, the artists suggested, for the first time, that progress was paradoxical. On the one hand, progress was inevitable and desirable. On the other hand, it involved losing a significant part of the past, a part which had associations and meaning for people. This paradoxical view was not a protest against progress, as the Arts and Crafts Movement in Victorian England had been. Not did it imply, as the Cubists had, that progress was ambiguous. The artists of the 1960s would unite the aesthetic of the mechanical age with the technology of the new electronic era. This attitude carried over to a reevaluation of industrial space. Loft buildings that appeared to be artifacts began to take on a distinctly "artistic" aura. The fact that many artists lived in lofts – as they had, indeed, since the 1930s – merely confirmed the loft buildings' new character.

HISTORIC VALUE AND COMMERCIAL VIABILITY

A new appreciation of the "historic" value of old industrial buildings developed along with the perception of their aesthetic quality. At the beginning of the 1940s, for example, Siegfried Giedion had noted sadly that the work of architect James Bogardus, who designed many of New York's distinguished nineteenth-century cast-iron buildings, was languishing in obscurity. Also to Giedion's chagrin, the warehouses along the Saint Louis waterfront, dating from about the same period, had recently been torn down to make a park. [26] In large part, the lack of concern about industrial buildings was due to the usual nonchalance about objects (and, at that time, works of art) that were not so old as to be either historically or financially valuable. Historic preservationists call this attitude "the grandfather clause": only objects built outside living memory – before "our grandfathers' time" – take on a "historic" aura. Certainly, buildings that were still used for their original purpose, especially factories where many real grandfathers had worked (and which they found either too uninteresting or too painful to remember), did not strike Americans as "historic." But after World War II, just as artists started to appropriate the industrial aesthetic, so historic preservationists began to defend industrial spaces from the wrecker's ball and to advocate their re-use. [27]

This shift occurred for several reasons. First, almost a century had passed since the first modern factories were built in the United States and the first "grandfathers" had gone to work in them. The distance of time lent the factories enchantment. Second, some factories, like their technology, appeared to have become obsolete. Disuse, as we have also noted, lends enchantment. Third, the change in attitude toward nineteenth-century places, including loft buildings, reflected a gradual American acceptance of the prevailing European view toward historic structures. In contrast to the successive American approaches that tended toward a rather pristine view of the past — the "Washington Slept Here" syndrome, "restoration," and "re-creation" — European "preservation" emphasized the desirability of keeping old buildings in continuous use. The Europeans made little effort to purge historic structures of architectural additions and stylistic "corrections" that represented, in their own terms, "historic" accretions. William Morris, the socialist theorist of the Victorian Arts and Crafts Movement, for example, had defended the beauty of buildings that seemed to grow organically, and his own home outside London is still a historic hodgepodge of building styles and materials. By the 1950s, Americans were willing to take up where Morris had left off a half-century before. American preservationists began to write about changing the use — without purifying the structure — of old buildings in order to keep them socially and economically "viable." [28]

A major obstacle to the spread of this preservationist philosophy was that it contradicted the logic of real estate developers, who worked on the basis of the axiom "Tear it down — build it up." Were old buildings to be preserved for changing uses, instead of demolished and replaced, the developers' profit margins might dwindle to nothing. So historic preservation seemed to threaten the pillars of modern capitalism as well as the burgeoning skyscrapers of the post–World War II building boom. To counteract the developers' resistance, preservationists had to create a public constituency for their goal. This was not easy. Particularly in the United States, where since the first New England settlements the abundance of land had encouraged people to abandon their homes and move farther West as they used up natural resources, new places had always represented new chances. The absence of ancestral homes and roots, the youth of the American culture, the relatively open social structure, and the growth, after 1900, of mass production of consumer goods — all suggested to Americans that preserving the past was either silly or pretentious. Indeed, until the 1960s, when the federal government began to fund historical projects on a large scale, support for historic preservation was confined to small community-based groups, patrician associations that were based on geneology (like the Daughters of the American Revolution or the Colonial Dames), and individual wealthy philanthropists (including John D. Rockefeller, who funded the reconstruction of Williamsburg, Virginia, and Henry Ford, who paid for the preservation of Dearborn Village in Michigan). [29]

By the early 1960s, urban renewal plans and private redevelopment had destroyed — or threatened to destroy — so many landmarks in so many cities that people began to speak of a sense of loss. Here was a counterpart to the artists' paradoxical view of mechanical progress: urban redevelopment damaged the "quality of life." The contribution of old buildings was invaluable, a preservationist wrote in 1966, because they "add to the variety and beauty of life that is daily more mechanized and stereotyped." [30] As cities like Philadelphia and Saint Louis destroyed their nineteenth-century architectural heritage, and famous, well-used buildings like Penn Station and the Metropolitan Opera House in New York were replaced with more anonymous office buildings, the sense of loss that some people felt turned into shock. Intellectuals and patricians who still lived in or frequented the old city centers tried to express these feelings through the institutional means at their disposal — schools, art societies, civic beautification groups. In 1963 Nathan Silver organized an exhibit of photographs of old New York buildings, most of which had already been demolished, at the Columbia University School of Architecture. The point of this exhibit, he explained in a subsequent book of photographs, *Lost New York,* was "that the collective picture of some vanished first-rate architecture would make a sobering reminder of how much finer a city New York could have been with its all-time best buildings still intact." Silver and his associates were sure that the more people saw such an exhibition, the more pressure they would bring to bear on real estate developers and urban planners. Essentially, historic preservationists wanted legislative protection for specified landmarks, and enlightened procedures for recognizing and registering them. They also wanted to retain the social and economic context — again, the "viability" of old places, which might include an individual building, a cluster of buildings, or an entire district. [31]

While it was possible that such restrictions on real estate development would harm the financial interests of some upper-class people, primarily the heads of banks and big businesses that wanted either to build or to invest in building new corporate headquarters, many patrician types supported historic preservation as they continued to support municipal art societies, museums, symphony orchestras, and civic beautification. If these people, or the intellectual and cultural figures with whom they were allied, also owned property in or near "landmark districts," such as Society Hill in Philadelphia or Beacon Hill in Boston, they also stood to gain financially from increased property values. Nevertheless, a stumbling block to preservation remained in the question of how to compensate developers and builders for the profits that they would forgo if opportunities for new construction were limited. The city of San Francisco paid particular attention to this issue in the early sixties when a patrician group founded by three prominent San Francisco matrons to conserve the open beauty of the Bay gradually developed into the San Francisco Plan, a policy backed by the full force of state power. [32] By itself, the "stick" of state power seemed an overly negative inducement. So San Francisco's "carrot" to developers took the form of shifting intensive new development downtown, toward the Mission District, and encouraging the commercial redevelopment of Fisherman's Wharf and Ghirardelli Square, along the Bay. The San Francisco compromise became the model for a *modus vivendi* between preservationists and developers in many cities. On the one hand, the preservationists got to keep in continuous use the low-rise, nineteenth-century buildings (including the Ghirardelli Chocolate Factory) next to the waterfront, but on the other hand, developers got to renovate and lease these facilities for "viable" commercial uses. And the high-profit, high-rise development was certainly permitted elsewhere.

The San Francisco model continues to be copied selectively. Ghirardelli Square has spun off clones along the waterfronts of Boston (Quincy Market and Faneuil Hall), New York (South Street Seaport), and Baltimore (Harborplace). Significantly, the developer of these three much-touted renovations is James Rouse, who earlier in his career made a fortune by developing suburban shopping malls. Rouse's key to establishing the commecial viability of historic structures in cities is derived directly from the "branching" principle of the typical suburban shopping center. While the physical context of each project is unique — because it is the original, nineteenth-century structure — the retail stores that rent space in the renovated buildings are the same assortment of "gourmet" and "ethnic" food shops, crafts boutiques, bookstores, and fancy fast-food stands like crèpe or oyster bars. The Harborplace development, for example, which opened in 1980, includes branches of an Ocean City, Maryland, fish restaurant, a Newport, Rhode Island, "continental" restaurant, a New York "pasta" restaurant, and a Washington, D.C., Indian restaurant. The commercial viability "rider" on which the general acceptance of historic preservation depends has created, in effect, a coast-to-coast chain of red-brick shopping centers. Their stock-in-trade is entirely predictable. Just as the residential re-use of loft buildings established "loft living," so the commercial re-use of old markets, factories, and warehouses has developed a similar style. The organized appreciation of the unique that began as a strictly local and elitist affair has become part of a national, middle-class culture.

THE MIDDLE CLASS IN THE ARTIST'S STUDIO

At the same time that historic preservation began to attract a broader group of supporters, the work of living artists started to arouse a great deal of public interest. Like the loft buildings in which they were often located, artists' studios appealed to the public's imagination. But in contrast to buildings that appeared obsolete, the studios seemed dynamic. The reason was not that artists were working harder than they had before but that their work was perceived differently. This happened because of changes in the work and changes in the price structure of modern art.

First, from the mid-fifties on, works by living American artists commanded increasingly high prices. Scarcity had something to do with this. On the one hand, as *Fortune* magazine carefully pointed out as early as 1955, the supply of Old Masters and even new masters (like Picasso) was rapidly drying up. Thus people who wanted to invest in "blue-chip" works of art had to broaden their interests. On the other hand, the death of Jackson Pollock, the famous New York Abstract Expressionist, in 1956, increased the money value of his work as well as that of his contemporaries in the New York School. When a new generation of abstract painters — Rauschenberg, Jasper Johns, Frank Stella — began to attract a wider circle of newly affluent art collectors, their prices also rose. By the end of the 1960s, the better-known artists were making enough money to buy their own loft buildings, and their old landlords, to whom they had given paintings in payment for rent or repairs, were counting their blessings.[33]

The second reason that living American artists achieved a historic new status had to do with the substance of their work. Because of both their subjects and their style, the Abstract Expressionists began to be perceived as more serious — more philosophical, more intellectual, deeper — than artists had before. The artists themselves encouraged this impression. They discussed their work in terms of existential pain and existential choices. Like the European philosophers who were also trying to distinguish between being and nothingness, such New York artists as Mark Rothko and Barnett Newman were reducing the artist's elements to the barest essentials. They pared their expression to bands of stark color or even shades of black. The best artists no longer did representational work (still lifes with fruit or landscapes with bathers); rather, they were painting, sometimes very self-consciously, portraits of the modern soul. For his model — and this was, incidentally, a male-dominated approach — the artist took himself. But people outside the studio understood that in wrestling with this image, the artist represented everyone.

Art critic Harold Rosenberg, whose work during the 1940s and 1950s contributed greatly to the clarification and exhaltation of some of these artists (especially Pollock's "rival," Willem de Kooning), called this new sort of aesthetic representation Action Painting. "Action Painting has to do with self-creation or self-definition or self-transcendence," Rosenberg wrote at the end of the fifties, "but this dissociates it from self-expression, which assumes the acceptance of the ego as it is, with its wound and its magic. Action Painting is not 'personal,' though its subject matter is the artist's individual possibilities." Because the style was abstract rather than literal, an attempt to "act out" the artist's creation of a new self rather than to reproduce a chair or an apple, Action Painting freed artists from their Sisyphean task of representing *what is*. This meant "liberation from the 'nature,' society, and art already there. It was a movement to leave behind the self that wished to choose his future and to nullify his promissory notes to the past." Of course, the immediate past from which these artists sought liberation — or escape — was the common vision of horror and holocaust shared by survivors of World War II. This was compounded, for the many artists who since WPA days had had contacts and alliances on the Left, by Stalinism abroad and McCarthyism at home. At any rate, the abstract painting of the New York artists held the attention of the American public as never before. Rosenberg's essays about the Action Painters described a living reality. They "were not only theories," as journalist Tom Wolfe breathlessly puts it, "but . . . hot news, straight from the studios, from the scene." [34]

No longer a mere work place, the artist's studio had indeed become "the scene." It was in the studio that the artist constantly re-created his self, and by transferring that moment to canvas, represented everyone's favorite *angst*. Although the artists who succeeded the Action Painters were less serious about the *angst,* they remained perfectly serious about the activity of art creation. In the mid- to late sixties, for example, the Conceptualists presented the process of making art as a work of art in itself. Like the "Happenings," which had combined art and theater in many loft-studios several years before, Conceptualist exhibitions were really performances, in which the artists exhibited themselves. Strangely enough, this did not repel the increasingly middle-class public that was interested in the artists. They attended the exhibitions, some in out-of-the-way places, in even greater numbers. Just as the artists became more willing to invite the public into their studios — to watch the process of art creation or self-creation firsthand — so the public became more interested in watching the artists work. Eventually, the consumption of art in the artist's studio developed into a consumption of the studio too. In 1968, the "Downtown Ten" Art Show exhibited the work of ten New York artists in their lofts. People had to walk from one loft to another to see the work and the artists. It was a novel situation — even more redolent with artistic ambiance than the late-fifties openings of the Tenth Street School of Abstract Expressionists, when an "uptown" art public used to go from one artists' co-op gallery to another in search of the most bohemian or most avant-garde showing. By the late sixties, the seed had been sown: people began to think of the art studio as an exciting place to live. The artists' success in attracting the art public to their studios became the success of the studios.

Ironically, the more artists become a distinctive social group that both lives *for* art and lives *off* art, the more the middle class appropriates their styles and their studios. The rise of the market in living lofts is not the first case in which this has happened. In Paris around 1900, artists began to live in distinctive studio-houses, which had a top-floor studio with large windows and living quarters on the floor below. In order to take advantage of the best light, and to fit the most housing into the available space, the architects sited them assymetrically. This inadvertantly created entire small developments — or colonies — of artists' ateliers. Between the 1900s and the 1930s, during the height of Paris's reign as art capital of the world, there was a boom in building of studio-houses. Modernists like Le Corbusier designed them. The interesting point is that non-artists, or people who were peripherally involved in the Paris art world, wanted them too. Critics, dealers, and collectors — in short, a significant segment of the middle class — took them over, "finding that the standard two-story studio with its double-height window made for an uncommonly exciting living room." [35]

From housing for artists "living poor" outside the mainstream of society to luxury housing for an urbane, "artistic" bourgeoisie, living lofts reflect an interesting expansion of middle-class culture. By this point in the twentieth century, the cultural style that is associated with loft living — the "loft lifestyle" — shows a middle-class preference for open space and artistic forms of production, as well as a more general nostalgia about the "smaller past" of the great industrial era. The market in living lofts, along with the movement for the historic preservation of buildings that are not terribly old, suggests how quickly these sentiments about space and time can be exploited for their commercial possibilities. The integration of an industrial aesthetic into the new cult of domesticity also reflects the commercialization of cultural change, besides obvious social changes like the end of the "mechanical age" of industrial society, the professionalization of leisure activities, and the dissociation of many middle-class women from household chores. So loft living takes it place — with "brownstoning," "parenting," and simply "Living," as a weekly section of the *New York Times* is called — among the cultural gerunds of our time.

While an explanation that relates culture and commerce — or space, time, and self — seems, at last, to make the demand for living lofts thoroughly understandable, it has broached an issue that places the rise of the loft market in quite a different perspective. The idea that artists were entitled to help in getting loft-studio space developed as an integral part of the explosion of state support for the arts in the 1960s. At the same time that art became involved in the expansion of state power, the power structure within the art world was also changing. Competition over patronage and the emergence of new, middle-class patrons of the arts affected the production of artwork and the artists. Just as art no longer "shocked the bourgeoisie," so artists themselves were becoming more middle-class.

4

ART IN THE ARMS OF POWER

It is inconceivable that living "like an artist" would have exerted any appeal to segments of the middle class if significant changes in the social position of art and artists had not taken place since the end of World War II. From a marginal and often elitist aesthetic concern, art moved into a central position in the cultural symbolism of an increasingly materialistic world. Artists enjoyed more visibility in the mass media as well as at prestigious social gatherings, and since the most prominent artists were also selling their work at the highest prices, it is reasonable to suppose that their visibility was connected, in some measure, with their commercial viability. But at the same time, public discussion transformed policy toward the arts into a national priority. Just as artists' prices and their dealers' commissions depended on which country "won" the Venice Biennale, so—in a larger sense—did national prestige. Artists began to be regarded as social assets rather than bohemians, and their work acquired important new patronage. Through state funding, they started to earn a steady living at their work. This more or less brought the idea of the Works Projects Administration (WPA) of the Depression into a liberal society that was based on economic growth at home and political expansion abroad.

There have been two periods in the twentieth century when the relation between art and society was fundamentally altered: the 1930s and the 1960s. Prior to the Great Depression, between 1900 and 1930, artists—or at least the most noteworthy artists in the art capitals of Paris, Berlin, New York, and Moscow—began to make a living from their art work. During the Depression, for the first time, artists were recognized as part of the labor force. In the United States, this recognition entitled them to get jobs with the WPA, jobs which encouraged artists—again, for the first time—to organize themselves in work-related groups. Often these were unions, like the Federation of Modern Painters and Sculptors. The friendships that artists formed in those years of working together on large projects rather than alone in their studios outlasted the Depression. Many of the New York artists who met at the WPA — a group of two thousand that included Mark Rothko, Willem de Kooning, Jackson Pollock, Arshile Gorky, and Adolph Gottlieb — continued to meet informally. Several of their social circles eventually developed labels by which they became known to the art public: a group that coalesced around the studio of German painter Hans Hoffmann; "the Ten," which included Rothko and Gottlieb; the "Whitney [Museum] Dissenters." In time these groups also became known by a locale — their studios and the bars that they frequented — which emphasized their collective identity. The most prominent of these groups after the War was the Tenth Street School of Abstract Expressionists. Their nearby hangouts were the Subjects of the Artist School, The Club, and the Cedar Tavern (described in the diaries of Anaïs Nin), and the two critics who hung out with them were Harold Rosenberg and Clement Greenberg. Loosely but definitively associated after World War II, these artists became known as a meta-group — the New York School.[1]

The moral seriousness and political purpose that made 1930s art, especially Social Realism, so useful to the government during the Depression were transformed by the affluence that followed World War II. The international expansion of a more highly developed American industry, and the greater sophistication of a public that had renewed its contact with European cultural forms, changed artists and the art they produced. The dominant mode of artistic expression, as we have already seen, became abstract, contemplative, rueful. New York supplanted Paris as the capital of the art world. Artists, that is, the more distinguished among them, developed the status of cult figures. If this didn't immediately make them rich, at least it made them famous. The public followed their careers in exhibitions, visiting the Tenth Street artists' co-operatives as often as uptown galleries, and in magazines for both the *literati* who read Rosenberg's or Greenberg's essays and the merely literate who wanted to know, as *Life* asked about Jackson Pollock in 1949, "Is he the greatest living painter in the United States?"

By the 1960s the new affluence and sophistication had opened up the art market to a broader group of consumers, who were more middle-class than the patricians that had predominated in art buying up to this time, and a less elitist group of art gallery owners, who frankly pursued new art and new artists and directed them toward a waiting public. In style the art of the 1960s was more ironic that rueful, more reflective than contemplative, more influenced by Pop than by High Culture. The oracular dominance of the New York School ceded to a pluralism in New York art. Younger artists, outpriced by property values in Greenwich Village but also put off by the success of postwar masters, moved away from Tenth Street. Working alone again, in studios all over Lower Manhattan, including the area that eventually became known as SoHo, artists multiplied in number. They seemed to feed off the nervous energy of the city's — and America's — expansionary outlook. Art world joined art public in creating what Harold Rosenberg described as "the American Art Establishment," and it is this pervasive blend of commercialism and elitism that Calvin Tompkins acknowledged when he wrote in 1980, "Sixties art makes SoHo possible. We are still drawing on energies generated twenty years ago, and that knowledge lends the SoHo scene its diffuse, uneasy glamor." [2]

Glamor on the one hand; power on the other. Between 1960 and 1965, as new styles and subjects flourished in an increasingly commercial art world, an idea grew that the arts deserved more institutional support than either the vagaries of the marketplace or the passion of traditional patrons of the arts could offer. In part an isolated idea and in part an idea whose time seemed to have come, state support for the arts quickly captured the public's imagination. Once Congress accepted the notion of a national arts council with discretionary powers, the state's long lack of involvement in large-scale artistic activity — a hiatus that had lasted from the end of the WPA through the 1950s — became a deluge of grants and an array of agencies, which led to a rapid expansion of that part of the labor force that made its living off art. But there were elements of control in this largesse. Integrally connected with the explosion of state support for the arts were local labor markets. So strategic thinkers in the business community also had a vested interest in regularizing arts employment along with the rest of the service sector. Moreover, the expansion of government's role in creating arts employment benefited the state. Funding for the arts generated competing constituencies that looked to the state, as well as to arbiters in the art world, for recognition. Under these conditions, it becomes important to know the social framework in which art is produced, perceived, distributed, and "consumed."

POWER IN THE ART MARKET: MUSEUMS VERSUS GALLERIES

By definition, if not also by custom, it would seem that the functions of art museums clearly differ from those of art galleries. Surely, museums are agents of *culture* and galleries are agents of the *marketplace*. If the functions of the former are educational and curatorial — to show and to tell — then the functions of the latter are to show and to sell. Until the early 1960s, museums and galleries coexisted peacefully on the basis of this division of labor. Their respective tasks — and raisons d'être — reflected both the breadth and the narrowness of the art public up to that time.

In the nineteenth century, the increasing number of citizens who enjoyed some higher education enlarged the public that could appreciate art, or at least those widely accepted art forms that were said to make up a nation's cultural identity. Duly appropriated and accredited by a nation's rulers, this cultural heritage became the stock-in-trade of public museums, where an increasingly professional staff arranged it in a more or less encyclopedic display of Art and Progress. In this sense, the private museums of Renaissance and Enlightenment patrons of the arts and sciences were transformed, under the aegis of the state, into national collections. This does not mean that nineteenth-century museums were "popular" institutions. The British Museum, founded in 1759, did not readily admit the public until 1800, and the Metropolitan Museum of Art in New York, which opened its doors in 1870, initially refused to include in its collection work by American artists. In America, the lack of a history of state patronage — due to the absence of a centralized state — made all the public museums that were established dependent on private contributions to build their collections. On the one hand, museums solicited donations in the forms of both artwork and money. On the other hand, museum trustees, as well as, for many years, museum directors and curators, represented the typical upper-class pillars of local society. So the "best" art in the museums reflected patrician support and patrician sensibility.[3]

But beginning in the 1860s, and again in the 1880s, the expansion of an affluent and cultured, or possibly pretentious, group of middle-class art buyers encouraged the emergence of a new type of middleman in the art market. The art dealer, like his clients in the industrial bourgeoisie, worked both ends of the market relation: production and distribution. The people who made art found it advantageous to sell their work in a gallery because the dealer relieved them of meeting the demands of individual patrons and regularized the conditions under which they were paid. In Paris in the 1870s, for example, art dealer Paul Durand-Ruel worked out a fee system for the Impressionists whom he represented, in return for the exclusive rights to all their work. By 1900, gallery owners like Ambroise Vollard were paying their artists a yearly income and, in addition to mounting periodic exhibitions, were organizing other ventures, like the publication of limited editions of hand-printed texts with their artists' illustrations. Moreover, passing through the art dealer's critical screening process freed artists from the double bottleneck that had limited their access to the art marketplace during most of the nineteenth century. First, dealers eliminated the obstacle of judgment by their peers, who decided what art would be admitted to the state-sponsored annual exhibitions, or *salons,* which were so important in giving a public showing to the work of living artists. Second, dealers reduced the make-or-break quality of judgment by the critics, whose published reviews of the *salons* could establish an artist's reputation — and sales.[4]

Art dealers also provided a service for collectors. They sold taste, status, and expertise as well as art. By showing a small number of works in the privacy of a "gallery," the dealer evoked the high culture of an aristocratic private collection and the erudition of a museum within the familiar commercial milieu of a shop. The dealer's prior selection relieved new collectors of the anxiety that they might feel in making an uninformed choice. By the twentieth century, when dealers guaranteed the quality and the provenance of the works that they sold, this offered further reassurance. In short, through their dealers new collectors could acquire whole collections of art without investing either the time or the effort that was put in by traditional patrons. But the art dealer also provided a service for old-style patricians. If they had to sell off some of their property, then disposing of a piece of art through a gallery was discreet as well as profitable. Indeed, the combined functions of the early art dealers lived on in those galleries where the sale of art coexisted with a business in second-hand goods.

This embryonic marketing system worked so long as the art public remained fairly small and observed the conventional aesthetic distinction between old masters and living artists. Essentially, people considered old art valuable and new art ephemeral, decorative, or "photographic." Old Masters were bought by the old rich and conserved by museums for the public's edification. Living artists were supposed to juggle aesthetic and commercial standards without making too much of a scandal or taking themselves too seriously. The few early-twentieth-century collectors who specialized in contemporary art were generally newly rich rather than patrician, and sometimes eccentric in the seriousness with which they treated artists. Exemplifying this new sort of patronage were the Arensbergs in New York, Gertrude Stein's family in Baltimore (and Paris), and Gertrude Vanderbilt Whitney. The divided view of old art versus modern art supported the division of labor between museums and galleries. To be accepted by a museum implied canonization: it established the aesthetic value of an artist or an artist's work. However, to be represented by a gallery established commercial value and assured living artists, to some degree, of making a living.

Between 1910 and 1920 the pace of collecting modern art sped up. Like everything that was labeled "modern" at the time, modern art began to excite collectors as well as the wider public. In part, the attraction to modern art reflected the general current of the times and the rejection, finally, of a stagnant, academic art. But the public had also been prepared for modern art by the proselytizing efforts of a few art gallery owners, who were themselves involved in making art. The photographer Alfred Stieglitz, for example, started a gallery in New York in 1914 that showed contemporary European art (like Picasso's) and attracted adventurous young American artists such as Marsden Hartley and Georgia O'Keeffe. The 1913 Armory Show, which introduced abstract painting to the New York art public in a massive, and massively shocking, exhibition, also enlarged the audience for modern art and the number of potential buyers.[5]

Apart from this exhibition, there were not many places where people could view a selection of modern art, so modernism remained a somewhat elitist taste. However, by the 1930s a few small circles of rich, educated and well-traveled Americans who hoped to arouse greater public support for modern art succeeded in establishing museums that took the representation of modern art as their special mandate. For the first time, new museums like the Museum of Modern Art (1929), the Whitney (1930), and the Guggenheim (1939) – all in New York – featured the work of living artists. Each of these museums developed a specific constituency among the artists whom they patronized and the public to which they appealed. Together, they generated the kind of excitement about modern art that had been restricted to the new galleries and to particularly scandalous exhibitions. From a marketing point of view, the establishment of museums of modern art not only certified the aesthetic worth of contemporary artists but also helped to drive up the commercial value of their work. This blurred the original distinction between art museums and art galleries.

For different reasons, both the old public museums and the new modern art museums assumed an educating role in society in addition to their primary task of conserving the best or, later, the most representative works of art. The establishment of the earlier museums coincided with an expansion of citizenship rights to the lower classes – including the middle class, which for the first time in many European countries won the right to vote – and an explosion of political consciousness among many national and ethnic groups. Class consciousness and ethnicity presented a threatening prospect to the rulers of many nineteenth-century states. To counter their potential for fragmentation and conflict, the leading social classes that dominated these states encouraged a redefinition of national culture that stressed unity, conformity, and a certain amount of patriotism. Public institutions were enlarged and revamped – "modernized," we would say, if we weren't aware of the ulterior motive – to facilitate social integration. In cities, where crowds and riots have always been particularly disruptive, an intensive program of construction and instruction established museums, along with schools, parks, and zoos, as part of the public's cultural "curriculum." Later, during the waves of European and Asian immigration to America in the 1900s, so many new citizens entered the mainstream of American society that the public museums intensified their educational role. Together with the more dynamic new means of mass communication, which included movies, radio, and even advertising, the museums helped process the immigrants into a unified vision of American culture.

The missionary work of the new modern art museums that opened around 1930 operated on a more elite level. Because they were established primarily by individuals of "advanced" cultural views – the little group formed by Alfred Barr and architect Philip Johnson at the Museum of Modern Art (MOMA), Solomon R. Guggenheim at the Guggenheim Museum, and Gertrude Vanderbilt Whitney at the Whitney – they had to create a constituency among the local patricians who traditionally supported art museums. The founders of MOMA, for example, assiduously cultivated the Rockefeller family and made a serious collector of modern art out of the young Nelson Rockefeller. On another level, Leo Castelli and Sidney Janis, who became prominent New York art dealers in the 1950s, also received their "art education" there, through the museum's comprehensive collection and well-documented exhibitions. Inspired by MOMA's professionalism as well as its missionary zeal, they brought some quality of the museum to the art gallery. "What [Janis] did was of enormous importance," Castelli has said. "He really taught me that a gallery should be run like a museum — he had that kind of rigor."[6]

In the aftermath of World War II, the trends that had shaped the art market since the nineteenth century were intensified. Public attention shifted even more decisively from Old Masters to living artists and from art museums to art galleries. In Europe, the financially pressed upper class began to sell off their collections. But in contrast to the 1880s, when they sold primarily to affluent bourgeois collectors in their own countries, the Europeans now sold to affluent Americans or to a rising social group of international business leaders around the world. As in the earlier period, the acceleration of art sales greatly benefited the art galleries, whose dealings grew in number and scope as well as marketing technique. Through their efforts the art market became truly international. The enlargement of the market, and the more active role of dealers in it, soon led to an energetic search to uncover all the sources of Old Master paintings, the market's most volatile and most desirable item. Competition over the high commissions that were involved, as well as the reputations that were made by the hunt and the sale of famous paintings, encouraged some dealers to be manipulative. New galleries, known for their brashness or their hucksterism, sprang up alongside the established concerns. Frank Lloyd, for example, a concentration camp survivor whose shrewd manipulations propelled the new Marlborough Galleries into the front ranks of international art dealing, acquired some notoriety not only for trying to control the supply of Old Masters but also for trying to control their distribution so as to drive prices up. This in turn affected the market in works by living artists. Limitations that were imposed on the distribution of these works — imposed first by dealers alone and then by dealers in association with the artists' widows — enhanced their commercial value.[7]

Dealers skillfully used their role as intermediaries between artists and the market to sharpen their power. On the one hand, as they mounted increasingly significant exhibitions — annual exhibitions, in particular, which were at least as comprehensive and even more avant-garde than the museums' — they took over the museums' special forte. On the other hand, the dealers' unique ability to raise an artist's market value, often by negotiating with a museum to include the artist's work in its collection, gave them special influence over this work. Admittedly, the galleries had a symbiotic relation with the museums as well as the artists. Just as the artists supplied the galleries with what they sold, so the galleries supplied the museums with what they showed. Moreover, as in all market situations, inherent (or aesthetic) worth became interchangeable with market value. Artists remained, of course, the source of modern art, but to get to the artists, museums as well as collectors had to go through their dealers. This dramatically changed the perception of museums in relation to galleries. Although the galleries obviously "represented" artists in more than a merely commercial way, the museums more or less "entombed" them — a morbidly respectful view which abstract artist Ad Reinhardt expressed at the beginning of the 1960s.[8]

The growth of the art dealers' power hardly pleased the other partners in the triad.* From the mid-fifties to the mid-sixties, museums suffered a crisis of identity and confidence, and artists alternately spurned and sought the gallery connection to the marketplace. MOMA, whose founders had taken as their specific task representing the avant-garde, seemed especially shaken by the galleries' successes. MOMA's vulnerability stemmed in part from its European bias and a complacency that its vast holdings in Picasso, Braque, and company already represented the best of the "moderns." When the center of world art production shifted to New York from Paris after 1945, the museum was caught short. Its dynamism foundered; its mission was challenged. Slowly MOMA's founders began to pursue the artists who were working in New York. They visited their studios, and they tried to collaborate more actively with their galleries. Either because they had initially missed the significance of New York art or because they found the Abstract Expressionists' ready dominance of the American art world sterile or banal, in contrast to the diversity of styles and absence of self-conscious theorizing in European abstract art, the MOMA group tended to concentrate on younger artists who became prominent around 1960. They quickly adopted artists Jasper Johns and Frank Stella, and significantly, both Johns and Stella came to MOMA's attention through their dealer, Leo Castelli. Although it was a curator who had worked for years with Barr and the other founders who made the key decision to include Johns and Stella in a 1959 exhibition of "Sixteen Americans," a new generation of art curators greeted the artists of the sixties with an enthusiasm bordering on hysteria. In some sense these curators became promoters rather than conservers of art.[9]

The exhibitions that these curators devised around particular artists or themes, or simply new American art, generated excitement. For some

---

* Indeed, the museums' criticism of galleries at that time, for creating a spectacle and driving up prices, resembles the art dealers' criticism of auction houses like Christie's and Sotheby Parke Bernet.

years, a museum exhibition of work by a living artist had had the effect of raising prices on the artist's other work. Now, however, museum exhibitions had an effect on the work itself. Artists were rumored to have created pieces especially for a 1965 exhibition at MOMA, "The Responsive Eye," which was supposed to choose from work that had already been completed. Another MOMA exhibition of large sculpture-collages made with found objects (or what Robert Rauschenberg called "combines") coined the word that then became the standard term for this type of work: the *assemblage*. Though nothing succeeds like success, even the curators were surprised, or maybe appalled, at theirs. As the editor of *Arts* magazine, Lawrence Alloway, reproached a MOMA curator in 1967, "In any case, it seems to me that you put on a show at the museum and then you were embarrassed by its success. On the other hand, what I liked about 'The Responsive Eye' was that it was an exhibition put on at a major museum which became an instant success in fashion magazines, humor magazines, teenage magazines, *Time* magazine, and so on." Yet this spectacle – provoking a mass public for modern art – is precisely what the curator resists. "What's involved here is pure publicity," he says. "And it's not the influence of art or fashion, it *is* fashion." [10]

In all the publicity for Pop Art, Op Art, Minimalism, Conceptualism, and other approaches of the sixties, it was hard to tell whether the artistic vision was bidding up prices, or commercialism was transforming the artistic vision. Market value had become thoroughly confused with aesthetic worth. Museums and galleries responded to this situation, finally, by forming an alliance for their mutual protection. The newer galleries, which frequently specialized in new artists, tried to steer museums as well as individual collectors toward the latest trends and to direct artists to their potential markets. [11] As curators acted more like critics, critics like curators, and gallery owners like both critics and curators as well as dealers, [12] artists simultaneously let themselves be wooed and tried to run away from it all. Certainly the artists' financial status, which reflected the greater market value of modern art in general as well as that of the newer approaches and the newer artists in particular, influenced their attitude. By the late fifties, the affluence of those original members of the New York School who were still alive sparked periodic mini-rebellions among them in the form of ill manners. When the "second generation" of Abstract Expressionists, who started to show their work in the early sixties, began to command even higher prices and more effusive critical acclaim, the older artists vented their disgust with the art world in public and private statements. Despite the younger generation's greater success – as a group – in the art market, they "grew up" firmly believing that museums and collectors colluded to maintain the high market value of the art that they held. So the artists' relationship with the galleries that sold to this market was, at the very least, ambiguous. [13]

Over the years, artists tried to thwart the marketing system that the cosy arrangement between museums, galleries, and individual "patrons" had established. They did this in several ways. First, they changed their product. They made art in forms that were so big, so unwieldy, or so "environmental" that they could not easily be transported to a gallery, let alone displayed there, among other works, or in a private collector's living room. Actually, artists had been creating big works—primarily painting large canvases and carving large sculpture—since the late 1940s. They were influenced socially and aesthetically, by the realistic murals of the 1930s and the detritus of industrial production that was increasingly available in the 1950s. Or perhaps, like Barnett Newman, they were painting a big idea. But during the 1960s, artists began to describe their big or bulky work as resistance to the market, rebellion against "easel art," return to the "real." You could buy, but you obviously could not own, work like Michael Heizer's excavations in the desert or Christo's fences and wrappings— "Earth Art," as some of this work was called, or "de-aestheticized art," as Harold Rosenberg termed it. However, Rosenberg also pointed out the essential fallacy in this artistic rebellion. "The uncollectible art object," he says, "serves as an advertisement for the showman-artist, whose processes are indeed more interesting than his product and who markets his signature appended to commonplace relics." [14] In fact, as the Conceptualists later confirmed, artistic processes could be highly marketable. Another way that the Big Art rebellion boomeranged—if it had intended to succeed at all—was that the galleries quickly accommodated to the new style and the new size of the work. The degree of specialization among galleries suggested that some of the most successful dealers who sold modern art had both the financial capacity and the dynamism to exhibit art in new ways, and to take their market along with them. Primarily, to meet the challenge of Big Art, these galleries expanded physically.

Several of New York's "uptown" galleries specializing in new art opened branches in the large loft spaces of SoHo, and many more brand-new galleries established themselves there. In 1968 the first SoHo gallery opened its doors; by 1978 seventy-seven galleries were doing business in the area. To some degree, this reflects the general expansion of the 1960s art market. Between 1960 and 1975 the number of galleries and dealers listed in the Manhattan yellow pages jumped from 406 to 761, with the greatest increase occurring between 1960 and 1965. But the dramatic increase in the number of art galleries in SoHo, which occurred largely between 1972 and 1977, testifies to the market value of the new art and the new neighborhood. Where artists innovated, their dealers were not loath to follow, and the style of the galleries varied with that of the artists. [15] *

The second way that artists tried to thwart the marketing system simply

---

* By the same token, what the market creates, the market can also destroy. A key art dealer whose branching out to SoHo in 1971 is considered to have helped "tip" the neighborhood to high-rent art, retail, and residential uses—André Emmerich—sold his SoHo loft space in 1979 because art in the eighties is getting smaller.

involved "voting with their feet," and changing galleries. If they couldn't find dealers who thought of themselves as artists and actively sought artists' advice – gallery owners like Peggy Guggenheim in the 1940s and Betty Parsons in the late forties and fifties – then at least they found dealers who were sympathetic, that is, "artists' dealers," like Castelli in the fifties and sixties. Although an individual artist's changing galleries often expressed a personal or a financial conflict with the dealer, a group of artists' leaving a dealer en masse made a collective statement about that dealer's position in the art market. The withdrawal of several of the original Abstract Expressionists (Rothko, Motherwell, Gottlieb, and Baziotes) from Sidney Janis's gallery in 1962 made such a statement against what they interpreted as Janis's pandering to the young pups of Pop Art.[16]

Aside from depending on a sympathetic dealer, artists also formed their own galleries. Artists' co-ops, as these arrangements are called, reflect the need for a collective "alternative" channel to the marketplace rather than a common style or approach. This type of gallery springs up from time to time, primarily among new or "unsaleable" artists. In the 1950s, for example, the New York School had their co-op galleries on Tenth Street, and in the 1970s many of the new galleries in SoHo were co-ops. However, as long as the artists who use them depend solely on the art market for their livelihood, the artists' co-ops enjoy but a brief success. Eventually, some of the artists are either picked up by professional dealers, who are glad of the "screening process" that artists' co-ops provide, or the co-ops themselves hire professional "directors" with the explicit goal of improving the gallery's position in the marketplace.[17]

These responses to the competitive art market of the 1960s and 1970s gave rise to a movement toward the "alternative space." As we have seen, artists had been living, working, and trying to sell their work in such space for many years. As far back as 1850 the French painter Gustave Courbet exhibited in a seminary chapel, a market hall, and a converted café in various provincial towns, and surely he was neither the first nor the last artist to take advantage of whatever places were available. But during the 1960s the use of alternative space accelerated. To some extent, it was identified as a movement – together with the decade's "de-aestheticized" aesthetic movements and "socialist" social movements. Like loft living, it was also identified with an artist's need for large space at low cost. Nevertheless, the *production* of art in alternative spaces was less important in making this model – or movement, or lifestyle – accessible to the public than the *marketing* of art in alternative spaces. A significant factor in the success of the alternative space – as in the success of the galleries that also set up shop there – is that it *projects the image* of artistic production. For an increasingly production-conscious art and an increasingly art-conscious public, this image was vital. Power in the modern art market began to derive from a closeness, or the appearance of closeness, to the artist's studio.[18]

THE POWER OF THE ARTIST'S STUDIO

Nineteenth-century patrons of art went to the artist's studio as a matter of course, to have their portraits painted and to negotiate commissions with the artist. But in the twentieth century several factors intervened between the artist and the patron and made their relationship less direct. First, the further development of the galleries' role in the art market enhanced the patron-dealer relation at the expense of the patron-artist connection. Second, the technical improvement and social acceptance of newer art forms like photography enabled them to replace painting in some documentary situations, like portrait-making, that previously had led patrons to employ artists. Unlike painting, photography minimizes the contact between patron and photographer to only one sitting, and the production procedure in the darkroom doesn't involve the patron at all. A third reason for the change in patron-artist relations had to do with the evolution, since the nineteenth century, of the "romantic" concept of the artistic process, in which the artist increasingly expresses his or her own vision and choice of subject rather than what a patron orders. Not only do these factors change the relation between artist and patron but they also make the process of artistic creation more mysterious. Because painting, in particular, becomes more abstract, and the image on the canvas reflects ideas or states of being rather than "real life," the place where the artist produces these images takes on a metaphorical significance. The studio becomes the place — perhaps the only place in society — where the *self* is created. For a public that is no less concerned than artists with questions of self-doubt and self-expression, the studio begins to exert tremendous fascination.[19]

There are at least two additional reasons why the artist's studio became so interesting in the 1950s and 1960s. First, in a culturally jaded and not overtly political society like the United States, there appeared to be only two cradles of innovation — science and art — and the scientist's laboratory was technically less accessible than the artist's studio. Second, newly affluent art collectors understood going to the artist's studio as a symbolic *entrée* into the upper class, a public or semi-public recognition of their elite status. By the late 1950s, when owning an Old Master was limited to the wealthiest or most patrician collectors, the new collectors learned to delight in ferreting out undiscovered artists — *potential* Old Masters — "at the source," that is, in their studios. Of course, new collectors merely joined a trek to the artist's studio that already included art critics, museum curators, gallery "talent scouts," and "uptown *culturati*" who had begun to frequent "downtown" parties. It is difficult to say whether it was the commercialism or the anti-commercialism of modern art that attracted the public to the artist's studio. But clearly, there was a new interest in getting *in*.[20]

For the broader strata of arts consumers who could afford the price of a ticket but not the price of a painting, access to the artist's studio was made possible by the development of a new art form, the Happening. Spontaneous and impermanent, "environmental" and object-oriented, and slightly abusive toward their paying audience, the Happenings of the late fifties and early sixties capitalized on the public's willingness to "participate" in the artistic process. So they were a somewhat more dynamic version of the environmental art (as was Tinguely's slightly later *Hommage à New York*) "in which all kinds of mechanically induced stimuli and forces play upon the spectator and make him no longer a spectator but, willy-nilly, a participant and thus a 'creator' himself." [21] Perhaps there was a didactic element in the Happenings, for they were created by an art history professor at Rutgers University in 1959 and were performed mainly by artists and art teachers as well as their friends in music and dance, the traditional performing arts. Musician John Cage, dancer Merce Cunningham, and artist Robert Rauschenberg had performed something like a Happening — which they called The Event — in a summer session at innovative Black Mountain College in 1952. However, the mixed-media group performance that distinguished Happenings from both "art" and "theater" came to have a distinctly "downtown" rather than an academic ambiance. Happenings took on the character of the "alternative spaces" where they were performed. In New York, the Happenings' locale included an art gallery on Fourth Avenue, the off-Broadway Living Theater Space, a coffeehouse on Bleecker Street, the avant-garde performance center in a Greenwich Village church, and Yoko Ono's loft near City Hall. [22]

Susan Sontag and others relate Happenings to the surprise element in Surrealism, so that they create, in Sontag's words, "an art of radical juxtaposition." But Sontag also understands Happenings as "environmental" in the same sense that artists intended their Big Art: a protest against the art market — "against the museum conception . . . that the job of the artist is to make things to be preserved and cherished" — and those people who make great sums of money by buying and selling the artists' work. In Happenings, a former participant recalls, "everything was itself, it wasn't part of something bigger and fancier. And the fancy people didn't like this, because it was all cheap and simple, and nobody could make much money out of it." [23]

Yet in retrospect, the Happenings' locale produced a greater effect on the public that did either their art or their motivation. In this sense, Happenings are important because they lured people who were outside the art world into the unconventional performance space, which was often, also, an artist's studio. Happenings made people aware, too, of the performance elements in modern artistic creation. Within several years, this aspect of Happenings influenced the presentations (or, really, the self-exhibitions) of Conceptual artists and also contributed to a growing perception of the artist as a performer and thus a celebrity. In a recent memoir, for example,

Andy Warhol recalls how four thousand students crowded into the opening of a 1965 Warhol retrospective in Philadelphia to see and touch him and one of his female "superstars." "I wondered what it was that had made all those people scream," he writes. "I'd seen kids scream over Elvis and the Beatles and the Stones — rock idols and movie stars — but it was incredible to think of it happening at an *art* opening. . . . But then, we weren't just *at* the art exhibit, we *were* the art exhibit, we were the art incarnate." [24]

While Happenings whetted the public's appetite for closer contact, the presentation of more static works of art — paintings and sculptures — also moved closer to the artist's studio. Betty Parsons's art gallery probably was the first, in the late forties, to have the look and the feel of an artist's loft. Apparently this was due less to a conscious choice of décor than to Parsons's empathy with her artists. The Tenth Street School's co-op galleries, in the 1950s, also necessarily reproduced the ambiance of the studio. But an exhibition like the 1968 "Downtown Ten" actually brought the public into ten artists' studios. By showing their art in their lofts, a writer commented at the time, these artists "offer the public the opportunity for a new intimate, personal involvement with the exhibition process." However, the dealers that opened informal, unadorned galleries in SoHo in the 1970s consciously exploited their resemblance to artists' lofts. The SoHo galleries represent the logical commercial means of bringing the public into the artist's studio. [25] *

The brief but dramatic history of the Fluxus Movement, a loosely knit group of artists that emerged in SoHo before the neighborhood got the name, links the subliminal appeal of performance in the artist's studio with the subsequent growth of living lofts. Street theater that tried to come indoors, or a Surrealist vision of the real world, Fluxus is fondly remembered by its former participants as having made the whole SoHo art scene possible. First, Fluxus established for that area of Lower Manhattan a reputation as the place where artists practiced an informal, participatory, street-smart aesthetic. Fluxus really embodied Sontag's description of Happenings as an integration of urban junk and the New York School. If the Fluxus group took part in the trend toward environmental art, then the changing factory district of SoHo was the environment that it both mined and mimed. "Fluxus activity was almost certainly the earliest conceptual and performance activity to occur between Houston and Canal Streets," Peter France recalls in a memoir of Fluxus that was published in 1979. "The surplus stationers that predominated on the stretch of Canal between Centre Street and West Broadway were going out of business, and plastic surplus merchants and job lot dealers were replacing them. The little

---

* The sort of presentation that brings the public into the artist's studio is still going strong. The Downtown Ten recently organized their fourteenth annual exhibition in artists' studios in Lower Manhattan, and forty artists who live and work in lofts on the Brooklyn waterfront mounted a similar effort in 1980.

machines and objects available in these junk stores fascinated the artists in the neighborhood. . . . It can be demonstrated that the visual aesthetic informing Fluxus work depends heavily on the *objet trouvé* sensibility nurtured by the Canal Street atmosphere." [26]

But the Fluxus group was also important because its members lived in lofts. Alison Knowles was the first of the group to move into a loft in the area, at Broadway and Canal Street, in 1957. Her teacher, Abstract Expressionist Adolph Gottlieb, suggested it. Over the next ten years a vision slowly grew among the Fluxists of creating an artists' community in lofts. The greatest dreamer of them all was their informal leader, George Maciunas. A recent arrival on the New York art scene from Germany, Maciunas dreamed up an art-performance-conceptualist fun house, which would be a home for the artists that were gathering in the city from countries all over the world. In Maciunas' project, which he called "Fluxhouse Number 2," artists would live and work in housing co-ops that were converted lofts. So in this eccentric vision of a self-proclaimed leader of a "fringe" artistic movement, the "artists' community" of SoHo took its first concrete form.

SOCIAL POWER: ART AND THE MIDDLE CLASS

The artists who moved into SoHo at the end of the sixties were different from artists like the Fluxists who had been living and working in lofts since the beginning of the decade. During the 1960s, works of art — and working at art — went through a fundamental transformation. Previously regarded as rebellious and bizarre, artists became so integrated into the mainstream of American society that they were practically indistinguishable from other groups in the broadly defined middle class. For the same reasons, *artist* lost its almost exclusively male connotation. "We're bohemians but we're not beatniks," a founder of the Artists' Tenants' Association stated in 1962, and the key to the transformation indeed lies in the artist's progress from "beat" to "bohemian" to "middle class." [27]

Only in part does credit for this change belong to the high prices that works of art by living artists began to command at the end of the fifties. Certainly these prices greatly raised the artists' standard of living. They even motivated some artists to buy back their earlier works and hold them as an investment. But high prices merely contributed to the artists' transformation. Far more significant was the regularization of their employment *as artists,* which enabled them for the first time in history to make a living off a totally self-defined art. The state played a crucial role in this transformation. From 1965 on, the number of art jobs in state-supported educational and cultural institutions multiplied enormously. Government grants for arts activities rose from nearly nothing to a multimillion-dollar "industry." Demand built up to make art an integral part of "public spaces." The state's contribution to artistic careers also took an indirect form through its support for higher education, which encouraged many more young people than before to go to college. In the sixties, more artists were college-educated than in any previous generation. The success of Frank Stella, who went directly from Princeton to an exhibition at the Museum of Modern Art, may exaggerate the trend, but still, as artist Larry Rivers now reflects, in the early sixties it became apparent "that one could go into art as a career the same as law, medicine, or government." [28]

In contrast to the original bohemians of nineteenth-century Paris, who had to live off parents, brothers, and lovers and whose financial insecurity at times resembled that of the factory proletariat, artists in the 1960s were brought into the white-collar labor force. The sense of upward mobility that this imparted to an artistic career, through regular promotions and wage increases as well as newly created honorary and administrative positions, recalls that of the "second generation" of literary and artistic bohemians in Paris around 1860. Once bohemianism was recognized as a transitional stage, mostly youthful, it was accepted "socially." As Balzac wrote in *Un Prince de la Bohème,* "The *bohème* consists of young people, who are still unknown, but who will be well known and famous one day." This was certainly an idea that the bourgeoisie could appreciate. [29]

The growing similarity between artistic and other white-collar careers also brought the "artistic vision" closer to an ordinary middle-class world view. The irony of Pop Art and the paradox of loft living, for example, reflected a kind of social comment and personal "lifestyle" that the middle class of the 1960s could understand. If artists, critics, and curators persisted in theorizing, then the other college-educated members of the middle class could follow the argument — or at least, as in some art history courses, pretend to follow it and look at the Kodachrome slides. In any case, the arguments about the different approaches — such as Jasper Johns's famous flat brushstrokes — depended more on "a way of doing" than on "a way of seeing." They were essentially arguments about technique. Therefore they attacked or defended the artists' professionalism rather than their artistic vision. Underneath the theorizing lay a basic consensus about what the artists saw. They saw the same world that the middle class saw: a "continuous past" made by rapid social and technological change, the passing of industrialism and the devaluation of industrial work, and a mass production of art objects and cultural standards. In these conditions, art no longer either contradicted or negated the value of social existence, especially the life of the middle class. Instead, art found its function in representing this existence and its implicit existential *angst.* Far from "shocking the bourgeoisie," art became the aesthetic vision of the bourgeoisie. "Art today is a new kind of instrument," Susan Sontag wrote in the mid-sixties, "an instrument for modifying consciousness and organizing new modes of sensibility." No longer particularly ascetic or philistine, the middle class accepted art as part of "a new (potentially unitary) kind of sensibility."[30]

The new view of art as "a way of doing" rather than a distinctive "way of seeing" also affected the way art was taught. On the one hand, the "tremendous production emphasis" that Harold Rosenberg decries gave rise to a generation of practitioners rather than visionaries, of imitators instead of innovators. As professional artists became facile in pulling out visual techniques from their aesthetic and social context, they glibly defended themselves with talk of concepts and methodology. On the other hand, the teaching of art as "doing" made art seem less elitist. If almost anyone can be taught to follow a technique and thereby reproduce "art," then anyone, anywhere, can legitimately expect to be an artist.[31]

All in all these changes had the combined effect of making art both more "professionalized" and more "democratized." In both senses, working in the "arts field" became accessible to people who previously had had no special artistic purpose or vision. This opened art as a career — or as Larry Rivers notes, as one career option among others — for such people. Even more important, it opened art as a *second* career for people who had not yet been integrated into the labor market in a significant way. In this sense, the recent attraction of women, especially college-educated, middle-class women, to arts-and-crafts careers is relevant. By the late sixties and early seventies more than a million adults in America identified their occupation as in some way connected with the creative arts. While at the beginning of the sixties, estimates of artists working in New York City ranged from one thousand to thirty-five thousand, census data at the beginning of the seventies shows around one hundred thousand of them living there. The question of whether they do good art is less important, socially, than their belief that they are artists. "Art is anything with creative intentions," the former chairman of the National Endowment for the Humanities, Ronald Berman, caustically remarks, where the word " 'creative' has . . . been removed from the realm of achievement and applied to another realm entirely. What it means now is an attitude toward the self; and it belongs not to aesthetics but to pop psychology." In this situation, the ultimate and "impartial" arbiter of who is an artist — though not, of course, of what is art — is the state. Ironically, then, the "democratic" definition of art as a set of production techniques, the state-supported employment of artists as service-sector "producers," and the middle-class plunge into artistic activity have the effect of subjecting art to political criteria.[32]

But the arts-and-crafts movement of the 1970s also shows how deeply art has been incorporated into many middle-class patterns of consumption. To some degree, art sells as a pastime — the paint-by-numbers craze of the fifties, for example, or the Jackson Pollock abstract jigsaw puzzle of the sixties — and to some degree, art sells as fashion. "By the time the Museum [of Modern Art]'s big Op Art show opened in the fall [of 1965]," Tom Wolfe remarks, "two out of every three women entering the glass doors on West Fifty-third Street for the opening night hoopla were wearing print dresses that were knock-offs of the paintings that were waiting on the walls inside."[33] However, museum attendance figures suggest that relics from Tutankhamon's tomb, Scythian gold figures, and Picasso's life's work also "sell." A chamber music concert for which so many tickets are bought that some members of the audience have to sit on stage — that surely shows heightened interest in arts consumption. Ten years ago, two sociologists, Joseph Bensman and Arthur Vidich, proclaimed, "It is clear that artistic cultivation, sophistication, and consumption serve as a new basis for status and life styles in the broad middle sector. . . . This is a wholly new development and one which has replaced small-town, middle-class bourgeoisie Babbittry, not to mention the Protestant Church itself." Yet it is easy to over-exaggerate, as Bensman and Vidich do, this "cultural revolution" that has farmers' wives in Iowa snapping up "original" oil paintings in the aisles of the local Sears, Roebuck.[34] In fact, something *has* changed. But it is worthwhile to recall the failure of the brief attempt to sell "original" art on the mass market — at Sears and Korvette's — as well as the circumstances.

Independently, between 1966 and 1971, Sears and Korvette's established "galleries" that stocked, for the most part, signed lithographs by well-known artists such as Picasso, Chagall, and Miró. The quality of the Korvette's art selections was higher than that of Sears's, for Sears also sold oil paintings that were calculated to "go with" standard living-room décor. However, the Korvette's decision to market original art work derived from the personal commitment of its founder and chairman, Eugene Ferkauf, who was also an art collector. Indeed, Korvette's set up an art department in only one branch store — in contrast to Sears, which tried to sell art nationally — and this branch was close to Ferkauf's house. The Korvette's art department did not really look as though it belonged with the rest of the store. Located on an upper level with its own separate entrance, as the former store manager now recalls, the department had the ambiance of a Manhattan art gallery. The only problem was that it was neither a gallery nor in Manhattan. It was in Queens, one of New York City's Outer Boroughs. And it was in a discount store. The Korvette's art department failed because of the high cost of maintaining its inventory and the relatively low unit profit that it produced. For a gallery, its profit level may have been adequate, but it didn't generate the dollars per square foot that a store like Korvette's required. It also failed to attract the customers who shopped in the rest of the store — the real mass market that Bensman and

Vidich imagined. When Ferkauf retired in 1971, Korvette's eliminated the art department. Presumably, Sears's attempt to sell art on the mass market met with similar difficulties.[35]

At Korvette's, the people who profited from the mass marketing of art were the employees who, with their employee discounts, bought for three hundred dollars lithographs that have quadrupled in value. However, the reason for their success as middle-class consumers of the arts is that they bought *signed* work by *famous* artists. This suggests that at least since the 1960s, a strong undercurrent in middle-class arts consumption has been to buy art as an investment rather than as either a thing of beauty or a status symbol. Of course, by this point in our inflationary times, those motives are thoroughly mixed. A radio commercial for Christie's art auctions, for example, features a young ingenue who says, "Yes, mother, I know everyone shops at that store, but doesn't it make sense to start out with fine arts from someone's collection instead of some designer's ideas?" Self-expression, status, taste, investment — who can calculate the appeal of art? The interesting point about the attempt by Korvette's and Sears' to mass market art is that, at least at top management levels, someone realized that an arts constituency was out there. Meanwhile, at the highest levels of the state, an effort was also being made to define and to mold this constituency.

THE ARTS AND STATE POWER

During the 1960s the state's role in society grew enormously. Partly this growth entailed the idea that the state should be a collective patron — indeed, the biggest patron — of the arts. Instrumental in defining state patronage of the arts were three New York politicians: the late Governor Nelson Rockefeller, Senator Jacob Javits, and Congressman (later Mayor) John Lindsay. It was natural enough for politicians from this area to take an active role in channeling state support to the arts, for New York City has long enjoyed a hegemonic position in various art markets. But in addition, these three men were uniquely situated to discover — and exploit — the arts as a series of constituencies. Rockefeller and Lindsay belonged to New York's patrician elite; Rockefeller and Javits (or Mrs. Javits) were patrons of modern art; the three were, at the time, Republicans, and so they were linked to big corporate political (and philanthropic) contributors; and all three men represented diverse groups of "liberal" voters who did not definitively identify themselves with either major political party. To some degree, their personal and political positions as pivots between those groups conditioned Rockefeller, Javits, and Lindsay to be receptive to the notion of an "arts constituency."

However, they were also attuned to changes in the whole system of American electoral politics that had only just begun in the 1960s. These changes included the decline of party identification among voters, the rise of new social movements that influenced votes, the emergence of single-issue voting and pressure groups, and the development of recognizable constituencies that were no longer defined by traditional social criteria, like a "youth vote," an "anti-Vietnam" vote, and, in the case of Lindsay's first mayoral administration, an ecology-minded "bicycle constituency." In addition to changes in art, something happened in American politics between 1960 and 1970 that made state support for the arts defensible and smart. In 1961, Congress defeated a bill to create a federal advisory council on the arts which President Eisenhower had suggested as far back as 1955; but in 1977, according to former Congressman John Brademas, a long-time supporter of pro-arts legislation, "today the arts are politically saleable. Now a Congressman could get into more difficulty voting against the arts than for." [36]

In reality, the East Coast Establishment, to which Rockefeller, Lindsay, and Javits belonged — the round robin of exclusive corporate, political, and social memberships that was centered in Wall Street and Washington, D.C. — had already decided on a greatly expanded program of support for the arts. As early as 1957 the Ford Foundation had set up its first program on the humanities and the arts. The Ford Foundation's close links with other major foundations, corporations, and the state suggest that their example would eventually have an impact on state policy. Most of the political and conceptual groundwork for state patronage of the arts was laid between 1960, when Governor Rockefeller established a prototype agency, the New York State Council on the Arts (NYSCA), and 1965, when Congress voted to establish the National Endowments for the Arts and the Humanities. Rockefeller's friends and allies, Javits and Lindsay, rallied congressional support for this legislation, and another New York associate, foundation president August Heckscher, acted as an intellectual link between NYSCA and the White House, primarily by summarizing the NYSCA (and his own) philosophy in a special report on the arts for President Kennedy in 1963. The interpenetration of Javits's, Lindsay's, and Heckscher's efforts and ideas, in the political climate of the time, accounts for the quantum leap in state support for the arts during the 1960s. Looking carefully at what they said, we find that patronage of the arts was involved in the struggle for power between nations and within the state — a motivation that recalls the official concern with art and industrial design, and their influence on industrial exports, in Britain, France, and Germany prior to World War I, as well as the official encouragement of socialist and social realism in the Soviet Union and the United States, respectively, during the 1930s. [37]

After World War II, support for the arts became a useful tool in the propaganda efforts of capitalist states. Ideally, these states should place no restrictions on the art that they sponsor. It is sufficient – and necessary – that the state-supported art of the "Free World" appear to be totally *free*. Britain, which rose quite early to the Soviet challenge in art and culture, established a national Arts Council in 1945, under a policy that "was intended to show the world that in the so-called 'Free World' artists produce works of great beauty and imaginative strength, whereas the Soviet 'Socialist Realist' system produces only hollow, rhetorical, academic *art officiel.*" [38] The United States was rather slow to follow the British example. Although some business and government leaders saw in modern art, particularly in Abstract Expressionism, a stylistic representation of America at the "cutting edge" of world markets and world politics, politicians on the extreme Right remained suspicious of both abstract art and modern artists for expressing "communist" tendencies. Consequently, American artists in the postwar period began to depend on support from politicians of the Center and patrons in the corporate sector with whom these politicians were often allied. Indeed, when the U.S. government responded to the "peace offensive" launched around the world in the early 1950s by the Soviet Union, it was private institutions like the Museum of Modern Art and the Rockefeller Brothers Fund that provided artwork and the financial means to send it on traveling exhibitions to other countries. They also furnished the public justification for using modern art to represent the official American image. Among the cultural forms that received special promotion at this time were jazz and the fine arts. Both must have appeared impermeable by propagandistic intentions – jazz because of the predominance of black musicians, and the fine arts because of their association with high culture. In reality, however, these forms proved to be a subtle, and thus effective, means of reaching social groups in foreign countries that might be expected to harbor cynicism about, and even opposition to, American political and economic goals. The judicious choice of artists, and the well-planned preparation of exhibition material, paved the way toward acceptance abroad of postwar American liberalism. [39]

The government probably spent more money in sending art abroad and helping to set up organizations for "cultural freedom," which were often infiltrated by the Central Intelligence Agency, in foreign countries, than it did in promoting arts activities "at home." But at the end of the fifties the direct challenge of Societ space technology pushed the United States into a Sputnik reflex, which generated a massive reorganization of the state's educational and cultural apparatus, particularly in science.

For several reasons, it now seemed logical to extend the same treatment to art as to science. First, art – and artists – was no longer so political, or so leftwing, as it had been in the 1930s. War and prosperity, as well as generational change and disillusionment with socialists and Socialist

Realism, had changed artists' politics. Second, the success that the government had enjoyed in exporting American culture, and the prestige of painters like those of the New York School, made artists appear to be valuable national property. Third, as Susan Sontag noted in the early sixties, the traditional dichotomy between "the two cultures" was vanishing, so that aesthetics no longer seemed more esoteric or less useful than science. Finally, modernizing an educational system that historically was oriented toward the liberal arts required that the government work within existing institutional frameworks. The U.S. effort to upgrade the cultural curriculum — for a "stronger" young generation — enriched art as well as science, and athletics in addition to modern languages.

It was clear that some people in government thought that art did belong among items of high national priority. In 1959 a task force on the arts appointed by newly elected President Kennedy recommended that an "educational and cultural affairs" coordinator be established in either the State Department or the Executive Office instead of in the usual educational or cultural bureaucracy. Yet at the same time, Congress consistently rejected proposals to set up advisory bodies on the arts in Washington, D.C. Nevertheless, the theme of foreign competition resounded in the arguments of the small number of congressional representatives who were committed to state support for the arts. Speaking in favor of August Heckscher's 1963 report on "The Arts and the National Government," for example, Senator Javits said that a comprehensive national arts "program . . . will enable us — far better than we do today — to meet the challenge of the Communists' cultural ideas in the world, on which they are spending great amounts of money for their propagation and which represent the key aspect of their activities, which are designed to 'bury' the Free World." [40]

Aside from its importance in terms of the competitive goals of foreign policy, a national program in the arts also had some significance for domestic political struggles. A strong governmental presence in this area could help to maintain state power — especially in the concentrated form of the modern Welfare State — against opponents who wanted to reduce or dilute it. In this sense, the growth of state support for the arts contributed to state power in three different ways. First, it justified the strong state as a defender of general human aims and aspirations rather than a destroyer of freedom and civilization. Second, it maintained the New Deal principle that the state should encourage spending and employment. Third, the expansion of state-supported employment in the arts, as well as the increasing rationalization of employment conditions in art and culture,*

---

* This rationalization includes, eventually, standardization of wages (and the imposition of a legally guaranteed minimum wage), regularization of tax deductions and royalty payments, unionization, and financing for artists' health insurance and retirement pensions.

permitted the state to spread its control over the social reproduction of a previously unincorporated – or "autonomous" – part of the labor force: creative artists.

The terms that justified the strong state of the 1960s differed fundamentally from the terms that introduced the New Deal in the 1930s. Unlike the arts project of the WPA, the arts policy of the 1960s did not view art as an instrument of economic recovery. Instead, the new state patronage of the arts gave the Welfare State the role of improving the "quality of life." When John Maynard Keynes discussed this point, his terms were almost identical with August Heckscher's. Keynes envisaged "'individual and free, undisciplined, unregimented, uncontrolled' artists ushering in a new Golden Age of the arts which, he said, would recall 'the great ages of a communal civilized life.'" Almost a generation later, Heckscher speaks of a growing awareness in America that the society will be judged by "the quality of its civilization": "We have come to feel as a people . . . that we should have a higher degree of national well-being in proportion as the arts come into their own." The state must rise to the occasion – "the accomplishment of the true tasks of a civilized community" – recalling those "moments . . . when statesmen possessed the clear realization that the forms of art reflected the inner ideals of the social order."[41]

At this time, as a chapter in Heckscher's 1962 book, *The Public Happiness,* puts it, the state must go "Beyond Welfare." While the government has been "preoccupied almost exclusively" until now with economic issues, "at some point the concern with welfare could be expected to pass out of the political realm into the realm of administration, and politics should then have concerned itself with more interesting things." Dealing with these "more interesting things," the state appears "at its most creative. . . . It is then the great critic, shaper, judge; it sets the patterns and the style of the common life. . . . At such times the ruler becomes the great teacher, and imitation of his ways and his character is a force at work throughout the social sphere."[42] How could this appeal fail to sway a president who was looking for a national mission? Furthermore, Heckscher's is really a liberal version of the 1960s "transition to affluence" scenario that Herbert Marcuse and others hoped would lead to a more radical social transformation. In his own area, then, Heckscher played an ideological role similar to Arthur M. Schlesinger, Jr.'s, for Heckscher's depiction of patronage of the arts suggests that a strong state can continue to be a liberal state. This indicates the general political significance of state support for the arts in the 1960s, as well as the decline in such support during the 1980s.

Specifically, however, the state's role as patron suited the needs of ambitious politicians. As governor, Rockefeller planned so many public buildings, including a monumental new state capitol and many campuses of the State University, that he was accused of having an "edifice complex." As mayor, Lindsay appointed August Heckscher cultural affairs commissioner and threw open the city's parks to new cultural "events." And as president, both Kennedy and Johnson used the arts as a means of tapping public approval. Heckscher astutely recognized this element in connection with Kennedy's successes and failures. First the success: the 1960 inauguration. As Heckscher recalls today, the idea of inviting various literary and cultural figures to attend JFK's inauguration came from a Kennedy supporter who was working for the new administration in Washington, D.C., a woman whose family owned a department store in Cleveland. When the press gave a lot of favorable coverage to the new administration's "cultural tone," no one was more surprised than the administration. But Heckscher and other advisers quickly moved to ascertain whether this really implied a popular ground swell. They sent out a survey to communities across the country, asking what the government should do for the arts. Apparently the responses were encouraging. In 1962 Kennedy appointed Heckscher special consultant on the arts. But at the same time, the administration suffered a serious failure: the Bay of Pigs invasion. In *The Public Happiness* Heckscher offers state patronage of the arts as a means of restoring confidence in the state's leaders. He invites Kennedy to compare himself with King Ferdinand of Spain, who, according to Machiavelli, regained the allegiance of his dubious subjects "by providing them with great expectations." In Heckscher's view, the new state patronage of the arts could inspire a similar response.[43]

Yet it is important to note that these expectations are "spiritual" rather than material. In theory, a citizenry that imbibes of art and culture limits its appetite for economic gain. Again, Heckscher voices the liberal interpretation: spreading art among the masses should allow them to turn inward in pursuit of "harmony" instead of aggressively seeking an illusory idea of "comfort." Since some material discomfort is inevitable, people should be discouraged from pursuing "a meaningless quest," "to eliminate the last element of hardness or friction."[44] Undoubtedly Heckscher did not mean to condemn all social activism. But the notion that the arts could be used to *limit* expectations appealed to the big business leaders — primarily corporate executives, bankers, and lawyers from the Eastern Establishment — who became involved in business support for the arts during the 1960s.

The Rockefeller family connection between business, politics, and private foundations played an important role in generating this support. Just as Governor Nelson Rockefeller almost single-handedly built NYSCA into an umbrella agency for distributing the state's largesse, so his brother David Rockefeller, head of Chase Manhattan Bank, and the family's philanthropies, the Rockefeller Brothers Fund and the Rockefeller Foundation, created the financial and organizational infrastructure that an expanded collective patronage of the arts required. It was no easier to

generate support for the arts in business than in Congress, but the precedent that the state established clearly prodded the business community. In
1962, two years after Governor Rockefeller set up NYSCA, a closed
meeting of the Conference Board, a national group of corporate executives, invited two arts organizations to discuss their funding problems
with the group. The following year, the Rockefeller Brothers Fund
appointed a special panel — which included August Heckscher, who had
just submitted his report on the arts to President Kennedy — to study "The
Performing Arts: Problems and Prospects." The panel's report was published in 1965, almost simultaneously with President Lyndon B. Johnson's
proposal that Congress establish a National Foundation in the Arts and
the Humanities. Two weeks later, the New York Board of Trade, an
association headed by David Rockefeller, formed an advisory committee
on the arts. In 1966 David Rockefeller proposed that the Conference
Board establish a permanent Business Council on the Arts — which it did in
1967. Around this time, the foundation of which Heckscher had served as
president, the New York-based Twentieth Century Fund, took over the
work of the Rockefeller Fund's panel, in which Heckscher had also participated. The Twentieth Century Fund commissioned a more thorough
study, by two Princeton University professors, on "The Performing Arts:
Economic Dilemma." When the federal government had to set up the
bureaucracy of the twin national endowments, after their creation in 1965,
high-level arts administrators began to circulate among positions in the
Rockefeller Foundation, NYSCA, and Washington. After all, who else
had the experience in large-scale patronage that the new policy required?

Certainly the business community could be expected to harbor expectations about this policy that both compared and contrasted with the state's.
In general, top-level leaders in business and the state — perspicacious
planners like David and Nelson Rockefeller — saw the arts as a way of
reestablishing cultural and political hegemony, and a means of absorbing
unemployment. While state intellectual Heckscher spoke of using art to
recapture society's "basic coherence and purpose," business leader Rockefeller placed a somewhat different value on art. To Rockefeller, the arts
offered a replacement for the "unproductive and aimless activities" that
new leisure time and new affluence had spawned. Although Rockefeller
invokes the "humanist revolution" of the Renaissance, his sense of public
purpose really evokes the shadow of social control. Similarly, a 1968
speech by C. Douglas Dillon, another member of the Eastern Establishment, on "The Corporation, the Arts, and the Ghetto," says that art can
"provide a voice for the youth who live in the poverty areas," as well as
overcome the "voicelessness, isolation, depersonalization" which are rife in
society as a whole. This approach recalls President Kennedy's message to
Congress in June 1963, in which he established an Advisory Council on the
Arts. At that time, Kennedy referred not only to the uplifting quality of

the arts but also to the Labor Department's gloomy projections of declining job opportunities in art-related fields. Although in the sixties young people were starting to enter art careers in far greater numbers, there were neither jobs nor grants to support them once they got past the entry level. Youth unemployment, smoldering urban ghettos, a crumbling social consensus — these conditions made wider support for the arts appear to be an urgent response to potentially severe social problems. "With urban malaise spreading," a researcher reports without any sarcasm, "a small group of business leaders, men like David Rockefeller, Arnold Gingrich of *Esquire,* George Weissman of Philip Morris and Dr. Frank Stanton of CBS, recognized and promulgated an important concept — that a so-called amenity, such as the arts, was in reality the very lifeblood needed to inject hope, purpose and beauty into a troubled society." [45]

As early as 1960, before there *was* a policy of state or corporate support for the arts, a shrewd observer could guess that as usual, the gift horse hid ulterior motives. "Anyone who speaks of using art to further domestic or international relations is out of his mind," Abstract Expressionist Ad Reinhardt wrote at the time. [46] Yet there were at least three clear-cut benefits that business and state leaders could expect to derive in exchange for their support of arts activities: the creation of service-sector jobs, political donations, and tax deductions.

First, providing jobs in the arts offers a relatively cheap way of satisfying social demands. Indeed, from the point of view of *lowering* expectations, employment in the arts is better than other kinds of work. It carries a relatively low salary and a relatively high prestige. It promises a sense of satisfaction that is inherent in the work itself, or in the social status of art, rather than the status of the jobholder or the job. Moreover, despite their increasing professionalization, the arts still lack a well-defined career hierarchy. Compared to most industrial and some white-collar work, many art-related occupations (like painting or dancing) don't have a formal seniority system, or a wage-labor situation like being hired or being fired. So expanding jobs in the arts could be expected to produce a fairly amorphous and relatively quiescent labor force.

Second, state support for the arts could be expected to generate different kinds of political contributions from different types of art constituencies. On the one hand, as Senator Javits apparently reflected when he proposed including symphony orchestras and operas in pro-arts legislation in 1963 (in the Keogh-Curtis bill, which pertains to tax deductions), the patrician boards of directors of established cultural institutions should feel some gratitude toward legislators who cater to the interests of their groups. On the other hand, artists who enjoyed the direct and indirect support of the state could also be expected to show their gratitude during political campaigns. As these campaigns come to rely more and more on public contributions, artists, especially those whose work has a proven market value, can contribute more than a merely symbolic presence. If artists donate to a campaign work that can be reproduced cheaply, like Robert Rauschenberg's or Andy Warhol's silkscreens, then the campaign can make a handsome profit on their sale. In 1980, for example, Senator Edward Kennedy's presidential campaign made four hundred thousand dollars from the reproduction and sale of work by Rauschenberg, Warhol, and thirty-nine other artists. This represents a much higher profit margin than, say, Governor Jerry Brown's rock concerts. And it looks much more refined than soliciting a cash contribution. Once the state stepped up its funding of local arts-and-crafts activities, this too increased the number of arts constituencies that could be considered as owing loyalty to the legislators who funded them.

Probably the most complicated of these give-and-take relationships involved the issue of tax deductions for contributions to cultural institutions. Here the constituency joins patrician patrons of the arts, who are often art collectors; the major cultural institutions — the biggest museums and the local symphonies — which they sponsor; and the artists who have achieved the highest market value. Like all tax deductions, these benefit the wealthiest people, who naturally can afford to make large contributions. Their tax-deductible cultural contributions may take two forms: financial contributions, in either cash or gifts of goods and services, like a wing of a museum, and contributions of works of art. The federal tax laws permit an individual to buy a piece of art for his or her collection and, after a year or so, to donate it to a museum — taking at that point a tax deduction on the new, and usually higher, market value. Of course, a museum must agree to accept the work in question. So there is some possibility that a collector might suffer the financial consequences of poor aesthetic judgment. However, quite early in the history of these tax deductions, museums and the patrician collectors to whom they were closest worked out a system for minimizing the risks to each. On the one hand, collectors risked buying an expensive piece of art and then having the museum reject their choice. On the other hand, museums risked being inundated with pieces that were either unsuitable for or incompatible with their collections. The solution was to have museum curators *advise* collectors on their potentially tax-deductible purchases.

Both museums and collectors stood to benefit from the piggyback acquisition process. Moreover, at least as early as the 1950s, museum curators tried to derive an additional benefit from the system by convincing rich collectors to buy controversial pieces — which the museum's board of trustees would not agree to purchase — and donate them, after the specified time, to the museum. Some of these collectors may have been members of the board, but they were more amenable, as individuals facing a potentially large tax deduction, than the board as a whole to investing in unknown or untested artists.[47] Significantly, museum acquisition, even by donation rather than purchase, drives up an artist's market value, so that this system benefited the artist as well as the individual collector and the museum.

The higher-priced artists also took advantage of these tax deductions by donating their own work to museums. They then benefited in two ways: from the deduction itself and from the museum exposure of their work. In 1969, Congress changed the form of this subsidy to artists by limiting tax deductibility to the cost of materials rather than the market value of the finished work. But the Tax Reform Act of 1969 did not affect the deductions of wealthy collectors. They continued to enjoy a state subsidy for their art collecting by taking deductions on the donated work's "fair market value." This system contributed further to the already rising prices in the heady art market of the sixties.[48]

Despite the socially progressive legislation of much of the 1960s, Congress never attacked the basic principle behind tax deductions for "cultural" contributions. Periodic conflicts did break out, however, over the amount of tax deductibility that rich collectors should enjoy. In 1963, just before Heckscher submitted his report on the arts, Representatives Keogh from New York and Curtis from Missouri introduced a bill to *raise* from 20 percent to 30 percent the ceiling on the tax deductibility of contributions to libraries and museums. This percentage applied to the cash or market value of the donation. In the House, Lindsay defended the Keogh-Curtis bill, and in the Senate, Javits added symphony orchestras and operas to the institutions for which donations would be tax deductible. Naturally, every arts constituency lobbied to be included. Patron of the arts John D. Rockefeller III suggested that ballet and repertory drama companies and community art centers be added to the list. In his report, Heckscher supported an across-the-board 30 percent tax deductibility on donations to all cultural institutions.[49] Certainly the tax advantages enjoyed by corporate and rich individual donors remained part of the bedrock of private American philanthropy toward the arts. Once again, the motivations behind patronage joined with motifs of privilege and power.

The policy of state support for the arts in the 1950s and 1960s drew upon a multitude of motives and a number of social bases, from competition in the cold war to tax advantages for wealthy patrons. It welded together old constituencies, such as patricians and the cultural institutions that they patronized, and new constituencies, including artists in the labor force and arts-and-crafts activists. The state played on the competition between these constituencies over funds and on the competition between museums and galleries over middle-class investment in the arts. In this process, power in the art market was rapidly translated into social power, economic power, and state power. The enigmatic content of much contemporary art became a paradoxical symbol of both power and powerlessness, illustrating art critic John Berger's remark that "diagrams of aesthetic power lend themselves to becoming emblems of economic power." [50] In this maelstrom of motivations and constituencies that linked as well as separated different social classes, a new concern for assuring the conditions of arts production arose. For this to happen, the pattern of patronage had to change; it had to combine the traditional functions of art patrons with the functions of the Welfare State. Without this change of patronage, the New York loft scene of the 1970s could not have been created.

5

FROM ARTS PRODUCTION
TO HOUSING MARKET

Providing space in the city for artists is more complicated than it appears. Although the idea originates in philanthropy — as a payment or a subsidy in kind rather than in money — it often has the effect of enhancing property values, and so it becomes a springboard for real estate development. This phenomenon is not peculiar to New York. By the mid-sixties, even local elites in Sun Belt cities, notably Dallas and Los Angeles, planned to redevelop their downtown around an arts presence. The early-twentieth-century "civic centers," which were planned and built by earlier local elites, suggest a precedent for concentrating cultural facilities near, but not in, the downtown area. The more recent construction of Lincoln Center for the Performing Arts in New York, in the late 1950s, set another important example. Although Lincoln Center's destruction of housing stock in stable, low-income communities was not really defensible, its construction of arts facilities was deemed socially acceptable. Moreover, the amenity that a concentrated arts presence offers to middle-class and upper-class arts consumers makes it possible to charge high prices for the housing that is eventually built nearby. Lincoln Center demonstrated that placing infrastructure for the arts in a devalorized area can work wonders for real estate development. Ten years later, the lofts of SoHo provided unexpected confirmation of this rule.

To a degree, as the discussion of the artist's studio suggests, an arts presence is attractive for purely symbolic reasons. However, the history of modern art markets and state support for the arts indicates that the symbolism is also connected with motifs of power. There is yet a third factor that explains the value of an arts presence to contemporary cities. This refers to the crucial role that arts production — involving the creation as well as the presentation or the performance of artwork — plays in deindustrialization. Both materially and symbolically, artists' lofts serve as infrastructure of a very special sort in the transition from an industrial to a deindustrialized urban economy. On the one hand, they are a place where "post-industrial" production is really carried out. On the other hand, they embody the switch in orientation from an industrial political economy to one that is dominated by the service sector. As both site and symbol, the artist's loft serves a purpose in a world city of a new type: the capital of banking, finance, and art markets. In this sense it is not surprising that declining manufacturing centers like New York have hailed artists as an "industry." Moreover, art is a growth industry for a period of economic no-growth, a sector in which quality, not size, is determinant. "The arts may be small in economic terms even in this region," says Dick Netzer, pro-arts advocate and member of New York City's powerful Municipal Assistance Corporation, "but the arts 'industry' is one of our few growth industries. . . . The concentration of the arts in New York is one of the attributes that makes it distinctive, and distinctive in a positive sense: the arts in New York are a magnet for the rest of the world." [1]

Nevertheless, in the course of subsidizing artists' physical infrastructure, there emerged several contradictions between the intentions and the consequences of state support. First, artists' access to loft space was championed by two constituencies with different sets of goals: an upper-class group of patrons of the arts and patrician politicians, who wanted to promote artists and save old buildings, and a middle-class group of urban homeowners — including artists — who wanted to protect their neighborhoods. Eventually the success of both constituencies opened up loft areas to real estate developers. Second, the spread of loft living to a larger middle-class group of housing consumers caused a conflict in the loft market between two basically "nonproductive" uses: arts infrastructure and housing. In time, competition over the finite amount of space in old loft buildings turned the artists' subsidy into the pivot of a new market. Third, the people who moved into lofts and created their own, loft dwellers' constituency defended their right to live in lofts but opposed real estate development. To their chagrin, they found they couldn't have it both ways. A subsidy for artists' housing finally created demand for a market in living lofts.

A HOUSING SUBSIDY FOR ARTISTS

Until the late 1960s there was no history of funding housing for artists. Just as artists no longer worked exclusively for a particular patron but sold their work on the art market, so they were also expected to buy or rent the housing and studio that they could afford. Although successful artists like Rodin and Picasso, or de Kooning and Calder, could afford to set up comfortable establishments, most artists suffered from a perennial search for cheap but well-lighted space. In New York, the last philanthropist who set up living and work space for artists was nineteenth-century real estate developer James J. Johnson. The Tenth Street Studio, which Johnson built in 1857, had large, loftlike spaces that accommodated studios for portrait sittings (as well as prop rooms for the costumes and accessories that portrait sitters of the day required) and adjacent living areas. After serving as headquarters for the most famous Greenwich Village artists of the 1860s to the 1880s, the Tenth Street Studio was eventually sold on a co-op basis to its artist-tenants. Significantly, the period when it became a co-op — the 1920s — was when gentrification priced most working-class and artist residents out of this part of the Village.[2]

Years later, in the wake of August Heckscher's report on the arts, the Federal Housing Administration (FHA) allocated funds to subsidize artists' rent payments wherever they happened to be living. However, this subsidy turned out to be impractical, or impracticable, for several reasons. On the one hand, artists did not race to apply for funding. They were probably unwilling to submit to the rigid administrative regulations that the FHA imposed, for example, on room sizes and room divisions. On the other hand, the local governments that administer FHA funds were probably reluctant, in the face of greater complaints from ghetto communities, to use the money for a small, unproven arts constituency. Otherwise, the artists who most needed rent subsidies may have had incomes that actually fell below the "moderate" minimum income levels mandated by FHA guidelines for aid recipients. So until the middle of the 1960s, neither individual philanthropy nor national state support had made a significant advance toward subsidized housing for artists.

The breakthrough came in the form of local initiative and institutionalized philanthropy. Again New York was the incubator. Around 1967, George Maciunas had the notion of getting a rich patron of the arts to subsidize his dream of Fluxhouse Number 2. He approached the J. M. Kaplan Fund, a private foundation established and run by members of the Kaplan family, wealthy collectors and amateurs of the arts, and was granted a $20,000 loan to buy three loft buildings in SoHo. Although Maciunas succeeded in setting up only one of three projected co-ops, the Fund eventually "forgave" the loan. But around the same time that they encountered the visionary Fluxist, the Kaplans had also begun to wrestle with the practical problems of artists' housing. An Argentine artist with whom the family had a longstanding patronage relationship needed larger quarters, partly because of his family and partly because of his sculpture, and the Kaplans wanted to help him without overstepping the patron-artist tie. They thought that a low-cost loft co-op might solve all the problems. So the Kaplan Fund bought a loft building on Greenwich Street, in the West Village, and immediately resold it at cost to a group of twelve artists that included the Argentine sculptor.

Evidently encouraged by their success, the Kaplan Fund bought a much larger building in 1969 with the intention of repeating the experience. Westbeth, as the vacant office building beside the West Side Highway at Bethune Street was soon called, was renovated and converted into nearly four hundred large living and work spaces for over a thousand tenants. But the Kaplans' philanthropic intention of making an artists' housing co-op in Westbeth seems to have coincided with certain interests of both national and local political elites. First, the Fund had been encouraged to buy Westbeth by Roger Stevens, who succeeded August Heckscher as President Johnson's special adviser on the arts and then served as chairman of the National Council for the Arts, from 1965 to 1969, and chairman of the National Endowment for the Arts, from 1969 to 1972. Stevens had already made a fortune in the private sector, from the 1930s to the 1960s, as a real estate developer. In addition, the Kaplan Fund's work on Westbeth enjoyed an unusual degree of support from the city, state, and federal governments. Not only were the Kaplans personally well connected in all three capitals, but this was also the period when the New York arts Establishment was ably represented by Javits in Washington, D.C., Rockefeller in Albany, and Lindsay at City Hall. Finally, the Kaplans may have been well placed to realize this sort of patronage because they held extensive properties in Manhattan, and the strategic placement of artists' housing could not have damaged their own real estate interests.[3]

Although the impetus for subsidizing artists' housing in loft neighborhoods originated in the upper-class patron-artist connection, the idea became popular because of the active support of a middle-class arts constituency. This constituency played the midwife's role in the curious sequence of events that led up to the birth of the Greenwich Street co-op. Their background is significant to the story. At the end of the fifties and the beginning of the sixties, a number of middle-class families had bought homes among the Federal-style brick and mid-nineteenth-century brownstone townhouses in the West Village around Greenwich Street. The residential properties that these new homeowners so proudly renovated abutted the area's warehouses, printing plants, and garages — the commercial and light industrial facilities which, together with the houses, created the ideal type of mixed-use neighborhood that Jane Jacobs praises in her book *The Death and Life of Great American Cities*. In fact, this was the neighborhood where Jacobs lived at the time. The middle-class families who were her neighbors formed the base of the grass-roots movement for neighborhood preservation that she inspired. It is important to know that the area's residents owed their mobilization to a plan put forward by Mayor Wagner. Sharing the objectives of local business and political elites in many declining cities of the Northeast and Midwest, Wagner wanted to have the West Village declared a "blighted area" in order to qualify for federal urban redevelopment subsidies. Once the area established an entitlement to Title I funds, the city could use the money to build low-income housing there. Isolated between the unused piers on the Hudson River and the warehouses of Greenwich and Hudson streets, the "projects" would be practically invisible. Nor would they encroach upon potentially revalorized Lower Manhattan land. Needless to say, this plan sparked opposition among the West Village's middle-class homeowners. They saw that if the projects were built next-door to their homes, their modest investments would be eroded by declining property values and their mixed-use neighborhood would be destroyed by blockbusting real estate agents. Organized by Jane Jacobs, the West Village homeowners fought City Hall. When Wagner ran for reelection as a liberal in 1961, he was forced to concede the issue.

This initiation into local politics left two imprints on the West Village. First, the old Jane Jacobs constituency remained mobilized and formed a new, more permanent base in the area's Reform Democratic Club and the community board. Second, the homeowners remained sensitive to issues of neighborhood preservation. When buildings in their purview were put up for sale or vacated, they were vigilant. In 1967 the local city council member started a chain reaction when she heard that a loft building in the neighborhood was going to be auctioned off by the city government for payment of back taxes. The chain ran through the West Village liberal constituency's organizational links and personal connections to the J. M. Kaplan Fund. At the auction, a Fund representative bought the loft building on Greenwich Street with the idea of turning it over to an artists' co-op. Before the Fund announced its intention, however, a Committee for Artists' Housing from the community board issued a call for artists' housing in the West Village. With great timeliness, the Kaplans were able to respond to this call.

Aside from the developers of Lincoln Center, the West Village homeowners showed a new awareness, at least implicitly, that an arts presence would affect real estate development in the city. The middle-class constituency was most concerned about two issues: the use of space and property values. Fearing disruption by, on the one hand, high-rise new construction and, on the other hand, subdivision of existing units, the homeowners sought a strategy that would counter the spatial consequences of current housing market trends. But as the homeowners' fight against Mayor Wagner had suggested, they also wanted to maintain the emerging middle-class character of the neighborhood without either increasing or decreasing property values. So in this sense, too, the West Villagers wanted a strategy to fight market forces. The artists' presence in the neighborhood as both producers and residents seemed to hedge all bets. Because artists wanted to live and work in lofts *the way they were,* they offered the possibility of having a *stabilizing* rather than an *accelerating* effect on a neighborhood in transition. Surely this seemed reasonable at the time.

Initially, the same middle-class dream also dominated the efforts of SoHo's artist-residents to secure the right to their lofts. But SoHo was different from the West Village. In contrast to the narrow strip of land along the Hudson, SoHo took up a sizable chunk of the middle of the island. As a future gateway to a redeveloped Lower Manhattan, the area attracted the interest of big real estate investors and planners. There were also the zoning regulations that prohibited residential use in a manufacturing zone. So in order to assure a housing subsidy in SoHo, artists had to rely on the direct intervention of powerful forces: the upper-class arts constituency and their patrician politicians. "People with money saved SoHo," an early activist in the SoHo Artists' Tenants' Association says. Another SoHo artist recalls, "We all had 'uptown friends.'" He explains:

> We had gallery owners. Many of us worked in schools and universities. There were wealthy collectors we had sold to. There were some very influential artists in the area — Robert Rauschenberg, Robert Indiana, Julie Judd [wife of Minimalist artist Donald Judd] — who could call on curators and museum board members. Others of us had only an occasional wealthy person who had bought something from us. We all put together the names of who we could talk to and found that between us we had a rather impressive list. It ranged from people who had nothing to do with art, like the chairmen of the boards of banks, to curators and international art dealers. We started to call these people up to let them know, "Hey, there's a unique phenomenon going on right here that nobody knows about, and if we don't do something, it'll be destroyed." [4]

Despite initial misgivings about a common cause, the SoHo artists also allied themselves with the historical preservation constituency in the form of the Friends of Cast Iron Architecture (FCI). An offshoot of the patrician Municipal Arts Society, this organization was formed in 1970, in the midst of the struggle for "saving" SoHo. The group was made up of people with money and power. Several times during the 1960s, these people had suggested that a landmark "Cast Iron District" be declared in SoHo to protect the distinctive loft buildings on Greene Street from being torn down. But the big real estate developers who wanted to redevelop the area had held the historic preservationists to small-scale tactics. Once the artists joined them, the preservationists launched a real offensive. Artists did much of the archival research that buttressed the argument for a landmark district. "We compounded the developers' difficulties by using historic preservation," an artist-activist says, and when the smoke had cleared over the ruins of the developers' plans, an official landmark district remained.

SoHo artists also learned the value of the print media, beginning with the highly favorable 1970 article in *Life* magazine, "Living Big in a Loft." "Suddenly, following the *Life* story, we were a national phenomenon," an artist says. "We were too big for them to ignore. We became known personally. Then *I* could call up Donald Elliott [the city planning commissioner] and sometimes get through to him. We had a deputy mayor assigned to us." "We learned to use the foreign media," another artist recalls. "Stories about us appeared in newspapers in France or Germany. Our embassies sent them back to the State Department, and the State Department sent them to Mayor Lindsay." Facing a city administration that had visions of presiding over a world capital, the artists realized that these news stories had an effect on City Hall. "We made a policy decision to cooperate with publicity," an activist says. "Many of the group were against it and we agonized over it. We saw what publicity and legalization [of loft living] might lead to. But if we hadn't done it, SoHo wouldn't exist at all today."

Despite their anxiety, the SoHo artists enjoyed certain political advantages in the struggle. "One thing that has never been adequately acknowledged," an early activist says, "is the importance of John Lindsay. We had in the mayor a cultured, sensitive, educated man who understood the value of art in the life of this city. SoHo would not have been established under Wagner and certainly never under Beame. The Lindsay administration was absolutely vital to our success. Throughout the struggle, we had the support of Lindsay and his personal aides. It was aides to the mayor who told us how to argue our case before the Planning Commission." [5]

Although the artists' original patrician support had been based on elements of cultural patronage, their bid for open political support depended on an economic argument. The advice that Mayor Lindsay's aides gave them was "to show our worth in terms of money. Some of the artists balked," an activist says, "but the rest of us came up with statistics on art employment, tourism, supplies — numbers the commission could understand." In this discussion, Art evidently yielded to the arts economy. "When we worked for the zoning changes we never talked aesthetics," another activist says. "We let *them* talk aesthetics. We took the approach that we were workers who need to work where we live for both economic reasons and the nature of our work. We hit them with vacancy rates and employment figures. We offered to put property back on the tax rolls." A certain amount of organizational confusion also aided their efforts. "We had friends on people's staffs," an early SoHo loft dweller sums up, "especially on the City Planning Commission. . . . We used interagency negotiation and countervailing areas of responsibility to muddle bureaucratic efforts to harass us."

Moreover, by the 1970s, art suggested a new platform to politicians who were tired of dealing with urban poverty. "I'll tell you a nasty little story," an authoritative source on the SoHo artists offers.

At the final hearing where the Board of Estimate voted to approve SoHo as an artists' district, there were lots of other groups giving testimony on other matters. Poor people from the South Bronx and Bed-Stuy complaining about rats, rent control, and things like that. The board just shelved those matters and moved right along. They didn't know how to proceed. Then they came to us. All the press secretaries were there, and the journalists. The klieg lights went on, and the cameras started to roll. And all these guys started making speeches about the importance of art to New York City. Those same guys who had fought us every inch of the way! It was sickening.*

A PRODUCTION SUBSIDY FOR THE ARTS INFRASTRUCTURE

As the state on both local and national levels intervened more and more in the arts economy, the nature of the loft subsidy changed. It evolved from an indirect subsidy for artists' housing to a direct subsidy for arts production. This was consistent with the reasoning behind the city government's switch to support zoning for artists in SoHo. But it was also consistent with a general support for real estate development. Subsidies for arts production gave artists no claim to a particular place in the city. So they did not interfere with market forces. After the arts presence helped to revalorize a section of the city like SoHo, then the artists could take their subsidies and move to another declining area. Regarded in the short run as a bonanza for creative and performing artists, production subsidies for the arts infrastructure proved, in the long run, to be a cornucopia for housing developers. The use of lofts as performance spaces offers a good example, particularly in the development of the movement known as Loft Jazz.

Beginning in the early seventies, some musicians who played and composed "experimental," or "non-mainstream," jazz gathered to perform in lofts instead of bars or concert halls. To some degree, their work, like that of the artists who formed co-op galleries, was unmarketable. But to some degree, also, these musicians deliberately cut themselves off from the traditional access points to the jazz market. They didn't like the commercialism of hustling for record contracts and concert dates, and as Black Muslims, many of them didn't approve of the boozy atmosphere of jazz clubs. Loft Jazz was more serious, more provocative, and more self-consciously artistic than the jazz scene had been. In 1972, when the annual Newport Jazz Festival moved to New York, several Loft Jazz musicians organized their own "alternative festival," The New York Musicians' Festival. Significantly, their performances were funded by the National Endowment for the Arts and Mayor Lindsay's Parks Department. The following year, the Loft Jazz movement was incorporated into the regular Newport Festival program. Half the performances took place in three jazz

---

* The Board of Estimate, made up of the highest citywide elected officials, acts as a court of final appeal on land use issues. The South Bronx and Bedford-Stuyvesant, in Brooklyn, are racial and ethnic ghettos.

lofts: Ornette Coleman's Artists' House in SoHo, Sam Rivers's nearby Studio Rivbea, and a loft in TriBeCa. Because this part of the festival was billed as a "community" effort, the other concerts were scheduled in community centers in various neighborhoods. But the press conference that announced the festival within the Festival was held at Artists' House. There, the *New York Times* noted, the surroundings were much more comfortable than a smoky little jazz club. Artists' House was a large loft with pillowcovered parquet floors, where the audience could lean back, sipping wine, while they listened to the music.[6]

By the end of the seventies, Loft Jazz had died as a musical movement, but it lived on in the performing of jazz in lofts. Although the entrepreneurialism involved in establishing these performance spaces was no more formal than it had been, the organization of the performances became more institutionalized, thanks largely to new state subsidies on all levels. Generally the new jazz clubs were set up by a new generation of jazz musicians. Young and impoverished, educated, ambitious, these would-be performers lacked a place to operate. Like the artists who had already learned to combine living and work space, the musicians adapted lofts to their needs. Not only did they use part of their loft as a rehearsal studio, but they often rented it out for the same purpose to other impecunious young musicians. Eventually the need for practice space led to a need for performance space, and either for their own sake or in response to the entreaties of the other musicians, the loft tenants turned their premises into jazz clubs and little theaters. They kept rents and entrance prices low — and usually operated on the fringes of the local laws governing entertainment spots and cabarets — and in time they captured a following. They were known, they were written up in the entertainment guides, and they even got funding from the government. On the one hand, the more serious and avant-garde performance spaces were able to qualify for NEA grants. The more the performers showed college credentials as an indication of their professional training, or in the case of jazz, a degree from the Berklee College of Music or the New England Conservatory, the more qualified they appeared for state support. On the other hand, a variety of local mechanisms was developed to help with operating expenses. In New York City, for example, this sort of aid flows through the Theater Development Fund (TDF). TDF organizes the sale of discount tickets for theaters and other performance spaces that are supposed to be in marginal economic circumstances. Through a system of "TDF vouchers," a theater or a club is reimbursed for every discount admission ticket that it sells. In practice, a performance place makes more money from a TDF voucher than from an ordinary discount ticket, say, for students. TDF is funded by NEA, the New York State Council on the Arts, and corporate and individual donors. As the young owner of a club whose jazz performances are subsidized by both sorts of government grants acknowledges, "This cat named

Cy from Brooklyn turned me on. Can you believe it?! Exxon, Ford, and the National Endowment for the Arts are subsidizing my club!"

Unfortunately for such entrepreneurs, state subsidies and public acceptance failed to preserve their lofts as part of the urban arts infrastructure. Like artists in SoHo and the West Village, by their presence they helped to make their loft neighborhoods more visible and more acceptable to the general public. With live-in musical performers as "anchor," their landlords were able to convert their buildings informally to residential use. Performance companies and performance spaces were evicted in favor of residential tenants who could pay a higher rent and, eventually, for complete and legal residential conversions. Ironically, some of the building owners profited from the arts infrastructure in more than one way. In quite a few cases, the people who decided on a residential conversion had inherited or bought their building from the old generation of loft building owners, and these new landlords worked in the arts economy themselves. Many of them even lived in lofts.

But these building owners are only the cutting edge of a larger process of change. In many loft neighborhoods a new type of cottage industry combines with loft living and the arts infrastructure to create a mixed use that remains entirely within the service sector. Generally these loft tenants are graphics or clothing designers — who may farm out the actual production to workers in other areas of the city — and service firms from the low end of the tertiary-sector spectrum, like advertising agencies and architects. Particularly when rents rise in the traditional office market, these sorts of tenants seek cheaper space in marginal areas. Though a corporate headquarters could hardly move to a loft, in their case a loft address is chic. Meanwhile, the loft areas that have been disrupted by a variety of productive uses settle down to a more homogeneous variety of middle-class mixed use.

In this process of social and neighborhood change, a single loft building may represent, in spatial terms, a cross-section. For example, a building in Greenwich Village that was converted "illegally" to co-op lofts shows a mixture of uses on every floor: the ground floor is half residential and half a rehearsal space for a theater company; the second floor is half residential and half a dental equipment business; the third floor is split between two mixed-use lofts, one in which a nurse and an architect live and which the architect uses for his office, and one occupied by a stockbroker and a woman who runs a plant business in the loft; the fourth floor is entirely residential; on the fifth floor, half is a doctor's home, and the other half is a living and working loft for a graphic artist and a fine artist; the sixth floor is half residential, where the original buyer, an architect, sold out to a businessman, and half is for both living and running a catering business owned by a schoolteacher and a man who directs the food department of a hospital (this couple also has a loft in another building which they rent out for parties); on the seventh floor, half was sold by an architect to a doctor for a residence, and half is used by two men who live there and run a mail-order business in the loft; the eighth floor is divided into a living loft for a young widow with children and a living loft for a city planner with work space for her husband, who is a potter; the ninth floor has two living lofts. Such is the physical infrastructure that supports the conversion of an old manufacturing center to a new service-sector capital.

For a while, various sorts of "nonproductive" use can coexist in this infrastructure. The creative disharmony is interesting and sometimes even elegant. But sooner or later, a contradiction develops between the production of art and other, higher-rent uses. At that point, real estate development reasserts its dominance over the arts economy. The development strategy that has been repressed, delayed, or masked by the burgeoning arts infrastructure shows that in the final count, any use of space is expendable. Naturally, the reemergence or the intensification of a development strategy in the loft market arouses resentment and opposition among loft dwellers. The organizations that have been formed over the years to defend the interests of this constituency have had to formulate an increasingly anti-development opposition. But as the market has changed, so has the loft-dwelling constituency. Their stand on real estate development contradicts, to some degree, their own living in lofts.

CONTRADICTION IN THE LOFT DWELLERS' CONSTITUENCY

Since the early 1960s three different organizations have tried to express the common interests of loft dwellers in New York City: the Artists' Tenants' Association (ATA), which enjoyed a brief but active life in 1960–61 and a resurgence in 1963–64; the SoHo Artists' Tenants' Association (SATA), which during the late sixties inherited, in a sense, the earlier constituency; and the Lower Manhattan Loft Tenants (LMLT), organized on a wider geographical basis in 1978. Basically, the change from one organization to another reflects the spread of residential conversion throughout the southern half of Manhattan, from Battery Park to Times Square, and into Brooklyn and Queens, as well as the inclusion among loft tenants of middle-class people who have nothing to do with arts production. As the loft market has attracted these people, the strategy for protecting loft dwellers' interests has switched from demands for the defense of artists to demands for the defense of tenants. "We are mostly artists," says a founder of Lower Manhattan Loft Tenants, "but we feel that the early groups worked an artist's angle that won't work any more. We work with what is left of the artists' groups, but they are still looking for housing as a subsidy for artists from kindly landlords, and that won't work any more."

ATA's success at the beginning of the sixties was due to three factors, all of which grow out of the spirit and the reasoning of the time. First, ATA's early demonstrations seemed to be part of a general climate of protest which the public could understand. In the summer of 1961, artists marched in the streets, threatened to boycott art galleries and museums, and conducted a propaganda campaign through the mimeograph machine. However, in contrast to other social movements, they "were a safe kind of thing for people to pick up on," as an ATA organizer says. "We were considered very respectable demonstrators." Like the later artist-activists in SoHo, ATA also capitalized on the emerging significance of the arts in the urban economy, especially in New York. In the light of record-breaking auction and gallery sales of contemporary art, "we were all savvy enough to realize that money talks in this city, not culture, but we also realized that a lot of money was going into the arts." Finally, ATA succeeded in gaining its objective — legal access to lofts for artists — because, at the time, they represented no real threat to the dominant use, manufacturing, and there was no market in living lofts. ATA seemed to represent just a few artists who wanted space that no one else wanted.

By the end of the sixties, artists in Lower Manhattan lofts faced competition from real estate developers who wanted to tear down their buildings and restructure the built environment from ground zero to high rise. But by this point, many of the artists had invested time and money in their lofts. In contrast to the artist-tenants who had formed ATA, most of the artists who founded SATA in 1968 lived in co-op lofts where they were homeowners rather than renters. "We simply wanted to protect our homes," an early SATA activist says. "In the late sixties we were filled with fear," another recalls. "We felt certain we would lose our homes." A certain dichotomy appeared, however, between the interests of the artist-owners who ran SATA and the artist-tenants who largely refused to join. On the one hand, loft owners favored the rezoning of SoHo for artists' living lofts because they thought that they would benefit from a rise in property values. On the other hand, loft tenants preferred to remain "illegal" because they thought that after property values increased, rents would rise higher than they could afford.

This dichotomy accounts for some of the vacillation, or weakness, in SATA's position. In retrospect, the founders claim that they never considered the zoning issue as their top priority. Instead, they wanted to keep rents low and maintain the "excitement" of a mixed-use district. In fact they advocated a rent stabilization program that could be applied to rents on A.I.R. lofts, but the city administration refused to consider it. In response to SATA's demands for some sort of control on rent increases, the City Planning Commission proposed rezoning. Even at the time, the proposal raised doubts in the artists' minds. Some of the more astute SATA representatives countered with a proposal to rezone the whole city for artists' loft living instead of creating a special artists' zone in SoHo. Chester Rapkin, the urban planner and future CPC member who had studied the use of SoHo's manufacturing lofts in the early sixties, advised them against the rezoning. He predicted that it would cause rents to rise. But on this question the City Planning Commission was unmovable. Ironically, like the middle-class homeowners in the West Village who brought an artists' housing co-op into their midst, the SoHo artists merely wanted to stabilize their neighborhood. "The first people found things attractive as they were," says an architect who has lived in SoHo since 1968. "They liked living quietly among the factories. They didn't want a residential area."

Ten years later, when Lower Manhattan Loft Tenants was formed, the situation had changed, but the motivation remained the same. LMLT stands for mixed use and low rents. "We will remain illegal until a legalization comes along that is not necessarily development oriented," an LMLT organizer says, "that will allow us to keep a mix of manufacturing and residential uses, and that will keep buildings, which are a finite resource, available and affordable." For the first time, the market has put loft dwellers in a common position with manufacturers, because for the first time, they are both underdogs in relation to developers. "We can ally ourselves with manufacturers because we both fear development," the LMLT representative says. "We have the same needs. . . . We don't want fancy lobbies and fancy dogs running around. We are for residence *as the areas are*. We are not for residential development."

But it is now harder for LMLT to claim that loft dwellers should be protected because they are artists. Although surveys show that 85 percent of LMLT members are artists,* a lot depends on self-definition. The membership includes a large number of photographers, punk rockers, arts-and-crafts amateurs, and shoestring entrepreneurs who probably would not be able to qualify for A.I.R. certification. So LMLT deemphasizes art as a reason for protecting its position in the loft market. As its organizer says, "We don't want to toss out the non-artists like the bohemian stockbroker who has lived in a loft for fifteen years." Certainly time and numbers are, to a degree, on their side. Loft dwellers no longer fear eviction by the city government for illegal loft use. What they fear is residential conversion. Because of the dramatic rise in property values, loft residents have to contend with a much more aggressive strategy of real estate development. "The problems we see," says the organizer, "run the gamut of symptoms from basically the same problem. Landlords realizing that their property values are increasing and reviewing the use of their properties, and either co-oping, or raising rents, or selling to those who

---

* The figure is uncertain because membership includes both households and individuals.

will. We also see cases where landlords are letting their buildings fall apart
to discourage tenants or because they don't know what to do with them."
The problems of residential development that bedevil LMLT are the
organization's inheritance from the successes — or the Pyrrhic victories —
of ATA and SATA.

Between 1960 and 1970, as the national government, big corporations,
and various local agencies moved toward massive state subsidies for the
arts, it became logical for artists in New York to defend their access to
cheap loft space in terms of their position in an emerging arts economy. As
major producers in this economy, and symbols of a "higher" service sector,
the artists began to transform their lofts into physical infrastructure for the
creative process. But the arts presence had a contradictory and somewhat
unexpected effect. On the one hand, it buttressed the artists' claims for
support from two arts constituencies: traditional, upper-class patrons of
the arts and the new middle-class base of urban liberals. On the other
hand, the arts presence attracted an increasing number of non-artists as
patrons, public, and, ultimately, tenants. The property values enhanced by
the artists' presence rose so high that they effectively barred entry to the
loft market by people who tried to live off artwork or performance.
Although the three nonproductive uses of lofts — for arts production, service-sector cottage industry, and residence — for a time coexisted in the
same space, market prices tended to reinforce the strength of residential
use. As loft dwellers began to include more amateur or peripheral artists
than professionals, the social movements that they formed evolved from
demanding protection for artists to demanding protection for tenants. In
part, they made common cause with those manufacturers who still
remained. But the market to which they responded had changed. Like
ATA in the early sixties, LMLT in the early eighties was still organizing
demonstrations. Instead of demonstrating in the streets and in front of the
museums, its members demonstrated before City Hall and in the aisles of
Bloomingdale's, because the store's home furnishings department promoted the décor of a "SoHo-style loft." Despite its militance, the current
loft-dwelling constituency has a contradictory group interest: it is *for* loft
living, but it is *against* residential development.

This contradiction parallels other contradictions in the development of
the loft market. In the early days the upper-class arts constituency was
interested in helping the artists whose work they collected and preserving
old buildings from the wrecker's ball. The middle-class arts constituency
wanted to preserve property values and mixed use. Unfortunately for the
loft dwellers themselves, aesthetics did not restrain real estate development, and the middle-class dream of neighborhood stability turned out to
be an illusion. As Dick Netzer has argued, a small amount of public expen-

diture on the arts can have a great effect on the city. But what sort of effect can be anticipated? In New York, a relatively small investment, often at state expense, in the arts infrastructure created a new demand in nontraditional real estate markets. In this situation, developers proved capable of more than responding to demand.

6

DEMAND AND DEVELOPMENT
IN THE LOFT MARKET

While taste, style, and the image-making that surrounded the arts infrastructure in the 1960s created a certain subjective demand for loft living,
the market also grew in response to two objective factors. It depended,
first, on a hunger for large spaces at cheap rents in the heart of the city
and, second, on a desire for real estate properties that did not require a
huge investment either to finance or to maintain. Usually when people try
to explain how a market develops, they emphasize the first of these two
factors, that is, demand by consumers. Clearly, in conditions of urban
housing crisis, that is only reasonable. For some time, general factors like
land prices, construction costs, and interest rates have affected activity in
the building industry. In particular, competition from more profitable
uses, such as office space, has diminished the incentive to build housing.
This situation has an obvious effect on housing markets. In New York
City apartment houses, for example, vacancy rates are low and rents are
high. Prompted by New Yorkers' complaints, Mayor Edward Koch once
admonished, "If you want to live in Manhattan south of Ninety-sixth
Street, you're got to pay for it." Or as Alan H. Wiener, manager of the
New York office of the U.S. Department of Housing and Urban Development, noted more precisely in 1981, "There aren't likely to be many rental
units coming on the market that will be available for most people earning
under $50,000 a year." That sort of response, by high elected and adminis-
trative officials, underscores the strength of consumer demand in the New
York housing market. In view of this demand, it is not surprising that
middle-class people have been willing to settle in, or settle for, lofts.

But in the early sixties, loft living represented still more of an acquired
taste. Of course there were many artists living and working in lofts;
however, not all of them required a large space for their work. Besides
painters like Frank Stella, who did work on big canvases, and dancers and

musicians who needed practice or performing space, there were also artists who found lofts convenient because of their nearness to the manufacturing areas and industrial suppliers that inspired their art. The Canal Street aesthetic of the Fluxists, for example, made them instant consumers for living lofts. They were joined by people who were not engaged in any creative or performing process but who, like the early-twentieth-century patrons of the Modern movement in architecture, in Paris and London, became identified by force of circumstances with an aesthetic avant-garde. As architectural historian Reyner Banham describes these spiritual ancestors of the early loft dwellers,

> The clientele of Modern architecture was composed of artists, their patrons and dealers, and a few casual visitors to the architectural section of the *Salon d'Automne*. The consequence was, first, that they would nearly all require at least one large, well-windowed north-light room, to use as a studio or gallery, secondly that their private lives were apt to be so eccentric as to put anti- typical demands on functional planning, and thirdly that, although a few were as munificent as the Princesse de Polignac, most of them were of only moderate means and needed very economical structures.[1]

Most early loft residents were similarly "eccentric" and "economical." Employed in relatively new service-sector jobs or self-employed in the interstices of the service economy, they were not restricted by objective needs to living in traditional residential communities. First, because quite a few worked at home — in either home offices or middle-class, cottage-sector industry — they could utilize large open spaces that were built for heavy use. Second, they didn't have to look for proximity to a commuting network of either highways or mass transit. Nor did most of them have children, so they didn't have to search for child-oriented infrastructure like good school districts, clean streets, and playgrounds. Furthermore, they were self-sufficient enough to take care of their needs without the usual amenities of a city neighborhood: grocery stores and dry cleaners, next-door neighbors or nearby relatives. Finally, they were relatively immune to the Levittown aesthetic and mainstream standard of domestic consumption promoted by magazines like *Better Homes and Gardens*. More relevant than the notion of "urban homesteading" on which descriptions of the early loft market rely, this style of life and its mini-mode of domestic production really suggest that for this time and place, loft dwellers generated a form of "subsistence housing." Like many forms of subsistence, the loft model was eventually upgraded into a luxury market, but at the beginning, moving into a loft required only a small initial investment.

It is interesting that much of the money for this investment came, directly or indirectly, from government and from the service sector. On the one hand, many artists and performers used their grants as "seed money" to buy and renovate a loft. On the other hand, local civil servants, whose jobs generated a certain commitment to center-city living, especially when they were involved in urban planning or economic development, used the savings from their public-sector wages to invest in a loft. These groups were joined by a number of small-time or first-time investors in income-producing real estate. Not really professional developers, they nonetheless had the money and the interest to view lofts as a viable investment opportunity. So the loft market began by pulling together a heterogenous yet typically middle-class group of artists, professionals, bureaucrats, and shoestring entrepreneurs.

These people moved into the loft market in two senses: as residents, occupants, or users, to be sure, but also as investors. The size of their investment determined the strategy that they followed, individually, in "developing" their property. However, on a more or less collective level, the size of their investments also influenced development strategy in general in the loft market. The market's course from eccentric, owner-occupied lofts to standardized, large-scale residential conversions reflects the decisions of different real estate investors at least as much as it reflects the changing tastes of housing consumers. Indeed, it could be argued that in any real estate market, investors rather than consumers enjoy an advantage in initiating change. It is this objective factor of demand—the demand for *placement* rather than *place*—that largely determines what gets built, how, where, and when.

INVESTMENT STRATEGIES IN THE LOFT MARKET

From this point of view, the rise of the market in living lofts is only a variation on the general movement of middle-class investment capital into declining areas of older industrial cities. Its obvious parallel can be found in brownstoning, or the gentrification of working-class residential neighborhoods in or near the historic city center. Both markets—lofts and brownstones—have been influenced by several general conditions of the urban political economy. Beginning in the mid-1960s, a new consensus between local business communities and local political elites tended toward a reevaluation of the downtown areas that still suffered from a deliberately induced, chronic shortage of private investment capital. This presaged a change, in economic terms, from devalorization of these areas to revalorization. Around the same time, the onset of a fairly long wave of combined inflation and recession pushed up property values and construction costs throughout the United States. So it became more economical to re-use than to tear down old buildings. But there are also some specific conditions affecting real estate investment, especially in devalorized property, that drew middle-class money into the loft and brownstone markets.

First, the price of entry into a market in devalorized property is low. An availability of cheap buildings means that people who have only a small amount of money to invest can become landlords of apartment houses or loft landlords. Also, the relatively small size of these buildings offers the possibility of part-time involvement in property management. It isn't necessary to have a Rockefeller-size fortune or the expertise that such wealth can buy to deal with property that is not, after all, as big or as complex as Rockefeller Center. Moreover, this sort of investment is often profitable. A small investment in stable, middle-class rental housing might return a profit of 15 percent a year. Large investments often return 25–35 percent on equity. Around 1970, 15 percent was a good rate of return for a small investor. It was three times as high as the interest on an ordinary savings account, about the same as in the stock market, and, in the days before money funds, much less risky than stocks or commodities. Indeed, at that time, real estate seemed the most reliable risk for a nonprofessional, middle-class investor.

But profit is not necessarily the only motive for investing in real estate. Because of "bracket creep," some people might find it advantageous to take a loss. When inflation pushes the earnings of high-salaried professionals, administrators, or athletes into income brackets where they have to pay over half of their income in taxes, they look for a way to reduce — though not really to lose — their taxable earnings. What they need is a tax shelter. According to the U.S. tax code, investment in rental property offers such a shelter because a portion of the investment and maintenance costs on the property is tax deductible. Nor is the deduction exhausted in a single year. The accelerated depreciation that the tax code allows — especially the "double declining balance," which makes quick turnover of a property doubly advantageous — enables investors to "write off" their total investment over a period of several years. Then, as their wage earnings increase because of inflation, their tax shelter permits them to lower the amount of income on which they owe taxes. Even if they lose money on a real estate investment, they make a net gain because of the taxes that they save. Significantly, while center-city markets in devalorized property began to grow, inflation made all real estate tax shelters much more valuable to middle-income tax brackets. Between 1969 and 1979, for example, a middle-income family, which earned perhaps $15,000 in 1969 and $30,000 ten years later, found that the value of a tax savings of this kind increased by 48 percent.[2]

Although the low rate of return on loft buildings in the late 1960s made them a likely "loss leader" among potential tax shelters, the profits that were shown by converting these buildings to residential use soon turned their meaning around. The diverse motives of early investors and residents in the loft market yielded to a dominant concern: how to make a profit out of loft living. Along with the profitability of residential conversion, a short-term, declining rate of profit in other urban real estate markets led an increasing number of professional developers to lofts. Changes in investment priorities were reflected in spatial terms. From the mid-sixties to the beginning of the seventies, the diversity of small investors in the early loft market had created a certain amount of innovation and experimentation in the use of loft space. Around 1975, through the influence of the professional developers' housing criteria, lofts showed more conventional relations between space, time, and money. The legal clearance and bank financing that professional developers obtained paved the way to more extensive, as well as more intensive, development of loft buildings. Nor were these trends dampened by medium-term economic prospects. The costs of gut rehabilitation continued to decline in relation to the costs of new construction. A Chase Manhattan Bank study of economic activity in New York City during the first half of 1980 showed that conversions of old buildings made up half the construction projects begun in Manhattan. At that time, according to the city's Office of Economic Development, 11 percent of all loft space in Manhattan south of Fifty-ninth Street had already been converted to residential use and another 17.5 percent was "going residential."

The development of the loft market from subsistence housing to luxury residence shows how a variety of investors, with different strategies for capitalizing on their investment, can coexist within a single market. As in any ordinary housing market, these investors run the gamut from owner-occupiers or even tenants, who primarily get "use value" from their investment, to nonresident owners, who get "exchange value" from buying, selling, or renting out their property. According to the size of investments in the loft market, we can distinguish between several types of small or "retail" investors, on the one hand, and large or "wholesale" investors, on the other (see table 8).

Retail investors include rental tenants or owners of individual lofts, and owners of buildings who engage in no development strategy that would raise the value of their property. In other words, these are entrepreneurs who operate on a shoestring. At the very bottom of this category are the loft dwellers who divide their loft in two and rent out part of the space to someone else. In the early days of the loft market, when almost all loft tenancy was illegal, such sublets were common. In general, however, tenants and owner-occupiers make a capital gain only when they vacate their lofts. Renters profit from charging the next tenant a fixture fee, and owners profit, of course, from charging a high sale price. Superficially, this profit reimburses the tenant or the owner for improvements that he or she has made in the property. But to some degree, also, both owner and tenant are capitalizing on their advantageous position in the loft market.

Table 8
Investors in the Loft Market

Investors	Operation
Retail	
Loft tenants, owner-occupiers	Charge fixture fee, set sale price
Loftlords	Increase rent, initiate turnover, cut upkeep
Building owners (1)	Sell floors as raw space
Wholesale	
Building owners (2)	Hold or vacate building
Co-op sponsors	Sell floor by floor with major or minor improvements
Developers	Make residential conversion to apartments

In essence, they are collecting a fee from people who want to enter a highly competitive, sellers' market. For tenants, this means access to a long lease at a relatively cheap rent. For owners, it means a sale price that is determined not only by current conditions but also by anticipated values. Again, as in any housing market, people may use the profits that they make from selling their property to "trade up" in the market, by buying a larger or a better home at a higher price. Alternatively, they may use their profits to support some entrepreneurial loft investment.

Another category of retail investor includes loft building owners who treat their rental property as if it were in a poor neighborhood in the slums rather than in a stable, middle-class housing market. They derive their profit from the slumlords' typical exploitation of their buildings and their tenants. Like slumlords, they try to initiate a rapid turnover of tenants and equally rapid increases in rent without going to the expense of making improvements. Loftlords have been known to harass tenants to get them to vacate the building, to raise the rent by 50–200 percent, and to give leases that are too short to allow tenants the opportunity to recoup some use value from the improvements that they make at their own expense. Loftlords have also hidden behind the double standard of New York's illegal loft living situation. Until an acrimonious court case in 1979, loftlords tried to have resistant tenants evicted. Hypocritically, the loftlords chose "illegal residence" as the grounds for eviction.

The final category of retail investors comprises those who derive their profits from selling the unimproved space of their loft building on a floor-by-floor basis. Although the lofts are not legally certified for residential use, they are sold as living lofts. Both buyer and seller understand this, but for the buyer, the purchase price buys a certain amount of floor space as well as entry into the loft market. For the owner, these conditions offer the possibility of quick turnover, and profits to be used to expand entrepreneurial activity. Because many loft building owners saw the advantages of turning their property over in this way, the multiple sales of loft buildings over a short period of time contributed to a rapid rise in their market value.

In contrast to retail investors, wholesale investors begin their activity with an entire building rather than an individual loft, and engage in some operation to increase the value of their property. This operation constitutes, in one form or another, a speculative strategy. Even by holding a building, and especially by vacating a building, in anticipation that values will rise because of a new use, a wholesale investor is changing the market. By manipulating supply, the investor affects both prices and demand. This situation has little to do with making improvements to the property.

A second type of wholesale investor does make improvements. He makes structural as well as cosmetic improvements in order to sell the building, floor by floor, as "finished" space. For a larger investment of time and money, he stands to make a larger gain. Although investors of this type are essentially selling "co-op" lofts, they often refuse to make all the improvements that are mandated by the state for legal sales. The more complicated the financing arrangements — for both buying and selling the building — the more an institutional lender is required, and generally these institutions require that legal codes and approvals be satisfied in order to minimize their risk. Consequently, the sponsor of a higher-price co-op loft building may be held responsible for more improvements than the market alone implies.

Finally, the third type of wholesale investors comprises those who choose to make a completely legal, full-scale residential conversion into rental apartments. Surely this strategy requires the biggest investment, but it also offers the highest return. Moreover, construction loans and J-51 benefits may be so great that they really reduce cash outlays. Once they become the owners of what is, essentially, an apartment house, the developers start recouping their investment with the first apartment rentals. The risk of producing rental housing is cushioned, on the one hand, by the tax benefits and, on the other hand, by the tight housing market. This category of investors is limited to professional real estate developers.

Over time, the dramatic increase in market values led to the replacement of retail investors by wholesale investors. Though this is also typical of the brownstone market in gentrifying neighborhoods, three examples underline the extent of inflated values in the loft market. In 1968 Fluxus leader George Maciunas bought two attached, six-story loft buildings in SoHo for $12,000. Using unemployed artisanal labor, he installed bathrooms, kitchens, plumbing lines, and electrical wiring. Within a couple of years, Maciunas sold the buildings to six artists who had been renting lofts there. They paid $5,300 for each 2,400-square-foot floor and set up a co-op. To finance the purchase of the building, they took out a $25,000 mortgage at the prevailing low interest rates. When this mortgage

Eventually developers converted entire loft buildings to standardized, legal residences. This building in TriBeCa will feature apartments with mini-terraces.

is paid off in 1982, the owner-occupiers will be free of debt or free to refinance. In 1980, while monthly maintenance charges on each loft were still as low as $180, the market value of a loft in the building hit $180,000.[3]

Also in the late sixties, a New York real estate broker, a leading Abstract Expressionist painter, and a sculptor bought a loft building in NoHo. As the real estate broker recalls, "Arman [the sculptor], Gottlieb [the painter], and I bought a building on what is now LaGuardia Place for $80,000 — $30,000 of it in cash. We put up only ten grand apiece. Gottlieb took two floors, Arman took one, I took one, and we made a rental unit out of the bottom. Today the building would go for $600,000 to $800,000."

By the early eighties, it was not rare to find developers producing, for example, forty-nine large co-op apartments or ninety-five smaller rental apartments out of a single factory or warehouse conversion. In the latter case — a project on the Brooklyn waterfront — the developer paid $530,000 in acquisition costs and nearly $3 million for the renovation. In the former case — the conversion of a former piano factory near Times Square — the developers paid $1.5 million a month in interest payments on the mortgage loan and $40,000 in monthly interest payments on the construction loan while they marketed their apartments. In both cases, presumably, rehabilitation and the open floor plan enabled the developers to keep costs down.[4]

In the center of SoHo, the old buildings accommodate new uses. Avant-garde art, boutiques, and loft living have acquired a neighborhood patina.

DEVELOPERS IN THE LOFT MARKET

Within the category of wholesale investors there is a progression from amateur and small-scale developers to professionals who command greater resources and correspondingly greater influence in the development field. For this reason, interviews that I conducted with a representative sample of thirteen loft developers in New York in 1978 throw an interesting light on the professionalization of real estate developers, the localization of their markets, and the motivation that underlies their activity (see table 9).[5] Significantly, these interviews indicate that with more professional developers, commitment to lofts as such decreases even as more and more loft apartments are produced. While the amateurs admit to a fascination with artists or with the loft scene, professionals — including several second-generation members of real estate dynasties — tend to view lofts merely as a segment of the larger rehabilitation market. In their firms, loft development is often delegated to a junior partner, who is sometimes a younger family member just entering the development field. Similarly, in contrast to the small developers, who are *pulled* into the loft market because of the profits that they can make there, large developers are *pushed* into the loft market by rising costs of development in their traditional markets.

There is an interesting relationship between a developer's professionalization and equity that confirms in several different ways the old saying, "Time is money." First, less experienced developers have greater equity or "participation" in their projects. Basically they have to put up a greater proportion of the capital themselves because the banks will not trust them with a loan until they have built up a "track record." Experienced loft developers are able to limit their equity to 25 percent, though sometimes they prefer to finance their smaller projects themselves. Nonprofessional developers have to put up 30–50 percent of a project's total cost. For that reason, the small developers have to divest themselves of each property that they convert as soon as possible. In the loft market, this often means selling raw space as illegal co-op lofts. However, professional developers can — or even must — take the time to amortize renovation costs and interest on various loans. Usually this implies that they become landlords of rental housing. While rentals stretch out the period of involvement with a property, they also offer a constant flow of cash into the developer's coffers. But all developers do not necessarily manage their own properties. They may delegate management functions to a division of their firm or hire a managing agent. Equipped, then, both financially and organizationally for rental housing, the largest developers may hold such a property indefinitely. However, in today's market, they — like the small developers — find it to their advantage to get out sooner. Developers in this market now have a "turnaround time" of as little as two years. At that point they sell off the property as co-op apartments. As this scenario indi-

Table 9

Developers in the Loft Market, 1968–78

Primary occupation	Year entered rehabilitation market	Production (number of rehabilitation units)	Product			Prior experience in real estate	Years in real estate development
			legal/illegal	rent/sale			
1. Investor	Early 1960s	16	Illegal	Rent		—	15–20
2. Architect	1977	10	Illegal	Sale		—	1–2
3. Attorney	1977	12	Illegal	Sale		Attorney for loft tenants, artists	10
4. Real estate agent	1970–72	60	Illegal	Sale		Agent/broker	20
5. Developer	1973	30	Legal	Rent		Developer, manager	20
6. Developer	1976	100	Legal	Rent		Developer of rental apartments	10
7. Developer	1977	15 apartment buildings	Legal	Both		Developer of rental apartments	17–18
8. Developer	1973	180	Legal	Rent		Agent/broker, financing packager	10
9. Developer	1973	30–40 per year	Legal	Sale		Manager of apartments, office buildings	5 [a]
10. Developer	1976	400	Legal	Sale		Tenants' attorney	2
11. Builder/investor	1970	500 per year	Legal	Rent		New construction of rental apartments	20
12. Builder/manager	1965	400–500 per year	Legal	Rent		New construction of rental apartments	30 [a]
13. Developer	1969	550 per year	Legal	Rent		—	9 [a]

[a] Second generation in family-owned firm.

136

cates, all developers are sensitive to time pressures. While the clock on loan payments ticks away, they have to plan the project, vacate buildings that are not delivered empty, hire a development "team" (of architect, contractor, engineer, and other special labor), and apply for the necessary zoning variances, permits, and approvals. It takes two years to carry out a single conversion project.

As projects become more complex, they demand more complicated financing arrangements. The simpler projects of the small developers can be done with personal rather than institutional financing — family money, loans from friends, or a bank loan obtained through personal connections with a bank officer. Professional developers learn to construct a loan "package" for each project. This begins with a permanent or purchase-money loan from a local savings bank, which is used in turn as leverage to get a temporary or construction loan from a commercial bank. These have to be repaid more quickly than mortgages and carry higher interest rates. Together with the developer's participation, the loan package pays for projects of up to $1 million. For larger projects — which in loft conversions might total $4 million or $5 million — developers have to go to larger institutional lenders, mainly insurance companies. Increasingly, these large lenders demand participation in profits, or equity, in return for their participation in financing. Thus enlarging the scale of development projects has deepened the lending institutions' involvement in real estate development. The lure of investment in American real estate has brought some foreign money into the conversion market, too. With a foreign bank or investor as a joint-venture partner, even a small developer can undertake a large project. But through their dominant role in the local mortgage market, savings banks constitute the largest institutional presence in loft conversions. Like the developers who operate on smaller margins, the savings banks prepare the loft market before the larger investors step in.[6]

In contrast to the widespread assumption that housing consumers are attracted by neighborhood "character," as indicated by the highly original marketing acronyms of loft areas like SoHo, NoHo, and Dumbo, loft developers suggest no such criteria for localizing their investments. They describe their acquisition procedure in terms of building attributes and general housing market demarcations. All but the very smallest loft developers aim, in the first place, for the upper-middle-class housing market. Reflecting, perhaps, the long-term gentrification of much of Manhattan, they see their market as larger than the loft neighborhoods of the southern tip of the island. They seek properties for renovation and conversion all over Manhattan, from East to West, south of Ninety-sixth Street. So Mayor Koch's statement bears witness to developers' strategy. Several developers try to be more selective, specifying the East Side rather than the West Side, or a cutoff point at Eighty-sixth Street, in addition to Greenwich Village. Significantly, these developers move in two directions in the market. Either they trade up by using their base of operations to expand to areas where property values are higher, or they acquire cheaper properties in marginal areas and hope to sell more units by compensating for the location with a custom product. None of these developers has ever invested in the flagship loft neighborhood, SoHo. The early and problematic formation of the loft market there restricted development activity to extremely small, part-time developers, especially artists and architects. As the market became more established, building prices in SoHo rose too high to permit the continued entry of small developers. Meanwhile, large developers preferred to acquire bigger, better buildings to convert, in more proven middle-class neighborhoods.

Despite their hardly hidden or barely suppressed commercial motivations, developers tend to see themselves as playing a benevolent social role in the urban political economy. Of course, as sellers of housing, they are known to speak in hyperbole. The loft that they glowingly characterize as "beautiful space" may turn out in reality to be a hollow shell so decrepit that weeds seem to be growing through the gaping floorboards. But developers talk as though they performed a public service by producing high-rent housing in the Manhattan market. In particular, the smallest and earliest loft developers claim to be the benefactors of artists — not quite patrons of the arts, but close. "I was a catalyst," says one such developer. "I provided artists with the know-how and the confidence [to do a residential conversion]." Also, loft living "civilizes the environment," as a lawyer-developer who has illegally co-oped a loft building says. "It gives artists a place to do their work." The larger developers who do residential conversion for a luxury market claim that their development strategy benefits the middle class. By choosing rehabilitation over new construction, they hold costs down and, they say, pass these savings along to their tenants in the form of lower-than-market rents. So they enable middle-class housing consumers who otherwise couldn't afford Manhattan rents to live in Manhattan. To some degree, this claim is supported by J-51. The city stipulates that in return for the tax benefits, the developer must submit rents to local rent-stabilization guidelines. But it is the developer who sets the rent structure initially. The developer, not the city, judges what "market rents" are. In general, though, loft developers feel that by converting factory space to residential use they are helping New York. By building middle-class housing "I am trying to save the city," says a small illegal developer who is also a real estate agent. "I want to do something for the city," says the lawyer who produces legal co-op lofts. "I'm changing the landscape of the city." More down to earth is a developer who converts lofts into rental apartments. "I knew there'd be a market in this area for a luxury building with small units," he says of a fully rented project, "where people could feel a sense of space without huge amounts of floor space. I created beautiful apartments, blending the old and the new. I spent a lot of money on every floor."

Less surprising than a self-image as urban benefactor is the developers' ambivalent self-interest in regard to state intervention in the housing market. Subsidies for development are "in"; regulations on development are "out." Developers criticize all three branches of local government whose actions cost them both time and money: compliance with administrative ordinances of the Buildings and Fire departments, adjudication of disputes with tenants in Housing Court, and rent controls that are set by vote-currying city council members. (All this contradicts, of course, the tenants' view.) But zoning variances most arouse the developers' ire. The lawyer-developer of legal co-op loft-apartments describes his first experience with the zoning committee of a local community board in aggrieved terms. "Last night at the zoning committee meeting only three people showed up," he says, "and they tortured me. The people who come have a predisposition to come, out of opposition. . . . They kept wanting to know if there could be a commercial use for these buildings. . . . That's ridiculous!" Yet he suggests a way that experienced developers get around this impediment. They apply for the zoning variance *before* buying the building instead of *after*. Not only does this reduce the developer's costs in terms of both time and money but it also reduces the risks that banks see in the project, and so eases the way toward institutional financing.

Even a subsidy for development creates different constituencies among developers in a market according to how the subsidy affects their own activity. All the professional loft developers swear by J-51, for example, and state that without the subsidy they never would have chosen rehabilitation over new construction, or housing over other uses. However, the illegal loft developers who cannot afford the full-scale rehabilitation for which J-51 was written are more critical. An illegal loft developer says that J-51 "killed the artists and destroyed the small operators. *It brought in the real estate people.*" Another illegal loft developer, an attorney who drafted laws to protect loft dwellers before becoming a developer, criticizes the City Planning Commission's effort to legalize loft living. "This legislation kills the market. It'll cost the developer so much money to do what the law requires [to bring the building up to code], he might as well go ahead and do a gut rehab. The law has closed down the lower end of the market."

But as in any industry, the big operators survive regulation. They prosper by seeking larger subsidies and markets farther afield. Developers who build up expertise in renovation in the Manhattan loft market can transfer this experience to other declining urban areas or even to old industrial or mill towns. In those areas, historic and neighborhood preservation, on the one hand, and government grants, on the other, shape development strategy. "The economic development business," says the lawyer-developer of legal co-op lofts, "that's the next game in town. There's federal money — for the right applicants." As acquisition and construction costs in Manhattan continue to rise, developers who can cultivate political contacts in state capitals and in Washington, D.C., and are not reluctant to do the paperwork — who include notably, so far, former lawyers and architects who became developers because of the loft market — find that rehabilitation offers them a viable niche. "We're now looking outside the city," the legal lawyer-developer says. "If this experience is replicable . . . in any city that has buildings a hundred years old — then we're really into something."

CONSUMER DEMAND IN THE LOFT MARKET

While government subsidies and investor demand play major roles in shaping development strategy, developers also respond to "market forces." The spread of residential conversion was certainly a response to consumer demand. Yet it was also the result of some manipulation of that demand. When supply is reduced in one housing market, the unsatisfied demand that builds up there spills over into other markets. Although this notion has been used to explain the movement of inner-city housing consumers — faced with a shortage of decent housing in their neighborhoods — into adjacent enclaves of a different race and class, it also describes the movement of middle-class housing consumers into nontraditional urban housing markets. In other words, if "6 RMS. RIV. VU" were really available for a reasonable rent in Manhattan, then the market in living lofts would never have arisen. But in fact, rental housing in the whole country is constantly being reduced in each of the three crucial dimensions: there are fewer new apartments for rent each year, they are getting smaller, and people are paying more for them. Since 1974, in the United States, apartment size has been shrinking by perhaps as much as 5 percent a year. In New York City, where competition for rental housing is probably keenest, the last boom in apartment house construction took place in the early 1960s. From a production high that put around 14,500 new apartments on the rental market in Manhattan each year in 1961–65, the number of new units fell to 5,600 a year in 1966–70. By the end of the 1970s only 3,000 to 4,000 new apartments a year were built for the rental market.[7] The resulting low vacancy rates made apartment hunters resort to unusual or expensive stratagems such as sharing space with strangers and paying agencies finders' fees of up to 15 percent of the annual rent. Moreover, they have had to get accustomed to living in different sorts of spaces than the ones they have known. New construction in downtown neighborhoods features studio apartments with sleeping lofts, nooks, or platforms instead of separate bedrooms. "Luxury" units make do with small entrances instead of airy foyers, and eat-in kitchens instead of "junior" or second dining rooms.

Space has been reduced partly in response to demographic changes. In Manhattan, for example, where households are often made up of a single person or a childless, working couple, an architect who specializes in new construction for the luxury market has cut the size of his apartments by 10 percent over the past fifteen years. Another architect in the market, whose father and grandfather also designed luxury apartments in Manhattan, produces quite different apartments from those of his grandfather's time. "In 1929 Mr. Roth's grandfather . . . designed the Beresford . . . with eleven-room apartments, twenty-seven-foot-long hallways (called galleries), maid's rooms, and huge dining rooms. By comparison, Richard Roth, Jr.'s luxurious Tower East . . . has L-shaped living-dining areas three-fourths the size of the Beresford's, kitchens 40 percent smaller, and secondary bedrooms half as big." Luxury apartment residents also find shoddier workmanship and cheaper-grade materials than in the past. Parquet floors are prefinished, preassembled, and glued down rather than laboriously nailed strip by strip. Plastered walls have been replaced with plaster boards made of gypsum, and ceilings are sprayed with a sand-based paint rather than plastered.[8]

Nevertheless, rents for these spaces have increased steadily in both absolute and relative terms — in the dollars that people lay out in rent payments and in the share of their income that goes for rent. In New York City the *average annual increase* in rent held steady at 4.9 percent from 1950 through 1970, largely because of a comprehensive rent-control program, jumped to 11.4 percent between 1970 and 1975, with the dismantlement of that program, and declined slightly to 7.8 percent from 1975 to 1978. At all times, the rent increase was higher than the increase in the Consumer Price Index. Middle-class people used to budget 25 percent of their household income for rent payments. However, in cities like New York they now plan on spending at least a third of their income on rent. Significantly, the percentage of New York City households paying at least 25 percent, 30 percent, and 35 percent of their income in rent has risen consistently, along with the rents themselves, and the period of heaviest "rent burden" seems to have begun in the 1970s. In 1975 almost half of all New York City renter households paid more than 25 percent of their income in rent. In 1978 nearly half of them paid over 30 percent. These rent rises hit Manhattan particularly hard. Between 1970 and 1975, apartment rents there rose 11.5 percent a year. Over the next three years they rose another 27.9 percent. Finally, the relief from market forces afforded by rent control and rent stabilization since the end of World War II has diminished as the rent control program has been phased out.[9]

Under such conditions, the entry — or the burst — of middle-class housing consumers into the loft market could not fail to have an effect on loft rents. In 1968 most living lofts still rented for relatively modest rents by middle-class standards, generally for less than $200 a month (see figure 2). But within a year, rents rose abruptly. Fewer than half the living lofts that were advertised in the Sunday *New York Times* and the *Village Voice* — the main carriers of this sort of advertisement — still rented at the former rate. Most rent increases raised lofts to the $200–$300-a-month level. By 1970 there were disturbing indications that loft rents had only begun to climb. Rents of $300–$400 a month overtook lower rents, and by 1971 luxury rents appeared for the first time in the loft market. A few lofts commanded rents of $500–$800 a month. Partly this reflects an increase in value that was due to the legalization of loft living for artists in SoHo. But it also shows that both consumer and investor demand in the loft market were growing. Within two years, by 1973, the supply of the cheapest lofts had dwindled to nothing. About half the lofts rented for $200–$300 a month, and the remaining half were evenly divided among various middle-class rent categories. Although this date marks the creation of the historic preservation district in SoHo and a resulting further increase in real estate values there, similar increases appeared with only a slight time lag in all loft neighborhoods of Manhattan. After 1973 an increasing number of high-rent lofts appeared. In 1974 a few rented for $600–$800 a month. In 1975 lofts renting for up to $1,000 a month entered the market, and in 1978 the $800–$1,000-a-month rents dominated the market, closely followed, however, by $300–$400 lofts. But there was still almost an even chance of renting a loft for $600–$800 or $400–$500 a month. A spot check of the loft advertisements in March 1980 confirmed the general trend. By this time the median monthly rent ranged between $600 and $800. The *average* loft rent had reached $1,044, and a substantial number of lofts were clustered at the luxury level of $800–$1,400 a month.*

But these rents cover lofts of various sizes. To be fair, we should adjust the rent figures to reflect the size of the loft, and calculate monthly rents in the standard commercial terms of dollars per square foot. This adjustment shows an even more dramatic change (see figure 3). The lowest rent category (below $1.00 per square foot) — which is roughly equal to the lowest manufacturing loft rent at the time — disappeared forever in 1971, and the higher rent categories began taking over as early as 1969. Nevertheless, the 1969 rents remained within the accepted rent structure of commercial lofts. That is, living lofts were still a bargain by middle-class standards until 1971.

* Rents are easier to compare than the sale prices of co-op lofts because of the improvements involved in most co-op sales. Nevertheless, it is interesting that by June 1981 a 4,500-square-foot, top-floor raw space in the Lower Fifth Avenue area was advertised for sale at $450,000 — an astounding price for unimproved space in an illegal loft co-op — and the asking price of a luxury loft in Greenwich Village hit $1 million.

The adjusted figures show that residential loft rents started to climb through the ceiling in 1972 and 1973. At that time, the extraordinary rent of $7.00–$10.00 per square foot — equivalent to a retail store rental on a busy thoroughfare in a commercial neighborhood — appeared. From that point on, adjusted rents evened out, so that the moderately high $2.00–$2.50-a-month category dominated the market, together with quite a few cheaper lofts (at $1.00–$1.50 per square foot) and more expensive ones ($3.00–$5.00 per square foot). Again, a spot check in 1980 confirmed that rent levels that used to be considered extravagantly high now dominate the market. A large number of lofts clustered at the $3.00–$5.50 level, but a significant number also rented for over $9.00 per square foot, and the *average* was $5.65.

Yet the most important point about these rents is not that they are high or that they rise over time. After all, property values and housing prices do increase in an inflationary economy, especially in an international business capital like Manhattan. What is more interesting is that the rents indicate that the market in living lofts formed earlier than most people imagine. With the disappearance of bargain-basement loft rents in 1971, the market in living lofts was firmly established as a middle-class enclave. Clearly, by then consumer demand was so great that people would pay a high price to enter the market. After 1971, SoHo "tipped" toward higher-rent arts, retail, and residential uses, and the loft market spilled over into all Manhattan loft areas. However, these areas were no longer cheaper than SoHo. This suggests that in contrast to the prevailing view of SoHo as the "initiator" of the loft market, SoHo made its major contribution to loft living because it *anchored* the market that had already begun. In other words, the visibility of SoHo conditioned rents for living lofts to rise higher and faster. It accelerated consumer demand. It also encouraged residential conversion all over Manhattan. But the rent structure of the loft market implies that SoHo in itself never represented a neighborhood or a market. SoHo broadened rather than localized the loft phenomenon. The large real estate developers could see this as early as 1973. That is why they began to lobby the city council for the rewriting of J-51 to cover big conversions. But the public, loft tenants, and artists remained oblivious of the cumulative effect of market forces on the loft market.

DEVELOPMENT OR SPECULATION IN THE LOFT MARKET?

The issue of demand is crucial for determining the influence of speculation, as opposed to development, in the loft market. In its ordinary sense, *speculation* merely means that a product is produced in anticipation of demand. While this may be problematic for the individual speculator, who may not be able to sell the product on the market, it is not, by definition,

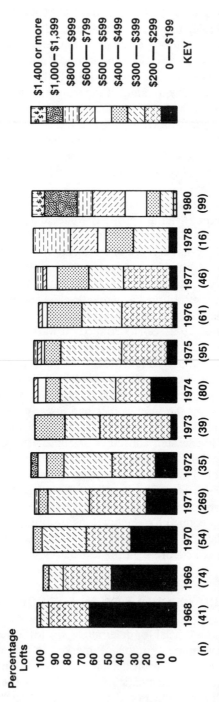

Figure 2. Rent structure of market in Manhattan living lofts, 1968–78 and 1980 – variation in monthly rents over time (in dollars per month). Data are from a 25 percent sample of advertisements for living lofts in *Village Voice* and *New York Times*, 1968–78 (first six months only, 1975 and 1978); and a 100 percent sample, week of March 1–7, 1980.

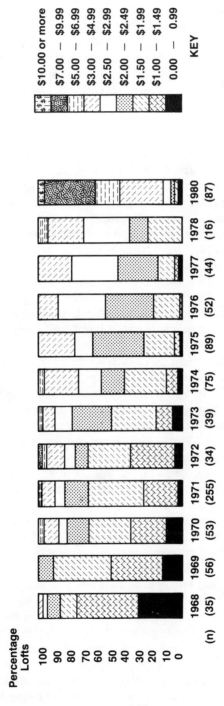

Figure 3. Rent structure of market in Manhattan living lofts, 1968–78 and 1980 – variation in adjusted monthly rents over time (in dollars per square foot). Data are from a 25 percent sample of advertisements for living lofts in *Village Voice* and *New York Times*, 1968–78 (first six months only, 1975 and 1978); and a 100 percent sample, week of March 1–7, 1980.

145

problematic for other people. But because in some cases speculation is suspected of having an unholy effect on price, on the one hand, and existing uses, on the other, it may create problems for certain classes of people and for society as a whole. Even in a general sense, the case of speculation versus development is important. As an economic activity, development is considered more productive than speculation. Developers produce economic value by making improvements in their property, by hiring workers and buying materials to build or to renovate, and, finally, by housing people who in turn go out to work. However, speculators who buy and sell property, reinvesting their profits in more real estate purchases, only keep the juices of capital flowing in that part of the economy that does not produce economic value — that is, in banks, insurance companies, and other institutions that are geared to making profits rather than products. As a social activity, also, development enjoys more legitimacy than speculation. The speculator derives a profit from guessing where to invest and when to sell, instead of from creating a competitive product that must often be sold under pressure.

In the loft market, development has evoked the negative connotation of speculation in several ways. First, the shortage of large spaces at reasonable rents caused pressure to build up in the middle-class housing market. With certain changes in social, cultural, and aesthetic values, this pressure spilled out or blew out into nontraditional housing markets. But demand would not have built up to such an intensity if developers in the middle-class housing market had not manipulated supply. In that sense, they acted like speculators. Loft developers also had an unnatural effect on prices. Because the supply of lofts in an old industrial center is, after all, finite, the intensification of demand for lofts enabled developers to charge monopoly prices. Particularly when housing consumers compete for space in historic buildings and landmark districts, they have no alternative but to pay the high price that a product in uniquely scarce supply commands. Although the creation of these conditions may have been an unanticipated consequence of public action, the developers who were able to buy up loft properties constituted, in effect, an oligopoly in the market. Moreover, when certain investors bought loft buildings and held or vacated them for future residential development, they were speculating, and this speculation had an immediate effect on market prices. Not only did the sale prices of loft buildings and the rents on converted loft-apartments rise abruptly, but so did the price of unimproved loft space — whose supply became subject to even tighter monopoly conditions.[10]

The relation between market price and investor strategy can be traced through changes in the ownership of particular buildings. As the loft market tipped, first, toward residential use and, then, toward high-rent apartment conversions, building owners seesawed between speculation and development. This can be seen, for example, in the recent history of an eight-story former loft building in the Lower Fifth Avenue manufacturing area. The building, with floors of 3,000 square feet, remained in the hands of its original owner until 1974. The owner had been able to refinance the mortgage regularly, in 1943, 1959, 1963, and 1971. Since 1959 the mortgage had been held by two local savings banks, and in 1971 the mortgage debt totaled $150,000. But in 1974 the owner sold the building for $120,000, which seems to be less than, or barely equal to, his investment in the building. The sale price was also lower than the total assessed value of the building and the land on which it stands. However, this situation is typical of New York City's chronic underassessment of land and buildings, which in turn symbolizes a general devalorization of center-city property. Three years later, without having made any improvements, the new owner sold the building for $525,000 — which was then more than double the assessed value. Merely holding the building, and perhaps vacating the building, over a period of three years resulted in a profit of roughly three times the investment. In 1978 the building was sold again. This time the sale price was $800,000, representing a profit of nearly $300,000 in a year's time, or a rate of return of 160 percent. Because the name of the owner who bought the building in 1977 reappears in the list of partners who bought the building in 1978, it is probable that he engineered the resale in some way. In any event, the new mortgages on the building — with higher principal and higher interest rates — were held by four local savings banks. The new owners converted the building to rental apartments.[11]

These transitions in ownership dramatize some of the problematic aspects of speculation versus development in the loft market. Especially remarkable are the effect of multiple sales on building prices, the savings banks' interest in generating new mortgage debts rather than maintaining old loans at the old rates, the preparation of downtown property for real estate speculation through underassessment for tax purposes, and the calculation that increasingly drew investment into loft properties, that is, the speculation that the dominant use would change from manufacturing to residence. Although early investors in the loft market were betting that their neighborhoods would remain the same, later investors were only buying in, in the anticipation that they would change.

The resulting displacement of small manufacturers, first, and arts producers, second, from the loft market is probably the most problematic effect of speculation in lofts. Even from the point of view of neoclassical economics, such displacement may be counterproductive. If users are thrown out of a market before a new demand builds up to fill the available supply, then a gap remains between supply and demand. Incapacitating equilibrium, in the neoclassicals' book, is as sinful as setting monopoly prices is in the radical perspective. Furthermore, there is a social question involved in the displacement of existing uses to satisfy potential demand.

Where can the old uses go? Revalorized urban property does not offer old, low-rent tenants ready access to new markets. Particularly when a productive use is replaced by a nonproductive one, or when a less productive nonproductive use like housing replaces more productive nonproductive uses like performance and creation in the arts, speculation poses problems for society as a whole. In this case the original infrastructure cannot be reconstituted without massive state intervention. But talking about subsidies to counter the effects of market forces reiterates the classic moral dilemma of state intervention in capitalist societies. The loft market represents only one small place in the system where that dilemma is felt.

7

SPECULATION AND THE STATE

Although people turn to the state for help in resisting real estate speculation, the state's position is necessarily more complicated than theirs. The changes that destabilize a neighborhood appear to most local officials as signs of economic growth. Particularly in cities whose economies are based on declining industrial sectors, a rise in property values seems to point to a renaissance, and redevelopment through "better" uses looks like a neighborhood's new lease on life. In general, though, local government has no quarrel with real estate developers. Government depends on the private sector to build the city. Through a kind of reciprocity, developers allow politicians to take the credit for it. But any relation that is ruled by mutual advantage also implies obligation. Operating in an economic system where capital mobility is the norm, both politicians and developers want guarantees. Developers want to know that the project they undertake today will not be subverted by external factors tomorrow. Politicians want the jobs and dollars that developers promise to last until the next election day. Somehow the mutual accommodation that develops seems more constraining for the state. The threat of capital flight makes officials soft-pedal regulations while accelerating concessions to developers who would otherwise — so they say — leave town. Especially over the past twenty years, subsidies in the form of tax advantages and zoning dispensations have formed the currency of exchange between developers and the state. Using these subsidies to contract with the private sector for change in the built environment takes the place of trying to plan development.

From the government's point of view, the weightiest argument against either speculation or development is that it imposes financial costs. If the "losers" in a development strategy must be compensated, if the development project requires state-financed infrastructure, and if, moreover, the "winners" demand subsidies to carry out their plans, then the state may wind up paying more than it anticipated and more than it can afford. In part this is because the state starts from the developers' premise, that

149

markets are chancy and risk should be controlled. Although this doesn't sound like classical free market economics, it does follow the standard operating procedure of contemporary capitalist states. Through the complicated mechanisms that have been negotiated over the past hundred years — mechanisms which include tax codes and loan guarantees as well as straight subsidies — government has learned to pay investors to invest. This means that the state socializes, or pays out of the public purse for, the costs of investment in all sorts of economic activity. Once the precedent has been established, it is hard to eliminate and nearly impossible to avoid applying it even in markets where profit seems to be guaranteed. The element of risk is taken for granted rather than demonstrated.

But this can't be made part of a public justification of the costs that the state incurs. For the public's consumption, the state does a cost-benefit analysis. This shows that for every dollar invested by the government in the private sector, a benefit is derived for the public good. In a period when the biggest benefit appears to be the promise of economic activity in place of disinvestment and decline, any sort of real estate development can easily be reconciled with public purpose. So in hard times as well as in times of prosperity, the state still functions, on the local level, as part of a "growth machine." [1]

The state's method of operation is fairly subtle. It both transforms the social climate that surrounds the built environment and institutionalizes the climactic changes that are thereby imposed on the positions of investors and consumers. It deals with success as well as failure. Just as it underwrites some of the costs of investment, so it recompenses some of the burdens of consumption. To any single group the state offers only partial relief. But in so doing, it implicitly adjusts conflicting demands and affirms its unique position as the arbiter of public purpose. The important criterion in the state's selection is whether intervention in the private sector will generate more investment in the economy and so keep the whole game in motion. However, the state's ability to influence the investment climate is limited by two key factors. First, the state relies on the developers' word as to whether a rate of return is satisfactory. Second, the state cannot directly affect demand for the developers' products in real estate markets. Given the areas of uncertainty on all sides, there is always an alternation of periods of growth and stagnation in local real estate markets.

Until recent years, the expansion of the urban economy, to which all local alliances were geared, depended on industrial growth within the city limits. [2] As capital investments are displaced into other regions and other countries, however, local government has to revise its strategy. As always, the maneuvering is complicated and even somewhat contradictory. The city has to facilitate a disengagement from industry on the part of big investors while demonstrating concern for retaining industrial jobs. It has to compensate for the loss of an important part of its tax base and prevent spillover effects from creating a wider disaster. In a local economy that is already fairly diversified, government tries to go with the flow of investments to more profitable nonproductive sectors. As the value of the unused or underused industrial plant and the urban infrastructure that supports it — streets, transit lines, public buildings — decline, the city tries to cut its losses by putting a value on alternate uses. Both led and leading in the ensuing process of social change, city officials opt, if they can, for a new investment climate. On the one hand, the city uses its considerable powers to isolate and shake off the vestiges of the industrial past. Zoning relates land use to new property values on a citywide basis, and removing property from the market through condemnation or legal takeover (that is, *in rem* proceedings) makes the use of individual properties compatible with general schemes. On the other hand, the three branches of city government tie up the loose ends that are involved in the massive switch. The city council changes laws and codes to reflect emerging investment practice, the city courts develop precedents based on new market positions, and city agencies deal on a daily basis with the resulting human casualties.

Certainly the intervention of the federal government has established many of the conditions in which new real estate markets rise out of old industrial ruins. Since the 1960s, for example, state subsidies for the arts have affected a demand for living lofts, and tax code revisions in 1976 and 1978 encouraged rehabilitation and re-use. But it is strategies of state intervention on the local level that really determine how successful the new markets can become. In the case of the loft market, four kinds of local intervention have had this kind of impact (see table 10). First, *rezoning* fostered change rather than stability and so helped dislodge remaining industrial uses from property that was ripe for upgrading to service-sector values. Second, local government helped to make new investment in old buildings more secure by both using traditional fiscal instruments and developing nontraditional juridical forms. The old means of revalorization were subsidies in the form of *tax benefits* for developers whose projects suited the public purpose. The new means were a rather complicated, indirect subsidy to developers that came through *local not-for-profit corporations.* These acted as the developers' silent partners by effecting transfer payments from the public to the private sector. The last strategy of local government intervention that has had a significant effect on real estate markets refers to *judicial decisions,* or the way the courts help to socialize consumption by legally recognizing, and thus socially regularizing, tenants' new rights and owners' new obligations. Although this refers especially to the quirky legality of New York City's loft situation, in general it sets a seal of sorts on the replacement of manufacturing by residential use in the center city.

Table 10

Strategies of State Intervention in Real Estate Markets for Urban Revitalization: Formation of the Market in Living Lofts

Strategy	Means	Example
Transformation		
Deindustrialization	*Rezoning*	City plans, zoning variances
	Holding off market	*In rem* takeovers of buildings with tax arrears
Revalorization	*Subsidies for development*	Tax abatements and reductions
	Silent partnerships	Transfer of property to nonprofit development corporations
Institutionalization		
Codification	Changes in laws, codes, and regulations	Buildings Code changes, A.I.R. certification, approval of co-op prospectuses
Socialization of consumption	*Judicial decisions*	Court cases on rights of tenants vs. owners/developers
Socialization of failure	Compensation and relocation	Advisory services, protection against harassment, assurance of financial settlements from developers

Note: The categories here are somewhat arbitrary. In real life, a subsidy or a legal change has more than one type of effect, and each "effect" has more than one "cause."

152

REZONING

The history of American cities and suburbs leads us to think of zoning as an exclusionary practice that aims to protect existing uses from encroachment by new ones. But in reality zoning is much more ambiguous. Theoretically zoning uses state power to protect the common good. "Its real purpose," says architecture critic Ada Louise Huxtable, "is to make a city a fit place to live." Yet she admits to some dismay about the project. "Something has clearly gone awry. New York's zoning has been turned into an instrument for maximizing real estate return through token tradeoffs." Why is this surprising? Once decisions on how to use land come under the control of public policy, making these decisions — or making exceptions to these decisions — becomes very lucrative. Particularly when political officials have to apply general regulations to specific situations, they seem as likely to bend the statutes as to enforce them. When broader groups of citizens have the opportunity to vote on zoning rules, they tend to use them to protect their position in the real estate market.[3]

Moreover, in the case of New York's living lofts, zoning *destabilized* real estate markets by progressively "ghettoizing" existing industrial uses and finally replacing them with higher-rent, service-sector tenants. Although successful manufacturers usually want to expand in the same area where they are already located,[4] the 1961 zoning resolutions forbade them to do that in most of Lower Manhattan. Like the earlier liquidation of working-class residential communities in adjacent areas, industry's forced march out of Lower Manhattan profited real estate developers in two ways: by creating a "demand" for new industrial parks in the hinterlands of the Bronx and Queens and by creating a "supply" of unused or underused space for redevelopment in the heart of the city. The selective rezonings of 1971 and 1976 busted the remaining clusters on which Manhattan's light industry still depended. Both materially and in people's minds, the traditional industrial centers in particular streets and neighborhoods existed no more, so that by the 1980s there was no public outcry about the number of living lofts that were breaking into the territory of the sacrosanct midtown Garment Center. In 1981 a new zoning change redefined the apparel district that had been established there under pressure in an earlier period in order to ghettoize low-class manufacturing use. After lengthy discussions in 1980 and 1981 between the City Planning Commission and the labor unions representing workers in the apparel trades, living lofts were legalized in an area that was designated as Garment Center East. Any use but manufacturing and business was prohibited in the Garment Center proper. Even in the mixed-use eastern portion, developers who acquired property to do a residential conversion had to obtain an equivalent amount of floor space and use it for manufacturing or commercial tenancy. Nevertheless, the legalization of residential use in adjacent areas to the south, as well as a number of as-of-right conversions to the west, effectively limited manufacturing to the Garment Center's existing borders. Any expansion that a manufacturer might contemplate would have to be made outside Manhattan, perhaps as far away as the new garment center in Atlanta.*

These zoning resolutions show how ambiguous the zoning mechanism can be. On the one hand, it is hard to prove whether rezoning primarily causes or follows a change of use. On the other hand, it is difficult to disentangle intention from effect. An architect who has lived and worked in SoHo lofts since the late 1960s complains that in this sense "zoning was never understood. It was *not supposed to make this* a residential area." In his and his colleagues' minds, the rezoning of SoHo for manufacturing and artists' living lofts would protect the neighborhood's existing uses. "We viewed the zoning change as a stalling action," he says, "to protect the manufacturers who were still here." In theory, zoning should have done that. But in practice, rezoning inserted a wedge in the *industrial* loft market that could be used to further *residential* use. "Zoning gave us respectability," the architect says of the 1971 laws.

Four years later, a different sort of zoning made the area more than respectable. After intense lobbying by SoHo residents, the New York City Board of Education created a special school district in 1975 that covers the area of SoHo west of Greene Street. In contrast to all other New York City school districts, there parents can choose which elementary school to send their children to. The reason for this is that SoHo, an industrial area that has no schools of its own, would ordinarily belong to the school district that includes Little Italy, Chinatown, and the rest of the Lower East Side. However, SoHo parents prefer the "progressive" and "magnet" schools of another nearby school district, in the West Village, to the Lower East Side's typically inner city schools. By making available to SoHo residents the "good" schools that upper-middle-class families prefer, the board of education confirmed SoHo as a middle-class enclave in the heart of the city. Even if the SoHo artists who lobbied for rezoning in 1971 did not intend this sort of effect, the same innocence cannot be claimed for the 1975 demand for redistricting.[5]

Whatever industrial uses remain unscathed by comprehensive and selective rezoning are often uprooted by zoning variances that make exceptions to the zoning rules. A variance can cover almost any sort of exception, from the size and shape of a building — too large, too tall, too bulky — to

---

* Significantly, by this time the city administration was moving ahead on plans to build a convention center in that area of midtown. The monumental project along the Hudson River that had been drawn up by architect I. M. Pei, designer of the Kennedy Library in Cambridge, would clash both aesthetically and socially with the traditional lofts of the Garment Center. The incompatibility was already indicated by rising property values that were totally incommensurate with manufacturing use.

the uses of particular floors. The issue "at variance" may be relatively minor, or it may be so extensive as to require practically blanket exemption from the rules. Where property values are high, developers use variances to enlarge the size of their projects without adding to acquisition costs. In the loft market, developers often apply for variances, first, because old loft buildings are basically small and, second, in order to evade the remaining zoning restrictions on nonindustrial use.

One developer's application for several variances on a residential conversion of a twelve-story loft building in NoHo offers a beautiful illustration of the use to which variances can be put. Though like the British Parliament they cannot make a woman into a man, they can change artists' living lofts into a housing complex and a shopping center for an upper-middle-class market. The variances for which the NoHo developer applied generally concern size, nonconforming use, and safety. In terms of size, the developer had bought a building that was so large — in lot size or square feet per floor — that the 1976 zoning resolution on NoHo specifically protected it for manufacturing use. So the building had to be exempted from this provision. The developer also wanted to enlarge the building by two floors — for a shopping mezzanine and penthouses. This required an exemption because the building was already considered oversize in terms of its height. Then, too, the developer wanted to maximize the number of rentable units by subdividing most floors into apartments that would be smaller than 1,200 square feet. But 1,200 square feet was the minimum size that the 1976 zoning mandated for artists' living and working lofts, which was, after all, the sole type of residential conversion that had been legalized in NoHo. The remaining four zoning variances merely deepen the irony. Because the developer wanted to get a high rent from stores on the street frontage, he asked for exemption from the zoning rule that reserves ground-floor space in NoHo for manufacturing use. He also asked to be exempted from certain fire safety rules in order to cut construction costs. Given the extent of these changes, it is not surprising that the developer hired a wheeler-dealer to argue his case. His law firm is Tufo, Johnson and Zuccotti, where the predominant partner, John Zuccotti, has been both city planning commissioner and first deputy mayor.[6]

Nor is Zuccotti's move from one side of the bargaining table to the other unusual in a world where elite members are known to circulate freely between business and government. In the old days before *Reform* became an acceptable word in the corridors of City Hall, real estate developers were appointed to the top city planning posts. Since the 1960s, developers have been replaced by professionals of another sort, who are mostly attorneys. This hardly jeopardizes the developers' interests. They merely hire the ex-officials when they return to their law firms. As attorneys the former officials represent the developers in their dealings with the city administration. There are several variations on this relationship. Zuccotti's predecessor as city planning commissioner, for example, now works as president of a private, not-for-profit development corporation in the heart of a midtown area that is being rezoned for big developers. Another prominent attorney, who specializes in negotiating zoning concessions from the City Planning Commission and considers himself, in that sense, a developer, keeps up a family connection in the field. His brother, a noted local power broker, was "a Brooklyn real estate lawyer with formidable political connections, who was more comfortable backstage at City Hall . . . as a lawyer, lobbyist, fund-raiser, and consultant." [7]

So getting a zoning variance can be an exercise in local power politics. But hiring a well-connected attorney is not the only way in which it is "political." Even institutionally the process is politicized. In New York City, for example, an application for a zoning variance can go by either of two routes, starting with the local community board or the citywide Board of Standards and Appeals (BSA). If the local board rejects the application, then the developer can appeal to BSA. Both in theory and in practice, the community board and the Board of Standards and Appeals represent different constituencies. Community boards of up to fifty members are appointed from among community leaders and volunteer activists in each area of the five New York City boroughs by the elected borough presidents. Half the members of each board are nominated by the city council representatives for the board area. Though they are appointed to two-year terms, they generally serve longer, at the borough president's pleasure. Recruited through a combination of self-selection, "connections," and service in local political clubs and neighborhood organizations, community board members form a heterogeneous and frequently divided microcosm of the city's communities. Nonetheless, they come closest in the political process to representing community interests. By contrast, the Board of Standards and Appeals hypothetically represents an impartial, professional interest. BSA is a group of six commissioners who must include two registered architects, two licensed engineers, and a similarly accredited city planner. These officials are appointed by the mayor to a six-year term. Their salary, which is over $40,000 a year, and their duties, which are mostly carried out at weekly meetings, make the office a political plum. The Board of Standards and Appeals is widely regarded as favorable to "real estate interests."

Indeed, BSA's record on granting zoning variances for residential conversion in the area of Manhattan where many loft buildings are concentrated — the community board district which includes SoHo, NoHo, and Greenwich Village — shows absolutely no opposition to developers' plans. Between 1969 and 1979, fifty-one applications for this kind of variance were submitted to BSA either directly or on appeal. Not one was rejected. Meanwhile, the local community board approved thirty-nine applications and rejected twenty-one. (In some cases, rejection by the local board was enough to kill the developer's interest, and he or she never appealed the decision to BSA. More often, the developer did appeal, and BSA reversed the community board's decision.) Significantly, however, the community board did not begin rejecting applications for zoning variances on residential conversions until 1976. In just a four-year period, from 1976 through 1979, the local board made nineteen of its twenty-one rejections. The reason for the turnabout is simple. For the previous ten years, members of the board had supported artists' lofts. Some members had been involved in the establishment of the Greenwich Street artists' housing co-op, and the board as a whole had promoted the rezoning of SoHo and NoHo. But the board learned from their experience, with some chagrin. Distressed by the chic scene and the high market prices that their action, in part, had created, the board tried to use the limited powers at their disposal to halt the overwhelming momentum of loft development.[8]

Nevertheless, the board was incapable of advancing the goal of neighborhood stability in the face of market forces. Its potential for pursuing an anti-development strategy is constrained by its organizational structure, by city politics, and by the attitude of its own members. Institutionally, the community boards are not set up as planning agencies, and their decisions do not have the force of law. Although they were created in the 1950s on the model of "home rule," and supposedly strengthened in the early 1970s as a sop to demands from the grass roots for decentralization, the community boards have only an advisory role. Thus, while they may express the community's indignation or the community's pleasure, they lack the statutory power that is necessary for community control. Nor is there much impetus for coordinating policies among them. Even in the two important areas where the boards have a chance of affecting decisions — budget and zoning — they show neither the will nor the way to shape policy. To some degree, the problem is due to the fact that board members have not bridged the large gap of aspiration and control that divides volunteers from professional politicians. No matter how sharp or how experienced they are — and the membership of the SoHo-NoHo-Greenwich Village board has included some very astute local activists — the board members do not have a vested interest in tackling controversial issues and battling the real elite. Some board members may relish a David-and-Goliath match against some powerful city agency or, more often, a local developer or private institution. But they really are not prepared to mobilize a struggle against capitalism, racism, or real estate development as social issues. In many ways they merely want to hold their own in the class structure. More and more, board members in a socially heterogeneous district represent single-interest constituencies that struggle among themselves over particular issues but rarely summon up the common interest to take on banks, developers, or the political power structure.

Significantly, the institutional procedure of land-use decisions really prevents the boards from constituting more than an obstacle to a developer's strategy. Developers already have the right to build projects that don't contradict the zoning laws (and to do as-of-right conversions). Because variances are handled on a case-by-case basis, even rejections can't exert an influence on general policy. And since BSA has the right to overrule local boards on these issues, they can hardly even set a precedent. Ultimately, community boards depend on the support of such elected officials as the city council members and the party district leaders in their area, the borough president, and, most of all, the mayor. Indeed, the board in the Greenwich Village area found it difficult to oppose a mayor who lived in the district and had been a long-time comrade in arms in liberal causes. On at least one occasion, the mayor's closest advisers telephoned board members and asked them to ease their resistance to residential conversion. In addition, the mayor publicly supports middle-class housing. Under these conditions, the board can not sharpen the anti-development thrust of its decisions.*

TAX ABATEMENTS AND TAX REDUCTIONS

Proponents of tax advantages for real estate developers argue that they are a necessary means of luring investment that otherwise would not be made. Despite precedents that go back to post–World War II urban renewal, this local development strategy grew, for the most part, in response to changes in federal policy toward cities in the early 1970s. At that time, short-term funding and block grants replaced subsidies for specific projects and long-range development plans. But real estate developers felt as though they had been left in the lurch. Whether Washington had intended to foster decentralization — through community development grants and revenue-sharing — or a diffusion of funds, the effect on the local level was to initiate a scramble for less cumbersome and more secure subsidies. The recession and inflation of this period also made developers insecure about investment capital, and local governments wanted freedom to maneuver around the rate of return on investments in their region.

---

* This community board did wage a fierce and persistent battle against New York University in 1977–78, when the University leased a square block of loft buildings in the Broadway Corridor to a national real estate developer, who threw out the manufacturing tenants in order to convert the lofts to high-rent apartments. The board succeeded in pressuring the university to aid the manufacturers in finding new space and to give them a relocation allowance. However, the board could not influence the university to reconsider the decision to convert the buildings to residential use. Nor could it stop the project, because this was an as-of-right conversion. Despite the crocodile tears shed over job loss, the Beame and Koch administrations did not intervene.

Moreover, tax abatements and tax reductions on development projects are supposed to be relatively cost-free to local governments. By merely forgoing a tax debt, the governments get development projects without having to give any money "up front" to developers. Nor are the voters asked to contract a public debt through a bond issue. Instead, the beauty of these subsidies is that in return for a mythical cost, they generate real benefits. The boon includes construction or renovation of buildings, higher property values, and revenue-producing wages and sales for the construction work. The greatest benefits, however, are supposed to come in the future. When the tax abatements expire, new property taxes will reflect the improvements and the resulting increase in property values. The city will be prosperous. Finally, by specifying what type of development qualifies for tax benefits, the city is able to contract for change in the built environment that suits the public purpose.

For those reasons, New York City's J-51 tax program has been defended as a valuable tool for redevelopment. Essentially, it removes the Catch-22 of penalizing a building owner for making improvements by raising property taxes on the renovated property. An owner who applies for J-51 gets a dual tax break. On the one hand, there is a tax *exemption* for twelve years on the increase in the assessed value of a building that results from the improvements. On the other hand, there is an annual tax *abatement and reduction,* by an amount up to 8.33 percent of the "reasonable cost" of the improvements, for a period of from nine to twenty years. Although this offers relief to the small landlord who would not be able to raise rents sufficiently to cover the cost of increased taxes, it really is advantageous to the developer who practices economy of scale. A gut rehabilitation, with its commensurately great increase in value, gets a better tax break than a minor improvement. It is also significant that by extending these tax benefits to residential conversions, the city administration defines them as a socially desirable form of upgrading.[9]

Specifically, conversions that qualify for J-51 benefits must meet certain conditions that are supposed to guarantee an increased number of apartments for middle-class housing at affordable rents. These conditions mandate larger than usual apartments, with separate bedrooms, at rents that are subject to the city's Rent Stabilization Guidelines. But there are special dispensations for the loft developer. "Loft-apartments" of at least 1,000 square feet do not have to have separate bedrooms, and apartments larger than 600 square feet (which is standard studio size) may eliminate two interior walls. Furthermore, the building owner is not inhibited by rent stabilization from setting the initial rents at market levels. So it is not surprising that with the crisis in real estate markets in the early seventies, large developers lobbied the city government to expand J-51 in 1975 and to renew it in 1978 and 1981.

Tax exemption and abatement programs like J-51 are generally discussed in terms of criteria that seem, on the surface, to be objective. One criterion of whether such a subsidy is effective is whether it generates economic activity. Another criterion is whether development projects would be undertaken without it. However, the basic problem with both criteria is that there is no way to measure or to verify the claims that developers bring forth to justify the subsidy. Without access to the developers' books, the city administration cannot really guess how essential a tax benefit has been to their calculations — or whether it has resulted in a windfall profit. Nor is there any honest way to tell whether, in the long run, a particular use is more stimulative of economic growth. To be sure, loft developers say that they would never have chosen rehabilitation over new construction were it not for J-51. But neither common sense nor the current market substantiates this claim.

Until recently, attempts to evaluate J-51's effectiveness suffered from a serious flaw. The data were either too incomplete or too heterogeneous to draw conclusions. Because they didn't separate J-51 applications from owner-occupiers and from large developers, analysts failed to distinguish between cases. The city administration blurred the lines of analysis in order to give the impression that the tax benefit helped the "little man." Moreover, the law was only amended to favor big projects in 1975, so for several years it was too soon to tell what its effects might be. Nevertheless, a study by two urban economists in the mid-1970s found that the rate of return on J-51-financed projects was as high as that on privately financed renovation. This meant that the subsidy was not the deciding factor in whether a rehabilitation paid its own way. Instead, the determinant seemed to be location. Any building in a "good" location could make up the costs of renovation in increased rents. Therefore, the researchers suggested, perhaps half the projects that received J-51 benefits would have been done even without them.[10] A second study, carried out around the same time, found, in answer to the other criterion, that J-51 did stimulate economic activity. But these researchers added another question that interested the city government. They asked whether the converted housing attracted new residents who otherwise would not have come to the center city. Their finding was that in this sense, J-51 was not particularly effective.[11] The last study of J-51 posed a fourth question: What type of projects most benefited from the subsidy? The results form a damning indictment. According to research done in 1981 by the staff of the city council president, J-51 subsidies have largely paid for luxury housing in high-rent areas of Manhattan. Since the law was rewritten in 1975, the number of new J-51-financed projects in Manhattan — which is the center of the city's high-rise rental market — grew five times more than that in Queens or the Bronx, and one-and-a-half times more than in Brooklyn. So owner-occupiers and landlords of low-rise, family housing in the Outer Boroughs benefited less from this state subsidy than did developers of expensive property in Manhattan.[12]

But would it not all be worthwhile if the subsidy generated more benefits, in a broad sense, than costs? "In this light," say some earnest urban analysts, "programs such as . . . J-51 may be seen not simply as subsidies to developers and to middle- or upper-income tenants, but as investments by the city government that may actually repay themselves through . . . broad stimulative effects."[13] Yet when these analysts compared the "stimulative effects" of J-51 with those of a similar state program that subsidizes new multiple dwelling construction (Section 421 of the 1971 Real Property Tax Law of the State of New York), they found that the forgone taxes made the city's program more costly. The 1981 study tried to work out these costs. With a hypothetical "sensitivity analysis," the researchers gauged how much money the city government spent on projects that would not otherwise have been done, in contrast to how much money it spent on projects that would have been done without the subsidy. They concluded that because of the long-term obligation to forgo taxes that the city incurs under J-51, New York loses a lot more money than it gains.

Perhaps the most important aspect of the growth question is qualitative rather than quantitative and social rather than economic. What kind of growth is encouraged, and at whose expense does it occur? Even the earlier J-51 benefits to small developers subsidized, in effect, a turnover of apartments to higher-income tenants.[14] By the 1980s the concentration of benefits in high-rent areas of Manhattan merely intensified the tendency. If we consider that in cities with chronically underfinanced budgets, forgone property taxes represent a significant loss in operating income, then it is clear that the people who really pay for this sort of "growth" are low-income city residents, whose access to public services is drastically reduced by the resulting budget cuts. Moreover, the benefits that accrue to the public sector from tax abatements and reductions differ qualitatively from those that go to the private sector. Developers derive concrete economic gains — which are as useful as direct subsidies — when the city lowers the tax bill. In addition, a tax abatement helps to assure bank financing. The public sector, in return, gets generalities. A recent study of a tax subsidy in Saint Louis, for example, found that the public sector gained "redevelopment of blighted areas," "increased non-property tax revenues," a "stabilized property base," and a lot of new office buildings and hotels.[15] What this essentially means is that tax subsidies are a tool to change neighborhood and urban character. This involves some legerdemain on the public officials' part about the public purpose that they serve.

Yet by itself a tax subsidy is neither big enough nor extensive enough to remake a city. Nor does it counteract market forces. When the wind blows hot on demand for loft-apartments, J-51 makes a viable project even more attractive. But when the market value of residential space falls, relative to other uses, J-51 does not sway a developer to counter the trend. By 1981, when the city council finally eliminated J-51 benefits for projects in the highest-rent areas of Manhattan, market forces had practically rendered the question moot. At that point, in these neighborhoods, it became more profitable once again to install commercial use. In contrast to the residential conversion of old buildings that dominated the 1970s, the new market of the 1980s tended toward condominium conversions for commercial users. And the city administration was anxiously exploring the tax advantages that it could offer such conversions.

Although it has never been proved that J-51 drove industry out of New York City, the tax subsidy played an essential role in the deindustrialization process. First, in the absence of a comprehensive urban plan, programs like J-51 serve as the flagship and the bellwether of the city's development strategy. Second, such subsidies have a "demonstration effect" on real estate development because they demonstrate both the viability and the visibility of certain kinds of projects. Third, the tax benefit has an "output effect" because it increases the supply of one type of infrastructure at the expense of another. All in all, in terms of social benefits, through a program like J-51 the city administration supports a new white-collar and professional work force in place of traditional blue-collar labor. The old New York labor unions' impotence in the face of residential conversion emphasizes this switch in public policy.

Other declining industrial cities seem to share the same strategy. They all use tax subsidies to shift the costs of redevelopment from developers to working-class and low-income taxpayers, and the benefits from the public to the private sector. In Boston, for example, tax subsidies paid for the redevelopment of a large waterfront area that includes Faneuil Hall, the Boston City Hall plaza, nearby federal and state office buildings, and loft buildings near South Station and the piers. Using some of this property for government buildings removes it forever from the property tax rolls, while the project helps to revalorize the neighborhood for private developers. Nevertheless, local officials justified the tax benefits that they granted to the developer of Faneuil Hall because of the future sales tax revenues that the area's boutiques and restaurants would generate. But in Massachusetts the sales tax goes to the state, not to the city. Furthermore, tax abatements on waterfront loft buildings that have been converted to residential use reduce the city's income from property taxes. Because the small businesses and manufacturers that had to leave those buildings confronted an increasingly tight real estate market, some of them probably left the city or went out of business and so cost the city revenue in commercial taxes. Like New York, Boston seems to lose in some incalculable degree from tax subsidies for real estate development.[16]

In larger economic and political terms, a declining city pays more than it gains from upgrading to a service-sector capital. On the one hand, no amount of real estate subsidies so far has reversed the overall direction of capital flight. Older downtown areas spend the most money to attract developers, and they leverage the smallest return on their investment.[17] On the other hand, city governments retain little control over development strategy. The state cannot compel the private sector to invest. Nor does public purpose have much meaning when there is no chance of popular control. In New York City, when a city council member complained to the housing commissioner that J-51 "may produce apartments of such a size, shape, and rent that the character of the building's tenants will change drastically," the commissioner shrugged his shoulders. He insisted that there was no place for community control in deciding where tax benefits for development should go.[18]

SILENT PARTNERS: THE CITY AND THE DEVELOPMENT CORPORATIONS

Local "development corporations" represent another kind of public entrepreneurialism that shifts the costs of redevelopment to the public sector and the benefits to the private sector. Set up under state charter as private but nonprofit organizations, these quasi-governmental bodies play middleman in the development process. With a variety of incentives at their disposal — depending on the terms of their charter — they aim at attracting and coordinating new investment capital. Supposedly they represent the public purpose more efficiently than do either government agencies or private developers because while their aim is "social," their *modus operandi* is "economic." In terms of both their membership and their sponsorship, they are primarily based in the business community. Their explicit purpose, as they often say, is to cut through the red tape of bureaucratic procedures and public approvals in order to facilitate development projects. It is inconceivable that the local development corporations would quarrel with the private sector's development strategy, because in many ways they *are* the private sector.

Despite constant intervention in real estate markets, capitalist states do not really feel comfortable in "usurping" the private-sector roles of landlords and developers.* So a local development corporation can take

---

* Even in countries with a long history of public housing, such as England, more conservative governments still question the principle. In France, the "mixed" public-private construction enterprises are run by the private sector. In New York City, where the massive abandonment of dilapidated apartment houses by their owners has made the city government the second largest landlord, the Housing Department has consistently shown that it is unable and unwilling to administer property.

both the financial and the administrative burdens of property management out of the government's hands. This type of organization is particularly useful for transfering property from public to private ownership. At one point, the state transfers property that has somehow come under its control to the development corporation. Because this is a quasi-public body, the state cannot be accused of making a giveaway to the private sector. Then the development corporation transfers the property, or the development rights on it, to a private developer. Although the developer derives a profit from his involvement, his intervention is justified because it conforms to the public purpose of fostering development. It is irrelevant to ask whether the development corporation pegs its strategy to the market, or whether the market is influenced by the corporation's development strategy. What matters is that, once again, public purpose is bent to suit private profit.

The redevelopment of the Federal Archive Building, a large, unused warehouse in Greenwich Village, highlights the role of a special-purpose development corporation, the New York Landmarks Conservancy, in making rehabilitation profitable for private developers. The Conservancy's raison d'être is to save old buildings that would otherwise be torn down. Symbolically, at least, this commitment to historic preservation also implies a commitment to neighborhood preservation. In the case of the Federal Archive Building, however, the community resisted the corporation's development's strategy. This raised the question of who determines the public purpose that the corporation represents — the community or the private sector?

There is no question that the Landmarks Conservancy serves the interests of the historic preservation and the patrician arts constituencies. Its gestation period was the 1960s of "Lost New York," when citizens' groups began to protest the demolition of landmark or favorite old buildings. By 1965 the city administration had established an official Landmarks Preservation Commission, but the upper-class Municipal Arts Society felt that the commission was hamstrung by political constraints. The commission, for example, had no power to compel preservation. So the patricians had a better idea: they would assist the market's invisible hand by making preservation no less profitable than new construction. The key to their thinking was the historic switch in preservation strategy from re-creation to re-use. They justified the adaptive re-use of old buildings by showing that with the proper renovation and choice of tenants, they could become economically self-sufficient. At the time, of course, this sounded like wishful thinking.[19]

When the Landmarks Conservancy was established in 1971, the collapse of the real estate market in new office construction began to make its strategy much more viable. In fact, the organization fit into the legal schema that Governor Rockefeller had devised during the 1960s when he created New York State's super-agency for economic development, the

Urban Development Corporation. In 1969 the state passed a Not-for-Profit Corporation Law, which made it easy to form smaller versions of UDC without involving the state legislature's, or the voters', participation. According to the Landmarks Conservancy's charter, the group has the right to own, hold, manage, lease, and sell property in its own name. In practice, it hires consultants, commissions plans, makes proposals, and selects a redevelopment strategy for each building that it takes under its wing. The Landmarks Conservancy also "assists" with the legal incorporation of the management organ that runs each renovation project. It assures and arranges the tenancy of the renovated buildings — "and in so doing," as a Landmarks Conservancy statement of purpose says, "it may attempt to transfer properties into more beneficient hands." Finally, the Conservancy "enlists the support" of public and private agencies, or lobbies, to make each project as visible and as viable as possible.

Although redevelopment and re-use may be consonant with the public interest, this kind of individualized attention to projects is rare in the public sector. Moreover, the Conservancy is more selective than a public agency. It operates in the fairly restricted market of New York City's designated historic landmarks. In Manhattan, these have included Grand Central Station, the Villard Houses that were incorporated into a new midtown hotel, and a former U.S. custom house (now a museum) in the Wall Street area. So the Conservancy tends to be interested in prime real estate locations. This helps to establish the economic viability of its projects as well as its own credibility in real estate circles.

However, historic preservation and re-use have been strongly aided by legal inducements too. In 1972 the U.S. Congress passed Public Law 92-362, which permitted, for the first time, the use of government-owned buildings for income-producing purposes. In 1976 the Public Buildings Cooperative Use Act legitimized the private redevelopment of public buildings for mixed public and private uses. The Tax Reform Act of 1976 initiated the practice of allowing deductions for the renovation of "certified historic structures" regardless of the use to which such buildings are put. This law's well-known Section 2124 extended the tax benefits to commercial properties and shortened the write-off period on renovations to five years. Adding the stick to the carrot, the tax code also prohibited accelerated depreciation on new construction that is carried out on historic structures. In 1978 a further Revenue Act granted investment tax credits for rehabilitating old commercial buildings, and two years later a Technical Corrections Act assured these tax credits to business partnerships that lease, often as a tax shelter, renovated properties. Such laws had an obvious significance for investors. The rehabilitations done on historic structures were worth $3.2 million in 1977, but in 1981 the renovation projects subsidized by the 1976 Tax Reform Act and the 1978 Revenue Act reached a value, according to an early estimate, of $795 million. By the

early eighties, Congress readied an increase in the tax credit for rehabilitating historic structures to 25 percent, plus depreciation of the building
and its rehabilitation costs over fifteen years. All together, these are important subsidies for redevelopment based on preservation and re-use.[20]

In light of the tax advantages that now accrue to the owners of certified
historic property, it is not surprising that the New York Landmarks Conservancy continues to attract support from the East Coast Establishment.
Its corporate donors belong to the highest circles of national and international capital. Its board of directors reproduces, in its interlocking cultural
affiliations, the directorates of the power elite. In 1977 and 1978, when the
Conservancy locked horns with the local community board over the redevelopment of the Federal Archive Building, the board of directors included
eight Wall Street lawyers; seven high-ranking professionals in arts administration, historic preservation, and the arts; four architects; three planners
and development consultants; two patrician women; two real estate
developers; an investment banker; a businessman; the vice-president of an
international auction house; and a U.S. senator. Nor was the Conservancy
distant from the city administration. Its executive director was a close
friend of the city planning commissioner.

The Conservancy's involvement with the Federal Archive Building dates
back to 1974. At that time, the large, dense building — an enclosed square
block, in effect, of 1.2 acres, or 520,000 square feet — was being used as an
archival warehouse by the federal General Services Administration. After
GSA moved its archives to a "horizontal" depot in New Jersey, it classified
the building as surplus property. Unaffected by the building's architecture,
which a *New York Times* critic calls the best piece of nineteenth-century
industrial brickwork in this part of the city, GSA decided to give the
building away. This was too good a property for the Landmarks Conservancy to pass up. As Geoffrey Platt, an architect and a vice-president of
the Conservancy says, "The Federal Archive Building . . . is a designated
New York City Landmark and is on the National Register. When we
learned that it was about to be declared surplus we leaped at this opportunity to prove our reason for being." But the Federal Archive Building also
sits on a valuable piece of property. Revalorized by the recent spate of
residential conversions in the surrounding West Village, this area is the
hub of a bustling arts-theater-restaurant infrastructure, as well as a
mainstay of the middle-class brownstone constituency. It is also the Main
Street of Greenwich Village's gay community.[21]

Between 1974 and 1975 the Conservancy commissioned a report on the
Federal Archive Building from a special research center at Columbia
University's School of Architecture and approved the research team's plan
for re-use. By 1976 the Conservancy had got Mayor Beame to request that
GSA turn over the surplus property, gratis, to New York City. The city
government would in turn lease the Federal Archive Building to the Con-

servancy. Because Congress had just passed the law enabling publicly owned buildings to be developed for mixed public and private use, Mayor Beame hastened to relate the Conservancy's role to the terms of that act. He wrote: "The Federal Archive Building will be redeveloped on behalf of the City of New York by the New York Landmarks Conservancy as a revenue-producing mixed re-use building to enclose a major new urban center. Bringing together in its mixture the life that is characteristic of this part of New York as such, the building will not become the private precinct of any one public or private user." [22]

But reciprocity has its limits. Although GSA was supposed to turn the building over to New York City for free, and the city then was supposed to turn the building over to the Conservancy for a negotiated annual rent that would be "comparable to taxes on redevelopment projects of this sort," and a "nominal" ground rent, the private sector could anticipate far greater returns. On the one hand, the developer, whom the Conservancy had the right to select, had to pay the city the same annual rent "*in lieu of taxes*" as the Conservancy did. This meant that the developer had very low acquisition costs. On the other hand, the developer had to pay a percentage of his "reasonable profit" as a "substantial" ground rent. However, this amount went to the Conservancy rather than to the city. Of course, the Conservancy's charter does not permit it to show a profit. So this income would be earmarked "to establish and maintain a revolving fund for New York City landmarks." Like any organization, the Conservancy defends its right to funding on the basis of its activism. In this case, the number of projects that it has already undertaken — "overseeing," by 1978, a million square feet of landmark property — and the number of projects that it has had to refuse "are inarguable proof of the Conservancy's need to grow."

In 1977, because of New York City's Uniform Land Use Review Procedure, which mandates consultation with the local community board on all important land-use decisions within the board's area, the Greenwich Village Community Board became involved with the Federal Archive Building. Once again, however, the public body lost out to the private sector. Although the community board had the right to propose, the Conservancy had the right to dispose. Over a three-year period, from 1977 to 1980, the community board's resistance to the Conservancy's ideas of development turned consultation into insult and development into donnybrook. The board and the Conservancy were at odds over two issues. On one level, the community board fought for a more significant public role in the decisionmaking process. On another level, it lobbied for "affordable" rents rather than luxury housing. The board also pressed for mixed use that would be weighted toward the existing community's social needs rather than toward retail facilities for the affluent newcomers that could be expected. Implicitly, the board advanced the same anti-development strategy — for mixed use and neighborhood stabilization — that it had advanced when it supported artists' housing in the West Village back in the 1960s.

In particular, the community board disagreed with the Conservancy's position in four key areas: the choice of developer, the way space would be used in the renovated building, the decisionmaking procedure, and the distribution of the public sector's share of the developer's "rent" payments. Although the board resented, from the start, the predominance of high-rent housing and retail space in any private redevelopment plan for the building, the terms of the bargain that had already been struck between the city administration and the Conservancy precluded either the board's initiative or its veto. From their position, as the board members saw it, they could only choose between equally undesirable alternatives. So they chose instead to stonewall. While the board withheld its approval from the project, it lobbied the developer that the Conservancy initially selected to provide more space in "semi-public," community facilities and more apartments at cheaper rents. When the developer protested that he had to make a "reasonable return" of 25 percent on his equity, the board suggested that he compensate for the profit that he would forgo by applying for federal subsidies. In this big new project in their neighborhood, board members obviously wanted to reproduce "their own kind." But they had no leverage to affect either market forces or development strategy. Like themselves, the middle-class people whom they wanted to see living in the Federal Archive Building — as the developer's architect shrewdly pointed out at a meeting with the board — were "people who are too rich to qualify for subsidies and too poor to pay market rents."

After two years of stalemate, the developer bowed out of the Federal Archive Building project. He had lost too much time and money in political foreplay. To circumvent the community board and to speed up the project, an alternate strategy for transfering the property to the private sector was devised. The second time around, GSA gave the property to the New York State Urban Development Corporation, the archetypal development corporation, with plenty of political clout. In turn, UDC leased the building to another developer who had been waiting in the wings. The mayor's advisers interceded with board members to stop their obstructionist tactics, and the board dissipated the final burst of its fury in an internecine dispute over dividing the community's share of the payments to the public sector. In the struggle over control of the Federal Archive Building project, the community board came out with a one-shot payment of $600,000 for "neighborhood preservation" — which was divided among community groups, an investment in city garbage trucks, and other good causes — and 60,000 square feet of "subsidized" semi-public space for rent at four dollars per square foot a year. The Landmarks Conservancy emerged $6 million richer in funding for the next fifteen years. The developer got 105,000 square feet of desirable commercial space and 347 highly marketable co-op apartments which average about 1,000 square feet apiece. Certainly this was not a bad deal for the private sector. But then, we began with the proposition that a development corporation does not aim to contradict the private sector's development strategy.

JUDICIAL DECISIONS

For the most part, the courts have intervened in the loft market to regularize the position of residential tenants. In doing so, they have helped to institutionalize the transformation of lofts from factory space into housing and the deindustrialization of the loft market. Unlike the city administration, the courts have never had the potential to halt the momentum of residential conversion. Commercial tenants enjoy the protection of the law only as long as their lease is in effect. When rezoning of a commercial or a manufacturing district forecloses the renewal of the lease, those tenants have no recourse to the courts. However, they can try to exert political pressure to expand their legal rights. In that sense it is the legislature — the city council and the state assembly and senate — that must deal with the human costs of development strategy, while the courts play a role in adjusting the benefits.

Yet over the past few years, as a more aggressive development strategy has replaced the passive investment orientation of most loft building owners, existing residential tenants have called on the courts for protection. Like relatively low-rent residents in any housing market, who are threatened by the incursion of higher-rent uses, these tenants plead for stability. But the courts can deal only with the aftereffects of a destabilized market. They cannot preempt a development scenario that runs on the energy of "market forces" and contradicts no laws. To the extent that the courts have been able to protect loft dwellers, they have defended them against loftlords rather than developers and against small developers rather than big ones. In other words, it's the two-bit villains that have been caught. Basically these loft building owners have been caught on the horns of their own greed. Loft tenants have won protection if they have been able to show that by renting them a loft their landlord carried out a de facto, though technically illegal, residential conversion. As New York Civil Court Judge Bruce M. Wright wrote in a 1979 decision, *Captain Crow Management* (owner) v. *Caligula Amusements* (tenant), "It is the fact of residential use which warrants protection, when that use is coupled with the landlord's knowledge and some active participation."

The court decisions that have set legal precedent in the loft market concern three simple issues: loftlord tactics, the eviction of existing tenants in order to sell or co-op the property, and rent stabilization. Needless to say, each issue becomes vastly more complicated in the context of real landlords and tenants.

Four key cases involve a single loftlord, Eli Lipkis, and residential tenants in two of his buildings in Lower Manhattan. In all four cases the courts decided in the tenants' favor. The impact of these decisions is that a landlord can neither evict a loft tenant for illegal residence — in the absence of a residential lease — nor collect rent from such a tenant without getting a certificate of occupancy for the building. In other words, these decisions protect residential loft tenants at the expense of the landlord — and imply the eviction of any remaining manufacturing tenants. The courts have pushed loft building owners who are inclined to rent lofts for living rather than manufacturing to go all the way to a "legal" residential conversion. There are to be no more halfway conversions that retain the possibility of manufacturing use. The net effect is to homogenize the residential market and generalize higher rents for all lofts.[23]

In another case, in which a newly formed artists' housing co-op in SoHo tried to evict a writer who had rented a living loft in the building for ten years, in order to sell the loft, the state supreme court ruled that a landlord could not evict a residential loft tenant whose lease had expired before getting a certificate of occupancy for the de facto residential conversion. Although the decision is quite similar to the court's earlier decision against loftlord Lipkis, lawyers regard this case, *155 Wooster Street Association* (owner) v. *Bengis* (tenant), as "cleaner" than the Lipkis decisions because there was no harassment or connivance on the owner's part. In *Captain Crow* v. *Caligula,* the judge also ruled that a residential loft tenant whose lease had expired could not be evicted because the owner wanted to co-op the building. But the case with the greatest potential for affecting relations in the loft market was *Mandel* (owner) v. *Pitkowsky* (tenant). In this case, the issue rather unexpectedly turned out to be rent stabilization — or the landlord's inability to raise the rent on living lofts without restraint. In *Mandel* v. *Pitkowsky,* the state supreme court followed the precedent of *155 Wooster Street Association* v. *Bengis* by ruling again that a residential tenant in a de facto residential building could not be evicted without a certificate of occupancy. However, in a surprise, unanimous finding, the court also decided that residential tenants in the building were entitled to the protection of rent stabilization. Because the tenants showed that the owner had knowingly rented more than six lofts in the building for residential use prior to January 1, 1974, the judges applied New York's Emergency Tenant Protective Act of 1974, which stabilized the rents on apartments that had not been protected before. Since this decision affected tenants throughout the loft market, loft building owners found themselves in the position of apartment house landlords, with all the restraints on rents and responsibilities for upkeep that owning an apartment house in

New York implies. Now that their loft tenants had the standard lease protections of apartment tenants in the rental market, many of them chose to sell out. They also lobbied the state legislature to rescind the advantages the courts had granted.[24]

Cumulatively, these decisions have had the effect of stabilizing the loft market — after residential transformation. To the degree that loft tenants compete for space in a sellers' market, the courts' intervention provides them with some protection. The courts cannot stabilize the market so as to stop development strategy where it now stands. But they can protect residential tenants in a residential loft market from being uprooted by the further advance of this strategy. They at least are firmly in place. In an interesting way, the courts' intervention in the loft market complements the evolution of the loft constituency. Just as loft dwellers are no more bohemian nor any more artistic than standard apartment residents, so their place in the loft market has been confirmed as a tenants' position rather than an artists' exception. They can now enjoy the regular rights of apartment tenants. Gone are the artists' claims to social support and the eccentrics' desires for benign neglect.

State intervention in real estate markets is part of a larger pattern of public entrepreneurialism that seeks to attract new investment to particular areas. Besides structuring the social and economic relations on which capital mobility relies, state power also affects the spatial forms that the movement of capital takes. The transformation of declining manufacturing centers into service-sector capitals starts with disinvestment, but it is affirmed and strengthened by the state's selective response. Betting on this response is part of the real estate developer's speculation.

In the case of the loft market, manufacturing tenants whose position was threatened by higher-rent residential uses found no relief in any part of the state's machinery. To a large extent, the dominance of "big capital" over small industries had already disabled them. Although recent city administrations paid an obligatory verbal debt to local industrial interests, they were really concerned with attracting "clean" service-sector jobs and expanding a desirable, expensive housing market. The rezoning of New York City, for example, has consistently eroded the spatial base of the small firms that make up the major garment and printing industries. In their place, city officials glowingly describe the growth of tourism, that "intersection of the best of the past with the worst of the present," as someone has remarked about a different part of the world.[25]

Because of a real reluctance to get involved in the ownership and management of what is, after all, private property, the state has developed or legitimized a number of devices for transfering development rights (and sometimes property) to the private sector. The state also aids development strategy under the guise of stimulating general economic growth. In addi-

tion to zoning, local governments provide subsidies for development, tax
abatements and reductions, and infrastructure improvements that further
developers' interests and shift the costs of development to the public sector. Local governments have also developed an ingenious collaborative
effort in which they act as silent partners of privately inspired but publicly
chartered "development corporations." These quasi-state organizations are
subject to few public controls. Indeed, the main reason for their existence
is that they offer private developers short-cuts through the roadblocks of
public policy. The development corporations also enrich themselves at the
public's expense. But because they spend their profits on "good works,"
who can tell where private enrichment diverges from the public purpose?
The New York Landmarks Conservancy is not the only nonprofit corporation that raises these suspicions. We could well have examined New York's
South Street Seaport Museum. On the site of the Fulton Fish Market, the
eighteenth-century houses of Schermerhorn Row, and the antiquated harbor which dates back to Dutch colonial times, the museum and the State of
New York have welcomed the developer of Faneuil Hall. They have given
him a seventy-five- to ninety-five-year lease on the waterfront, at a decent
rent, to develop a similar shopping center with a nautical theme. Though
he pays this rent to the South Street Seaport Museum, the museum owes $6
million to various local banks. The banks also have the right to select
developers for projects in adjacent areas. Once again, the profits from
redevelopment are channeled into the private sector.

Although the state's judicial machinery cannot initiate policy, the courts
can and do intervene to protect certain types of participants in real estate
markets. Judges cannot control rents where rent controls do not exist, and
they cannot compel landlords to continue renting lofts to manufacturers in
a nonmanufacturing zone. However, residential tenants in the loft market
have had their position regularized even in situations where residential use
has been considered illegal. In a sense, this furnishes the illusory stability
that people are always looking for in real estate markets. Yet in another
sense, the courts have confirmed the total destabilization of the loft
market. To put it simply, the ultimate effect of state intervention on loft
living has been to benefit urban redevelopment for the upper middle class.
From the worm's-eye view of the original loft neighborhood, the state acts
like a real estate speculator because the net effect of its intervention is that
people are displaced. But from the bird's-eye view of City Hall, this
represents the only possible development strategy.

8

CAPITAL SHIFTS AND THE
CULTURAL AVANT-GARDE
IN URBAN AMERICA

When it blows great guns and the rain comes down . . .
there is plenty of studio work to do, and plenty of fine
old lofts with improvised studio windows to do it in.
Outing, January 31, 1894

A close examination of the rise of loft living warns us not to take any style for what it superficially appears to be. Especially when the issue concerns "lifestyle," it is critical to distinguish between personal taste and its social sources, or between apparent nonconformity and social constraint. Certainly people always express the aesthetic values of their time and milieu. But the way that they individually appropriate collective goods also reflects the way that markets are structured and the relations between competing uses and users in those markets. The real estate market in living lofts that emerged in New York City during the 1970s seems to exemplify such competition. A market of small manufacturers slowly yields to demand for space by artists and artisans and middle- to upper-middle-class residents. The sequence of users converts loft space to increasingly "better" use and, in so doing, alters the quintessential form in which that space is used. This succession of uses and users in the market reflects processes of social change in the larger society. Not only does it parallel the gentrification of working-class neighborhoods in many cities but it also concretizes – through change in the built environment – the dislocation of industrial production from traditional centers of light manufacturing and it apparent replacement by higher-level, "post-industrial" activity. Demand in the new loft market is even keyed to change in dominant aesthetic modes. Technological changes in production processes influenced a more poetic appreciation of industrial design and a domestic appropriation of industrial products. Moreover, the loft-studios where some artists worked exerted an irresistible social and existential appeal. This demand also responds to economic changes within the middle class. Gains in the social position of the arts and the financial viability of art work, as well as an increase in the availability of middle-class investment capital, made it possible to capture the supply of lofts that a new market required.

Nevertheless, the market in living lofts was also formed by institutions and individuals that seem, at first glance, not to have been directly involved in market competition. These were the banks, the state, and the upper class. For years, selective disinvestment by the banks and selective rezoning by the city government had weakened industry's hold on center-city infrastructure. When their own plans for downtown clearance were foiled, the urban patricians and their politicians constructed an alliance based on state support for alternate uses that cut into the existing loft market and helped to displace those small manufacturers who remained. They were counting on a spillover, or blow-out, of demand from highly competitive middle-class housing markets elsewhere in the center city to exert further pressure on the loft market. This expectation also encouraged small-scale, middle-class investors to take the risk of entering loft areas and financing conversion to residential use. Over time, that enhanced the value of the patricians' large development projects and the properties that they owned nearby.

These considerations suggest that the real significance of loft living lies on a deeper level than that of the market — indeed, on the level of an underlying terrain that represents a space, a symbol, and a site under contention by major social forces. It is relations on this terrain that determine real estate markets. In that sense, the market in living lofts appears as the newest battlefield in the struggle for control over the city. While loft tenants are the obvious pawns in the struggle, they really act as surrogates for the interests of groups situated outside the market.

Such an interpretation contrasts with the usual account of the rise of loft living, according to which loft living is the spontaneous result of "market forces." The presence or supply of underused loft buildings supposedly inspired an inventive adaptation. Demand for lofts emerged among worthy, though unworldly, artists and performers. They settled bravely in the urban tundras and carved neighborhoods out of the wilderness. Just when they had succeeded in taming their cast-iron environment, a band of new arrivals — who were interested in domesticating an industrial aesthetic — moved in on their territory. Recognizing neither claims nor conventions, this wave of loft tenants bid up property values, started boutiques, and crowded the original settlers with their purely residential ethos. They outlawed mixed use. They had no sense of mission.

But that is mythology, not urban history. It only makes sense to the urban ecologist or the arts constituency. An ecologist finds in it proof of an ineluctable competition over territory, particularly when one side in this competition can pay market rents. A member of the arts constituency finds it a satisfying demonstration that though the artist seems to have achieved a new social status as hero, he or she is really still relegated to the position of society's victim. Neither version, however, can account for two apparent contradictions in the way the loft market was formed. On the one hand, loft living began as a "marginal" phenomenon, but in time it became chic. On the other hand, artists who moved into lofts were "powerless," yet they managed to win access to contested urban space. These contradictions can be resolved only by considering what the loft market means in the larger contest over urban terrain.

What is really at stake on this terrain is the heart of the city: the reconquest of the downtown for high-class users and high-rent uses. To some degree, this represents a simple matter of expansion. Corporations in an expanding service sector want to increase their office size and surround themselves with the amenities that they require. Their demand for space conflicts with that of other urban groups, especially the small businesses that cluster in low-rent concentrations throughout the downtown area. But the corporations' demand also reflects other calculations. To the extent that some of them are big property owners in the financial district, or profit from high-rise commercial development projects, they want to drive the value of that space up to the highest level. The continued presence of light manufacturing, jobbers, and wholesale markets on their terrain is both an irritant and an impediment. That is why they work so hard to bust these clusters. Furthermore, corporate demand for downtown space exemplifies a new view of a streamlined city. In this view, revalorization is made possible by changing the city as a whole to a "higher" use, notably, by converting it into a financial capital.

Certainly such a conversion strategy does not work *ex nihilo*. Yet in cities that already have an expanding base in banking and financial services, the private sector generates both a demand for spatial expansion and the capital to carry it through to the creation of new urban forms. The interests that are involved, and their influence, suggest a rather different program of redevelopment or revitalization than the publicity of the early 1970s diffused. Reinvestment, from the banks' point of view, or displacement from the losers', clears the terrain for a new use. The resulting forms reproduce a white-collar world that is expensive, nonproductive, and eminently profitable. Though loft living arose somewhat circumstantially on the downtown terrain, it expresses these priorities. So it is the terrain, rather than the space or form of lofts, that invests the loft market with significance. Nevertheless, the peculiar characteristics of lofts as a space and loft lifestyle as a form clarify the type of change that is occurring on this terrain. Revitalization really involves putting into place an accumulation and a cultural strategy. That combination suggests that we are at a historic turning point in the urban political economy.[1]

THE "ARTISTIC MODE OF PRODUCTION"

Shifts in a dominant class's accumulation strategy generally invoke new cultural norms in order to justify and facilitate the exercise of unaccustomed forms of social control. Nevertheless, the current linkage of accumulation and culture in urban forms seems more paradoxical — or perhaps merely more subtle — than most historical examples. In this case, the linkage is made through the use of art and historic preservation. The urban forms that are thus created, or, rather, preserved and adapted, become the basis of an Artistic Mode of Production. Far from being a response to aesthetic problems, the AMP really represents an attempt by large-scale investors in the built environment to ride out and to control a particular investment climate. The AMP originated in part as a response to contingencies. On the one hand, big investors faced an insurmountable degree of political opposition to the slash-and-burn tactics of the urban renewal that they, in conjunction with the state, had practiced. On the other hand, in some older cities there was a growing shortage of easily assembled large sites for redevelopment where bulldozing would still be effective. Developers were also pressed to find a supply of new urban spaces and cheap urban forms by several other factors: the rising costs of new construction, an overbuilding of suburban shopping centers, and the saturation, temporarily, of the center-city office market. Furthermore, uncertainty over the investment climate for new development held big projects in abeyance. This provided both the motive and the opportunity for the emergence of a seemingly modest redevelopment strategy based on the arts and historic preservation.

Yet the AMP also conformed to several long-term priorities in accumulation strategy. On the level of the national economy, investment had been shifting since the 1890s toward the production of producers' durables and consumers' products, and new forms in the built environment — in both cities and suburbs — reflected the dominance of capital-intensive, rather than labor-intensive, production processes and individualized, rather than collective, consumption. In this sense, the AMP can be understood as a response to greater "leisure" time and more "sophisticated" patterns of consumption. But it also suited an equally long-range pattern in the accumulation strategy of the American upper class. Since a small number of industrialists began to buy the work of Impressionist artists in the 1880s, they had a dual conception of modern art as both an investment and a means of socialization. Perhaps these ideas didn't really become coherent until after World War I, when a swelling population gave voice to the period's radical political ideas and appeared ready to borrow from Europe's revolutionary experiences. At the same time, however, the culturally elite groups in American society were increasingly exposed to abstract art and modern architecture on the Continent, and some of them were prepared to borrow from these revolutionary aesthetic experiences.

Nonetheless, the potential *social* use of modern art did not assume an urgency until the Great Depression. In conditions of economic crisis and social despair, a well-subsidized, well-diffused cultural "product" held out the possibility of reintegrating American society — as long as the artists who produced it could be brought within the discipline of the state. Indeed, the art, drama, and photography projects of the New Deal period appear in this light as an attempt to legitimize "America" by both documenting and transcending its current crisis. These projects also represent an effort to incorporate American artists into a depoliticized but socially constructive labor force. The documentary style that developed so fruitfully in all the arts at that time suggests an obvious parallel with the use of Socialist Realism in the Soviet Union, but the organization of American artists under the aegis of the state offers a broader parallel with the trends toward corporatism that emerged throughout Western and Eastern Europe during the 1930s.

Yet in contrast to art in these societies, and especially in the Soviet Union, art in twentieth-century America showed that it had a more directly "capitalist" use. Particularly striking was art's utility to urban real estate development. In burgeoning centers of international trade and finance, such as New York on the East Coast and San Francisco in the West, developers found that art, when it was set within the proper physical and institutional framework — the museum or the cultural center — could become a vehicle for its own valorization. The growing value of art also enhanced the value of related factors: the urban *forms* that grew up around it, the activity of *doing* it, and most important, the status of *consuming* it. These processes of valorization commanded — or even demanded — a wider public for art and culture than had existed until this time. Throughout the twentieth century, with a marked acceleration after World War II, that public of cultural consumers was expanded and integrated by a loosely linked system of art markets of varying degrees of sophistication and competition. The usefulness of avant-garde art to a general accumulation process derives precisely from the need both to expand and to integrate these markets.[2]

Such motivations suggest that there is a close connection, in late industrial capitalism, between *accumulation* and *cultural consumption*. So sectoral shifts in investment in the economy as a whole are related to social decisions to build up the urban infrastructure for art and culture, as well as to individual decisions to build up an art collection by members of the upper class and the corporations that they direct. Aside from the personal or collective advantages to be gained from buying art (tax deductions representing an institutionalized advantage for collectors of serious worth), the valorization of art has a *general* value for accumulation processes. Particularly in the large-scale shifts that are involved in deindustrialization, it has been essential to use cultural consumption to put accumulation strategy into place. The precedent seems to have come from developing a strong state policy in the arts as part of a wide set of national priorities. After World War II, American preeminence in world art markets facilitated and symbolized a transfer of cultural control and economic domination from Europe to the United States. The enhanced production of modern art in America not only absorbed investment and attracted art talent but also provided a tool for international political competition. As a proponent of government funding for sending exhibitions of American art abroad said at the time, "The arts of a country should be so integrated into the life of a country that any comprehensive exhibition going forth would act as a mirror. The stranger should be able to look into it and see reflected there the vitality, the creativity, the spiritual force of the country — yes, the confusion, diversity and materialism also." [3]

But eventually this strategy was turned inward, toward America's cities, where it has had an effect on their forms and their people. Certainly, over the years, state intervention in the arts at key junctures of the valorization process has had a great effect on urban forms. Recently, however, state intervention in the arts has been instrumental in changing the use of these forms and deciding between the claims of social groups that seek to appropriate them. This is particularly evident in the revitalization, or reconquest, of the heart of the city. In America's financial capital, New York City, the Artistic Mode of Production has been translating this strategy into a suitable social and built environment since the early 1960s. So far the visible effects fall into five major categories. First, by an adroit manipulation of urban forms, the AMP transfers urban space from the "old" world of industry to the "new" world of finance, or from the realm of productive economic activity to that of nonproductive economic activity. Second, the AMP transforms the local labor market. Third, it helps to lower people's expectations. Fourth, it reduces the immediacy of industrial society and its problems to a distant, historical perspective. And finally, it makes it impossible to consider a return to any version of the old urban-industrial infrastructure. Let us review this briefly.

By creating an arts infrastructure in the center city, the AMP occupies key spots in the terrain with a nonproductive use. Artists who think that they are pushing into niches here and there are really activating a mechanism of revalorization that destabilizes existing uses and their markets. Although the arts presence promises — and seeks — neighborhood stability, it becomes the pivot of new market competition. While this may be advantageous for some small property owners because of the turnover that is involved in the market, it benefits the big real estate interests most because it redefines the terrain on which several new markets may develop. In a somewhat different context from lofts, the construction of Lincoln Center for the Performing Arts on the near Upper West Side of Manhattan provided an important model. The ground for Lincoln Center was assembled from small parcels in a typical, though not terribly dilapidated, late-1950s inner-city district of low-income and ghetto housing. The assemblage related to urban strategist and public-sector builder Robert Moses's ideas about slum clearance. However, the notion of implanting on that spot a concentration of facilities for the performing arts came from the patricians with whom Moses was often associated. The Rockefellers, in particular, undertook the patronage of Lincoln Center and went about assembling a performing tenancy to fill the facilities. Their efforts to assure an audience that would pay for that tenancy continue to this day. In the meantime, from the late sixties to the late seventies, properties contiguous to Lincoln Center were cleared and turned into upper-middle-income housing. The success of this market changed the meaning of the West Side from drab to chic, secured the area for high-class residence, and enhanced the value of all West Side office market development.[4]

Because it provides a material base in the built environment, the AMP restructures local labor markets around low-wage, service-sector activity, part-time work, and working at home. The advantage of this sort of labor force, especially for those groups that dominate the private sector, is that it incorporates people who would otherwise be unemployed and dissatisfied. On the one hand, the AMP trains and absorbs bards and ballerinas from the *barrio,* and on the other hand, it attracts college graduates, particularly women, for whom, since the expansion of the educational system in the 1950s and 1960s, not enough high-level jobs have been created. Although a job in the arts suggests a choice of career, increased leisure time, and meaningful work, it also imposes costs. A large arts proletariat, for example, pays for its proximity to art markets by waiting on tables and working "off the books." An interesting example concerns two restaurants in SoHo: in one the owner hires only actors as waiters and in the other the owner hires only dancers. For the social ecologist, this is a laudable example of "symbiosis," but it really represents how the new AMP work force is exploited in a labor market that has been restructured around the low end of the service sector. Similarly, people who use their lofts for artwork or performance pay by running the constant risk that cottage industry will be evicted in favor of pure residential use.

Furthermore, the AMP accustoms the new urban work force to lowered expectations. As both space and form, lofts have been very important here. When center-city housing is necessary but expensive, landlords and developers can get away with providing raw space for a hungry market.

The individualized consumption patterns with which loft living has become identified — in a passage from asceticism to the new cult of domesticity — are costly to maintain. Also, the residential conversion of manufacturing lofts implies getting used to a more intensive use of urban space. The spaciousness inside a loft coexists with greater population density in the old manufacturing districts. It disappears, in any event, with the incorporation of loft spaces into more traditional apartment forms. But even in a general sense, as the liberal 1960s view of the arts suggested, satisfying demands for the "spiritual" life may dampen material aspirations. Dramatizing the arts distracts criticism from a strong state, an aggressive foreign policy, and the international expansion of national capital. It also compensates, at least in principle, for a no-growth situation in the economy.

The fourth use of the AMP is even more deeply ideological. Through the expansion of an ethos of historic preservation, it extricates the built legacy of the industrial city from the social matrix of industrial production. When the lofts that were used for light manufacturing are reduced to being considered as a cultural artifact, the image that their economic function is dead is reinforced. Without such a function, the urban-industrial infrastructure submits to the rules of the "picturesque." Indeed, the publication of *Lost New York* has been followed by picture books of *Lost Chicago, Lost Boston,* and *Lost New Orleans;* the obvious worth of their aesthetic appreciation should not obscure the effect on "market value" of their image of *social* obsolescence. While blue-collar labor recedes from the heart of the financial city, an image is created that the city's economy has arrived at a post-industrial plateau. At the very least, this displaces issues of industrial labor relations to another terrain.[5]

Even as the AMP destroys the ideological basis of the old built environment, it implies that the accumulation strategy that was vested there has been thoroughly exhausted. Certainly there are both objective and subjective limits to the value that can be squeezed out of an established and organized working class, a low turnover of lofts and loft buildings, and low-rent manufacturing use. By making revitalization depend on the conversion of urban forms to other uses, however, the AMP forecloses any reasonable possibility of expanding productive activity within the old infrastructure. Once the manufacturers' clusters have been busted, and their premises changed to residential or commercial use, there simply is no site where productive replacement can start up. This literally forces a complete conversion of the infrastructure, and the economy, to nonproductive activity. Though heavy industry and industrial expansion had long since been precluded from commercial economies like New York's, the small businesses for which location in Manhattan was still essential were now effectively excluded from the core.[6]

Despite the apparent rationale of instituting the AMP in such cities as

New York, it is surprising to see the alacrity with which it — or significant parts of it — has been adopted as an urban conversion strategy in places that either lack a suitable infrastructure or have a different set of problems. In Sun Belt cities, for example, local government and the private sector orient their redevelopment strategy toward a downtown that ceased to exist many years ago. In Los Angeles, the Victorian houses of Bunker Hill were demolished for urban renewal, which hasn't prevented new construction for upper-middle-class residence and office use from borrowing both the area's old name and its historic appeal. In Phoenix, the downtown's Skid Row changed its name from The Deuce to Heritage Square and was then resurrected through "historic preservation" and a new arts center for conversion to similar service-sector uses. Certainly the federal government's Urban Development Action Grant funds have had some influence on this strategy, but there has also been a calculation of what it takes, subjectively, to spark revalorization. Another Sun Belt city offers an exception that proves the rule. In Dallas the local business elite abruptly withdrew its support from a project to establish an arts infrastructure near the central business district after land values there rose so high that it seemed absurd to subsidize an artists' quarter in the area.

Cities like Seattle and Rochester represent a response to different pressures. In the early 1970s a crisis in the aerospace industry, which provides Seattle's economic base, caused massive unemployment. In the ensuing pall, business leaders and urban planners lobbied, under the baton of the local business council on the arts, for the city government to finance an expansion of the arts infrastructure. The resulting boom in arts production and arts consumption gained Seattle favorable publicity in the national media. Its self-declared conversion to a "quality of life capital" was supposed to generate new investment and new jobs. Finally, in Rochester, New York, site of the corporate headquarters of Eastman Kodak and IBM, a downtown that showed signs of Times Square squalor was fixed up with some of SoHo's appeal. An existing arts infrastructure was geared to the expansion of the Eastman School of Music, and the school's director lobbied for new zoning regulations to outlaw massage parlors in the downtown area. The Eastman School became the base of a new cultural district.

These experiences pose the question of whether the conversion strategy that works in a cultural capital can be transplanted outside the core. Certainly a demographic and occupational base for such transformation has been established, over the past fifteen to twenty years, by the professionalization and democratization of arts activity. In 1980, for example, 40 million Americans were engaged in some sort of artisanal production, and a quarter-million of these people lived off their earnings from this work.[7] But arts production alone generates neither investment nor economic growth. Nor is it realistic to conceive of a congeries of artists' quarters without a highly competitive art market and the concentration of capital that supports it. So there are really three issues that have to be considered in evaluating the AMP's effect on the urban political economy: what sort of base is necessary? what will it cost? and what are likely to be the contradictions?

Base

Essentially, two preconditions limit the effectiveness of using the AMP as a strategy of urban conversion. First, there must be a concentration of art markets where performance and creation are sold. Second, there must be a contiguity to property markets that are already experiencing demand for "higher" use. These preconditions establish a situation where art markets and real estate markets have a mutually reinforcing effect, which in turn affects the underlying terrain. Clearly a preference for artists over bulldozers develops at a specific conjuncture. Nevertheless, the multiple advantages of implanting an arts infrastructure appeal to the one group that controls both property and patronage — the patricians. As Lincoln Center shows, arts infrastructure, when properly managed, valorizes the nearby property that patricians either already own or readily acquire. It also accelerates the valorization of patrician and corporate art collections, thus making the tax benefits of art donations do double duty, in both reducing present income and increasing future income from real estate holdings. Finally, under the proper conditions — notably, an expanding public of arts consumers — an arts infrastructure may even pay for itself.

SoHo offers an interesting example of this process because the influx of arts consumers there made experimental art forms into a commercially viable concern. But "alternative spaces" have had the potential for this double meaning at least since the 1860s, when the Impressionists who had been barred from the *salon* of official art in Paris exhibited their work, under the government's aegis, at the *Salon des refusés*. For the artist and most of the public, alternative spaces represent a way of circumventing either official taste or "the market," and the pressures that each in turn applies. Yet in reality, alternative spaces serve as filters in a screening process that directs the most marketable or most accessible art toward established distribution channels. In fact, the most important *economic* impact of the successful offshoots of the avant-garde arts production that takes place in alternative spaces occurs when they are grafted onto mainstream arts production. So off-Broadway theater, artists' cooperative galleries, and jazz lofts are not merely *alternative* spaces. They are *adjuncts* to the dominant urban forms — "Broadway," "Madison Avenue," the concert halls at Lincoln Center — that support mainstream art markets.

This concentration of and contiguity to mainstream markets make possible a seemingly endless replication of SoHos, even in loftless districts of Manhattan. The example of Manhattan Plaza, on West Forty-second Street, is significant. In the mid-1970s, performing artists were given access to subsidized space to the west of the theater district because the city administration could not rent apartments in a brand-new, white-elephant housing project that it had just completed building there. In fact, artists were given preference over low-income neighborhood residents. The presence of artists and musicians, and the marginal, off-Broadway productions that they put on, nourished an ailing Broadway theater system that had been suffering from the high costs of new production. But it also anchored the western end of a plan for redeveloping Forty-second Street for new corporate headquarters and hotel construction. Once the performing artists are in place, a supporter of the project declares, "the buildings are full, the tenants have established a unique brand of camaraderie . . . and [the] 42nd Street Redevelopment Corporation plans are going full-steam ahead . . . includ[ing] the opening of a row of Off-Off-Broadway theaters on 42nd Street, across from Manhattan Plaza, the conversion of the West Side Airlines Terminal into a dance center, the creation of an equestrian rink, a skateboard park, and a Quincy Market-style Farmer's Market near the waterfront. . . ." [8] Yet no area illustrates the salience of concentration and contiguity to the redevelopment of the cultural and financial core so well as Lower Manhattan. The story bears a brief retelling from the perspective of this terrain.

From the beginning of the 1960s, New York patricians with the greatest interest in Lower Manhattan real estate lived with the realization that sites for future redevelopment would have to be cleared by different techniques than those that had worked in the past. Skirmishes with community groups were costly and unpleasant, financing was so onerous and complicated that it required new instruments of state support, and competition among developers and building owners in the office market was often so fierce that backing for commercial projects could not readily be assumed. For these reasons, the patricians relied on both subtlety and pressure to create a fresh supply of downtown space. As French sociologist Christian Topalov cogently remarks, "It's not enough that the developer 'invents' land; together with the state, he has to 'manufacture' it." [9] In Lower Manhattan, patrician real estate investors used three "manufacturing" processes to increase their supply. They continued to use, in part, the high-technology, expensive sort of new development that worked in the suburbs and in slash-and-burn urban renewal. This is exemplified by the mammoth twin office tower construction of the World Trade Center and the landfill in the Hudson River on which Battery Park City is built. But the patricians' demand for space also spilled over into adjacent areas — to the lofts of SoHo and TriBeCa as well as the brownstones of Hoboken, New Jersey, across the Hudson. There new markets emerged and altered the existing uses of infrastructure so that it complemented, rather than stymied, the patricians' plans. Finally, by strategically placing a small amount of patronage for the arts, particularly artists' housing, on the

Lower West Side, the patricians hoped to counter the obstacles to redevelopment in that area that were posed by low-rent neighborhood stability and low-density zoning regulations. Indeed, these two obstacles have proved so formidable, and the stakes of redeveloping the land along the West Side Highway so valuable, over the past twenty years that they have made the West Village into the Alsace-Lorraine of New York City real estate confrontations. But these three processes — high-tech, capital-intensive construction, replacing uses, and low-cost arts patronage as a tool of neighborhood destabilization — do not exhaust the patricians' means to make a supply of space available. As the biggest developers in town, they also influence the state to create the infrastructure that makes this space accessible. So patricians are responsible for the rezoning of SoHo, for example, or the PATH trains from Manhattan to Hoboken, which date from the same period as the plans to revitalize the Wall Street area.

Nor should the role of a large cultural institution on the Village's southern flank, New York University, be ignored. During the years when the Downtown–Lower Manhattan Plan was devised, NYU developed its own plans for expansion. Significantly, the most vulnerable land for the university's expansion lay to the south, in the manufacturing loft district and adjacent tenements occupied by working-class families of Italian origin that was known as the South Village. In the late 1950s, chairmanship of the university's board of trustees passed to Laurence Tisch, a member of one of the family dynasties of builders in New York City and a graduate of NYU Law School. Tisch quietly assembled the several square blocks from Washington Square Park to Houston Street, between LaGuardia Place and Broadway, and then, at no apparent profit, turned the properties over to NYU. During the next few years, the university built two high-density housing projects on the site for faculty and staff. Instead of creating the usual institutional barrier between urban areas, the architectural design that was implemented cleared an easy path from the lofts below Houston Street to the heart of the Village. Whether or not Tisch remained a silent owner of properties contiguous to the university, it is important that even at a time when demand for manufacturing lofts was high, NYU's expansion reduced the amount of loft space that was available. Moreover, by physically integrating Greenwich Village with the loft district south of Houston Street, the university made that space accessible to a different class of users.

The geographical and morphological expansion of Lower Manhattan's higher uses is particularly interesting in the case of Hoboken, where space was "liberated" in a deliberate shift from early-sixties urban renewal to late-sixties AMP. Initially, Hoboken had depended on anti-poverty funds from the federal government to deal with the problems of a low-income population. When demand for "downtown" urban forms spilled over into the loft buildings and brownstone houses of tiny Hoboken — which had already, around 1900, absorbed a spillover of *industrial* demand by Lower Manhattan's crowded manufacturers—the urban planners who were already there yielded to a desire to increase the arts and historic preservation constituency that had begun to form. Naturally this meant a change of tactics and funding, as well as a certain amount of displacement. These changes parallel the rise of the loft market in SoHo. Hoboken, too, started to attract new middle-class residents around 1966, and "by 1973," according to a planner who worked there,

> emphasis shifted from social programs to housing and capital improvements and the Community Development Agency moved to augment the local middle class by importing reinforcements from Manhattan and suburbia. . . . The strategy combined a determined public relations campaign and the mobilization of a local middle-class constituency anxious to welcome *new explorers* with the development of a two-pronged housing strategy. One element of the housing strategy involved provision of low- and moderate-income housing, the other involved assistance in marketing brownstone and row houses to *"people like us,"* i.e. *the supervisory staff of the Development . . . Agency.*[10]

Clearly the AMP works such a transformation in supply only when there already is strong demand. Though patrician developers may incite this demand, it reflects real middle-class needs and desires. Indeed, the contradictory interests of the two key social groups who are involved in the process of urban conversion—patricians and the middle class—are mediated by local real estate markets. Particularly in the new market that is created by the AMP, living lofts, and all styles established on the basis of a preference for the space-and-time values inherent in lofts, real estate establishes the interdependence of the accumulation and consumption strategies used by these two social classes. Significantly, the accumulation strategy of the patrician property holders who want to redevelop the downtown is supported by that of a whole range of smaller, middle-class investors. The urban forms that these investors finance typically provide facilities for the social reproduction of the labor force—industrial in the nineteenth century, service-sector today—that the patricians require. Just as the savings of grocers, contractors, and butchers built the cheap working-class housing around factory districts in Europe and the United States in an earlier urban era, so middle-class loft developers and brownstone owners shelter the employees, administrators, and professionals who work in the office towers that fill today's downtown.

The appropriation of this space for the social reproduction of the middle class is rationalized, in part, ideologically. The middle class is said to appreciate the aesthetics of forms that would otherwise be considered physically, economically, and socially obsolete. However, the middle class is not completely autonomous in their aesthetic choice. In their lives as in the patricians' plans, art and real estate are joined. Their investment in the "preserved" or renovated housing market situates the arts markets on which the valorization of the patricians' holdings depends. Ideologically penetrated, in short, by the AMP, members of the new urban middle class become consumers of both urban space and urban forms that pay for the patricians' redevelopment plans. So it appears that the new middle-class real estate markets really valorize the patricians' terrain. That is how the material base is constructed for urban conversion through the AMP.

Costs

It is vain to pretend that instituting such a base does not impose costs on cities as they are politically constituted and socially financed. Basically, the economic geography of a "converted" city changes to reflect an absence of productive workers and a dependence on nonproductive activity. Formerly responsive, on some levels, to the needs of a low-income and dependent population, local governments now become "captive cities" in quite a different sense. Subsidies flow to the service sector. Through tax abatements, location incentives, and debt service on municipal financial obligations, city budgets lose income and pay for the continued expansion of the banks and the large real estate developers. Banks' and developers' physical expansion through greater amounts of center-city space molds the forms of the built environment to fit their needs. Meanwhile, the municipality aids in creating a social environment that conforms to the image of a service-sector capital. Ideologically, city governments camouflage "deviations" from this new norm. Their cutbacks in social-welfare expenditures encourage a moral type of urban clearance. They enter into long-term debt in order to finance publicly new infrastructure — historic districts, highways and transportation lines, commercial developments of offices and hotels — that enhances the patricians' and the corporations' center-city projects. Institutions that are established to mollify urban residents' desire for community control either are too weak to confront this public sector/ private sector development strategy or are subverted at higher levels of decision. Their essentially consultative power is fragmented by such issues as zoning, which are reactions to market trends rather than initiation of public policy and which frequently pit capital against sentiment. Lacking an institutional base to deal with their own "preservation," communities and neighborhoods easily fall prey to quasi-public bodies that claim to represent the public interest. In reality, these organizations effect a socialization of the costs of development and a transfer of the benefits from the public sector to the private sector. Collectively, the "community" never really has a chance at autonomous self-reproduction.

Middle-class constituencies are particularly vulnerable to this sort of manipulation because of their integration in local markets as small-scale investors and small business owners. However, they pay a price for their market success. Turnover in the property market affects the neighborhood stability that they seek. Moreover, the attraction of outside capital to the special forms, services, or amenities that they provide overruns them. Their small businesses are soon surrounded by branches of chains whose high volume of sales is based on a standardized product, or by expensive shops that the original neighbors can't afford to patronize. In other words, there is a transition to either "McDonald's" or "Disneyland" in successful local service markets that complements the urban area's conversion to higher-class use. The mean between these two extremes is represented by the publicly subsidized implantation of private commercial developments like James Rouse's Faneuil Hall, Harborplace, and South Street Seaport, which utilize existing infrastructure to reproduce the suburban shopping center in the heart of the city. This type of downtown project has become so widespread that the editors of *Progressive Architecture* refer to it as "the Faneuilization of America." It is valid to ask, as they do, whether cities will continue to provide an adequate social base of consumers who are oriented toward the middle-class patterns such shopping centers require.

Clearly, blue-collar workers and their families no longer provide the traditional urban mass base of either production or consumption. Skilled and crafts workers, some of whom have already bought houses outside the city, are increasingly "pushed" out by a lack of the amenities that they seek, a decline of the services that they need, and the elimination of the necessity of having to live in the city because that is where they work. At the same time, unskilled and low-wage service workers who do find employment in the converted city are "pulled" into generally declining, semi-suburban neighborhoods within the city limits. While the crafts workers bear the costs of a suburban way of life, these low-level service workers endure the decay of the infrastructure of municipal services, including mass transportation, public schools, and sanitation. This work force is stabilized, to some degree, by passing on to them the costs of home ownership in their neighborhoods. Thus they in turn become a constituency for "neighborhood preservation." Like the middle class, they are encouraged in their belief so long as the space they occupy doesn't impinge upon terrain that is convertible to higher use.

The geographic dispersion of the urban work force mirrors the distortion of the multiple labor markets in which they are employed. Within the service sector, high-wage jobs at the top and low-wage jobs at the bottom proliferate. In manufacturing, highly skilled and precision work disappears, while sweatshop labor enjoys a resurgence. If there initially was a dual labor market, then deindustrializing the built environment skews its duality into a pair of dumbbells. Moreover, the gains that appear in business volume — in total sales, for instance, or value added — do not reflect a greater number of jobs. Indeed, the city is converted to an "import economy" through the employment of fewer people who are both better paid and less skilled than ever before. In this sense, the arts economy really is a microcosm of urban conversion. It replicates in older cities the skewed labor markets of Sun Belt cities, founded on the rapid growth of both high-level and low-level jobs in the service industries. Indeed, "with the arts now considered an industry," an urban planner writes, "artists have become the new industrialists, as important as any industrialists to the city's economic health and development."[11]

Yet it is fair to question closely the contribution that these new "industries" make to the urban political economy when they replace more productive, light manufacturing activities. Who in particular finds them beneficial? It is significant that in New York City the corporations in the sector that has expanded most — banking services — are enthusiastic supporters of the growth potential of the AMP. In a recent full-page advertisement in the *New York Times,* for example, Citibank said, "As bankers we'd like to remind you of two facts: last year, the arts, especially the performing arts, helped attract more than 16 million visitors to New York; these visitors, many of them from overseas, contributed a whopping $1.5 billion to our city's economy." Curiously, this assessment of the dollar value of tourism in the city in 1980 neglects the boost to foreign tourism in New York caused by international currency exchange rates, notably the fall of the dollar, until 1981. Also the volume of tourism in 1980 was roughly equal to what the value added in the manufacture of women's clothing in New York's garment industry had been in the early 1970s. Nevertheless, by 1980 so many manufacturing jobs had disappeared and so many banking jobs had been created that more people in the city worked in banking than in the garment trade.

Moreover, the promotion of banking, tourism, and the arts occurred simultaneously with a promotion of the city's apparel industry. The city administration issued special awards and organized ceremonies around the garment district as job loss accelerated. This was not intended as a eulogy. On the contrary, what was important for the city's "revitalization" effort was fashion rather than production. In fact, it was people like Calvin Klein and Geoffrey Beene who were being honored, not the Mannys and Harrys of traditional local industry. Furthermore, the designers whose showrooms are located in the Garment Center have many of their items produced in the factories of Hong Kong, and their popular hand-made, expensive sweaters knit in a cottage industry set up in working-class homes. Indeed, the trend toward high-price artisanal products for domestic and personal consumption has encouraged manufacturers to move production out of the factory and back into the artisans', or the knitters', homes. The city's promotionalism shifts public attention away from these conditions of manufacturing toward retaining the glamorous or the nonproductive side of economic activity. Particularly in an inflationary economy, this makes for higher profits and higher social status. But it doesn't compensate for loss in the total number of jobs.[12]

Moreover, enhancing the AMP in many cities accentuates the uneven level of development that divides New York or any other cultural and financial core from the periphery. The concentration of art and capital on which the AMP relies continues to fuel the necessary markets, and the internationalization of these markets continues to enrich the metropolitan core, at the continued expense of the periphery. For quite a few cities, this indicates that the expenses incurred — through subsidies and forgone property taxes — will never bear the anticipated result of generating economic development. In fact, as a greater tax burden falls upon their residents, developers and corporations will have less incentive to invest their capital there. Smaller companies and local capitalists have no choice — indeed, that is why they have begun to apply techniques of revalorization through the AMP to their own property — but the high-class service-sector industries that every city wants are predominantly international in their approach to location. The decentralization of industrial production throughout the world, as well as the internationalization of markets and careers, suggests the increasing segregation of economic activities according to a world hierarchy of cities. When cities, like individuals, assume a greater debt burden in order to "move up" in this hierarchy, they may never come out ahead. Instead, they become the captives of high-level real estate speculation, reflecting the investment strategies of international, rather than local or even national, economic elites.[13]

So the traditional function of the state on the local level — to arrange fiscal structures and physical infrastructure in such a way as to enhance the accumulation process — now changes to facilitate a *disengagement* from productive activity. Of course, city governments hope to compensate for this loss with a concomitant increase in service-sector investment. But their willingness to accommodate corporate *dis*investment shows how utterly dependent they are on decisions that are made entirely within the private sector. Similarly, the competition between localities that act as "public entrepreneurs" by luring new investment with tax benefits and outright subsidies indicates that local governments will undertake any restructuring that is deemed necessary by the private sector for service-industry expansion. This in turn suggests the emergence of a new coalition, on the local level, of corporate elites and middle-class property owners, including big real estate developers and small-scale investors. Such a coalition is well represented by the current "Fusion" mayoralty in New York City, where political ideology defers to a common cause based on protection of real estate investments and service-sector interests. This is what post-industrial politics look like in cities where there is no real possibility of creating or re-creating an industrial economy but hope for economic growth has not been abandoned. Necessarily, the "preservation" of neighborhoods and historic buildings that flows so easily into the depoliticized ideology of this transformation depends on a dynamic expansion of the service sector. That is not the least of the problems involved in reconciling growth with disaccumulation. So far, however, its costs have been marginal, affecting the displacement of low-income social groups and artists without increasing social protest.

Contradictions

Seeking inspiration in loft living, the new strategy of urban revitalization aims for a less problematic sort of integration than cities have recently known. It aspires to a synthesis of art and industry, or culture and capital, in which diversity is acknowledged, controlled, and even harnessed. This underlying motif — of power *in* diversity and power *over* diversity — engenders contradictions. Nowhere are such contradictions more apparent than in contemporary urban forms. First, the changes in the use of space that promise to reconstitute an urban middle class really effect the reconquest of the city's core for upper-class users. Second, the historic preservation that local businesses accept in order to compete with shopping centers and national chains turns all downtowns into versions of Faneuil Hall. Third, the revitalization projects that claim distinctiveness — because of specific historic or aesthetic traits — become a parody of the unique.

But it should not surprise us that the "preservation" promoted by one constituency becomes the means of another constituency's expansion. The meaning of ideas always changes when they are applied by different social groups. Particularly as they are mediated by the market, ideas about urban form provide vehicles for valorization. The basic problem, then, is not, as the Frankfurt School of social critique warned back in the 1940s, that capitalism eventually transmutes all ideas into commodity fetishes. Rather, the danger is that the realization of ideas in urban space re-creates an unequal distribution of the benefits that these ideas represent. The promotion of a historic infrastructure, for example, changes the nature of urban space. By giving value to old buildings near the downtown, preservation makes them into a scarce commodity and so creates monopoly rents. Alternatively, the uncertainty that surrounds their conservation — in the face of the predominant tendency to destroy and rebuild — can create a climate in which speculation runs rife. So, too, the promotion of an arts infrastructure changes the nature of urban space. Shifts of power in the art market transform the urban terrain.

Looking at loft living in terms of *terrain* and *markets* rather than "lifestyle" links changes in the built environment with the collective appropriation of public goods. This is entirely in keeping with the general interests of political economy. By studying the formation of markets, we get a more insightful view into the motivations that underlie broad social initiatives. In particular, this approach to the loft market makes four contributions to critical analysis of the capitalist urban crisis. First, it directs attention to *investors rather than consumers as the source of change.* In the case of the loft market, analysis is mystified by explaining change in terms of "urban pioneers" instead of the opening up of a new real estate market to middle-class investors. The creation of such a market reflects large shifts of investment capital toward and within the service sector. Second, real estate markets turn out to be important arenas of capitalist interaction not only because of the production and consumption that are involved but also because the markets integrate and differentiate social classes, and fractions of classes, in *investment hierarchies.* In modern cities, the loft market is fairly unusual because its formation integrates all levels of investment except that of the biggest developers. Third, studying capitalist cities in terms of real estate markets establishes that people negotiate distributive politics on the basis of sometimes curious conceptions of property rights. Thus the real meaning of *defending an urban terrain* involves both mediation by other groups and the unanticipated effects of such mediation, as well as negotiating a position in a market. Finally, studying state intervention by focusing on real estate markets illuminates *the hidden actors in "urban struggles."* Playing a vital role in the resolution of conflict, as well as in the definition of its parameters, are groups that are not directly concerned with either production or consumption in the contested terrain. In the loft market, the groups directly involved are upper-class real estate investors, small developers, politicians, manufacturers, and artists. But an important *mediating role* is played by patrician constituencies for arts and historic preservation and a middle-class homeowner constituency.

In many ways the emergence of loft living in New York was as unplanned a development as the city government and the real estate industry claim it was. But it was hardly "spontaneous." The preconditions for converting manufacturing lofts to other uses had been established as far back as 1945. They were set, in the long run, by the disinvestment of financial institutions from an infrastructure that served light industry and, in the short run, by economic and political factors that worsened the already shaky condition of competitive capital — the small businesses and small manufacturers that were ensconced in loft buildings. In terms of the cultural values that made loft living worthwhile, the real estate market in living lofts was set up to sell the social changes of the 1960s to middle-class consumers in the seventies and eighties. The creation of constituencies for historic preservation and the arts carried over a fascination with old buildings and artists' studios into a collective appropriation of these spaces for modern residential and commercial use. In the grand scheme of things, loft living gave the *coup de grâce* to the old manufacturing base of cities like New

York and brought on the final stage of their transformation into service-sector capitals. The form itself sets up a matrix of accumulation and consumption, cultural expression and social control, that changes the nature of urban space. As a real estate market, too, loft living acts as a vehicle for deindustrializing local capital and thus, paradoxically, for making the specific historical legacy of the built environment conform to world market trends. In the process, in each city, upper-class and middle-class constituencies lobby to protect their property rights on the urban terrain. But their different property interests give them unequal opportunity in the struggle. Although the middle class can sometimes protect their position in a real estate market, patricians have the opportunity to shift the ground under the whole terrain. This is the meaning of the urban revitalization that loft living represents. The question is, who among us will be left in the city to enjoy it and how much will we have to pay?

NOTES

1: LIVING LOFTS AS TERRAIN AND MARKET

1. Kristina Ford, *Housing Policy and the Urban Middle Class* (New Brunswick: Center for Urban Policy Research, 1978), pp. 6–7.

2. Ibid., pp. 100–105; New York City, City Planning Commission, "Residential Re-use of Non-residential Buildings in Manhattan," 1977.

3. Ford, *Housing Policy,* pp. 9, 60.

4. Ibid., p. 9.

5. In 1963, 23.2 percent of all new housing units planned in New York City received some sort of state subsidy; by 1970 this proportion had risen to 74.0 percent, and by 1971, to a high of 82.5 percent; by 1974 it had declined to 64.4 percent, which was still higher than in any year prior to 1970 (George Sternlieb, Elizabeth Roistacher, and James W. Hughes, *Tax Subsidies and Housing Investment: A Fiscal Cost-Benefit Analysis* [New Brunswick: Center for Urban Policy Research, 1976], p. 63).

6. Jack Newfield and Paul DuBrul, *The Abuse of Power: The Permanent Government and the Fall of New York* (New York: Viking, 1977), documents the large contributions made to political campaigns by the real estate industry and the equal largesse in the state's concessions on real estate deals.

7. Paul Goldberger, "Housing in Loft Buildings Key to New Urban Vitality," *New York Times,* June 15, 1977. Also the following *Times* articles: Alan S. Oser, "Zoning Revisions to Expand Loft Conversions Are Urged by New York Real Estate Board," Oct. 29, 1975; idem, "Former Army Induction Center to Become a Health Club," Mar. 1, 1976; idem, "Trials and Rewards of Building Conversion," Oct. 22, 1976; Carter B. Horsley, "A Push for a Residential Midtown," Dec. 12, 1976; Alan S. Oser, "Largest Split-Level Duplex Conversion," Feb. 4, 1977; Dena Kleiman, "The Bowery Would Be Chic, They Said – Ha!" May 29, 1977; "Mercantile Traders Move to Trade Center," July 2, 1977; Donald G. McNeil, Jr., "Nursing Homes in Conversion," July 17, 1977; Alan S. Oser, "Improving Greenwich Village Buildings," Oct. 12, 1977.

8. By 1977, after the J-51 extension had been in effect one year, only 43 of 1,023 loft conversions counted by the City Planning Commission had qualified for J-51 benefits. This number represents only 4 percent of all conversions but nearly half of all *legal* conversions (City Planning Commission, "Residential Re-use").

9. See Francis Godard et al., *La Rénovation urbaine à Paris* (Paris and The Hague: Mouton, 1973).

10. See David Harvey, "The Political Economy of Urbanization in Advanced Capitalist Societies: The Case of the United States," in *The Social Economy of Cities,* ed. Gary Geppert and Harold M. Rose (Beverly Hills: Sage, 1975), chap. 3; and idem, "The Urban Process under Capitalism: A Framework for Analysis," *International Journal of Urban and Regional Research* 2, no. 1 (1978): 101–31.

11. Eleanor L. Brilliant, *U.D.C. and the Conversion Process: Planning in the American Context* (Lexington, Mass.: Lexington Books, 1975); and Jane Jacobs, *The Death and Life of Great American Cities* (New York: Vintage, 1961).

12. For a similar interpretation of neighborhood as a "residual concept," see Harvey Molotch, "Capital and Neighborhood in the United States: Some Conceptual Links," *Urban Affairs Quarterly* 14 (1979): 289–312.

13. Jim Stratton, *Pioneering in the Urban Wilderness* (New York: Urizen, 1977).

14. For good examples of the pervasiveness of state intervention in real estate development, see William K. Tabb and Larry Sawers, eds., *Marxism and the Metropolis* (New York: Oxford University Press, 1978); Martin Mayer, *The Builders* (New York: Norton, 1978); and Leonard Downie, Jr., *Mortgage on America* (New York: Praeger, 1974). On local state subsidies to lure all kinds of investment, see Robert Goodman, *The Last Entrepreneurs: America's Regional Wars for Jobs and Dollars* (New York: Simon and Schuster, 1979).

15. This principle is documented in G. William Domhoff's penetrating analysis of the 1950s urban renewal policy of New Haven in *Who Really Rules? New Haven and Community Power Reexamined* (Santa Monica: Goodyear, 1978). Its absence from the framework of Robert A. Caro's biography of Robert Moses, *The Power Broker: Robert Moses and the Fall of New York* (New York: Vintage, 1975), damages that monumental work.

16. Carter Ratcliff, "SoHo: Disneyland of the Aesthete?" *New York Affairs* 4, no. 4 (1978): 64–72; and Michael Winkleman, "The New Frontier: Housing for the Artist-Industrialist," ibid., pp. 49–57.

2: INVESTMENT AND POLITICS

1. *United States Census,* 1950, 1960, 1970; Daniel Creamer, *Changing Location of Manufacturing Employment,* pt. 1, *Changes, by Type of Location, 1947–1961* (New York: National Industrial Conference Board, 1963); New York City, City Planning Commission, "Planning for Jobs," 1971. Cf. Peter D. McClelland and Alan L. Magdovitz, *Crisis in the Making: The Political Economy of New York State since 1945* (New York: Cambridge University Press, 1981).

2. City Planning Commission, "Planning for Jobs."

3. Robert Fitch, "Planning New York," in *The Fiscal Crisis of American Cities,* ed. Roger E. Alcaly and David Mermelstein (New York: Vintage, 1977), chap. 16.

4. City Planning Commission, "Planning for Jobs," p. 4.

5. U.S., Congress, Joint Economic Committee, *Central City Businesses – Plans and Problems,* 95th Cong. 2d sess., Jan. 14, 1979.

6. David L. Birch, "The Job Generation Process," mimeographed (Cambridge, Mass.: M.I.T. Program on Neighborhood and Regional Change, 1979).

7. Jane Jacobs, *The Death and Life of Great American Cities* (New York: Vintage, 1961). Her idea has been confirmed by Birch's far more rigorous study, which calls attention to the significance of job generation in manufacturing by differential branching, that is, the decision to open branch plants in one region or another, and in both manufacturing and service-sector businesses by setting up *small* shops.

8. City Planning Commission, "Planning for Jobs."

9. Michael R. Greenberg and Nicholas J. Valente, "Recent Economic Trends in the Major Northeastern Metropolises," in *Post-Industrial America: Metropolitan Decline and Inter-Regional Job Shifts,* ed. George Sternlieb and James W. Hughes (New Brunswick: Center for Urban Policy Research, 1975), pp. 77–99.

10. "Business in the Region: Structure and Performance in the Region's Producer Economy in 1972–75," *Regional Plan News,* no. 103 (April 1979): 6, 8.

11. Alan S. Oser, "Zoning Revisions to Expand Loft Conversions Are Urged by New

York Real Estate Board," *New York Times,* Oct. 29, 1975; also New York City, Department of City Planning, Zoning Study Group, "Technical Paper: Industrial Activity in Manhattan's C6 Zones," 1977.

12. *New York Times,* July 19, 1978.

13. These data were taken in 1978 from the real estate tax records of the Department of Finance, New York City.

14. Chester Rapkin, "South Houston Industrial Area: Economic Significance of Structures in a Loft Section of Manhattan" (Study prepared for New York City, City Planning Commission, 1963), pp. 225–28.

15. Ibid., pp. 122–23.

16. Ibid., p. 262; also *Regional Plan of New York and Its Environs. Economic and Industrial Survey: The Clothing and Textile Industries in New York and Its Environs* (New York: Regional Plan Association, 1925), p. 621.

17. Rapkin, "South Houston Industrial Area," pp. 252–56.

18. Fitch, "Planning New York."

19. For a history of this construction, see Robert A. Caro, *The Power Broker: Robert Moses and the Fall of New York* (New York: Vintage, 1975).

20. Rapkin, "South Houston Industrial Area," pp. 237–39.

21. Samuel B. Kuckley, "Rebuilding Manhattan: A Study of New Office Construction" (New York: Real Estate Board of New York, 1972).

22. *Plan for Rezoning the City of New York* (New York: Harrison, Ballard and Allen, 1950).

23. *Zoning New York: A Proposal for a Zoning Resolution for the City of New York* (New York: Voorhees, Walker Smith and Smith, 1958).

24. City Planning Commission, "Planning for Jobs."

25. For a detailed discussion, see G. William Domhoff, *Who Really Rules? New Haven and Community Power Reexamined* (Santa Monica: Goodyear, 1978).

26. Jack Newfield and Paul DuBrul, *The Abuse of Power: The Permanent Government and the Fall of New York* (New York: Viking, 1977), p. 144.

27. Ibid., p. 89; also Maynard Robison, "Rebuilding Lower Manhattan: 1955–1974" (Ph.D. diss., City University of New York, 1976).

28. Caroline F. Ware, *Greenwich Village 1920–1930* (1935; reprint ed., New York: Harper and Row, 1965).

29. Newfield and DuBrul, *Abuse of Power,* p. 89.

30. Ibid., and Robison, "Rebuilding Lower Manhattan."

31. Rapkin, "South Houston Industrial Area," pp. 286–87.

32. Ada Louise Huxtable, "Good Buildings Have Friends," *New York Times,* May 24, 1979.

33. Constance Perin, *Everything in Its Place: Social Order and Land Use in America* (Princeton: Princeton University Press, 1977), chap. 4.

34. Also Willkie Farr and Gallagher, "Housing for Artists: The New York Experience" (Study prepared for Volunteer Lawyers for the Arts, New York, 1976).

35. New York City, City Planning Commission, "Lofts: Balancing the Equities," 1981; Julia Vitullo-Martin, "The Real Sore Spot in New York's Economy," *Fortune,* Nov. 19, 1979, pp. 92–105; and "New York Banks are Found to Lag in Lending under Federal Program," *New York Times,* Mar. 17, 1980.

3: THE CREATION OF A "LOFT LIFESTYLE"

1. Robert Harbison, *Eccentric Spaces* (New York: Avon, 1980), p. 131. Alternatively, such spaces may be made to appear *as though* they had lost their function (and their human content); hence they become "picturesque." In English art of the late eighteenth and early nineteenth centuries, for example, "the rules of the picturesque allowed the intrusion of

steam engines or mills or mines [into landscape paintings] only if they were given an air of decrepitude or made to appear ancient and ruinous, and so harmless" (Francis D. Klingender, *Art and the Industrial Revolution,* ed. and rev. Arthur Elton [London: Adams and Dart, 1968], p. 74).

2. Jane Jacobs, *The Death and Life of Great American Cities* (New York: Vintage, 1961); Marc Fried and Peggy Gleicher, "Some Sources of Satisfaction in the Residential Slum," *Journal of the American Institute of Planners* 72, no. 4 (1961): 305–15; Herbert Gans, *The Urban Villagers* (New York: Free Press, 1962); Nathan Silver, *Lost New York* (New York: Schocken, 1967); James Biddle, Foreword, in Constance M. Greiff, *Lost America* (Princeton: Pyne Press, 1971).

3. Calvin Tompkins, *Off the Wall: Robert Rauschenberg and the Art World of Our Time* (Garden City: Doubleday, 1980), pp. 83, 211.

4. "Nine Artists/Coenties Slip," Whitney Museum, New York, 1974; Tompkins, *Off the Wall,* pp. 175–76.

5. Dore Ashton, *The New York School* (New York: Viking, 1972), p. 299.

6. "Living Big in a Loft," *Life,* Mar. 27, 1970, pp. 62–63.

7. "SoHo Artists' Bohemia Imperiled," *New York Magazine,* Aug. 24, 1970, p. 46.

8. "A Very Lofty Realm," *Progressive Architecture,* October 1974; Norma Skurka, "Landmark Loft in SoHo," *New York Times Magazine,* Nov. 24, 1974; *New York Magazine,* May 20 and Sept. 30, 1974.

9. *New York Magazine,* Mar. 8 and Oct. 11, 1976.

10. Bernardine Morris, "Built for Healthy Living: A Loft With Splash," *New York Times,* Mar. 9, 1978.

11. Mary Russell, "At Home in a French Factory," *New York Times Magazine,* Dec. 10, 1978.

12. *New York Times,* July 10, 1980.

13. Gaston Bachelard, *The Poetics of Space,* trans. Marie Jolas (New York: Orion Press, 1964), p. 72.

14. Harbison, *Eccentric Spaces,* pp. 22, 33; Burton J. Bledstein, *The Culture of Professionalism* (New York: Norton, 1976), p. 61.

15. See, for example, Orrin E. Klapp, *Collective Search for Identity* (New York: Holt, Rinehart and Winston, 1969), pp. 23–28; Yi-Fu Tuan, *Space and Place: The Perspective of Experience* (Minneapolis: University of Minnesota Press, 1977); Dean McCannell, *The Tourist: A New Theory of the Leisure Class* (New York: Schocken, 1976); Kenneth Frampton, "The Aura of the Past," *Progressive Architecture,* July 1974, pp. 48–79; Ada Louise Huxtable, "The Troubled State of Modern Architecture," *New York Review of Books,* May 1, 1980, pp. 22–29.

16. For example, Philip Slater, *The Pursuit of Loneliness: American Culture at the Breaking Point* (Boston: Beacon Press, 1970).

17. Siegfried Giedion, *Space, Time and Architecture* (Cambridge, Mass.: Harvard University Press, 1941), pt. 5; Thoreau, quoted in August Heckscher, *The Public Happiness* (New York: Atheneum, 1962), pp. 258–59.

18. Gustav Stickley, "Simplicity and Domestic Life" (1909), reprinted in *Roots of Contemporary American Architecture,* ed. Lewis Mumford (New York: Grove Press, 1959), pp. 302–3.

19. Siegfried Giedion, *Mechanization Takes Command* (New York: Norton, 1969), pt. 6; idem, *Space, Time and Architecture,* p. 289; Delores Hayden, *The Grand Domestic Revolution: A History of Feminist Designs for American Homes, Neighborhoods and Cities* (Cambridge, Mass.: M.I.T. Press, 1981); "A Romantic Solution," *Progressive Architecture,* November 1967.

20. Giedion, *Space, Time and Architecture,* pp. 265–66.

21. Kristina Ford, *Housing Policy and the Urban Middle Class* (New Brunswick: Center for Urban Policy Research, 1978), p. 25; Dena Kaye, "Revolution in the Kitchen,"

Mainliner, April 1980, p. 82. There has also been an anti-gay backlash in cities where gays have been an active presence in gentrification (see *Advocate,* Aug. 7, 1980).

22. Stephen Koch, "Reflections on SoHo," in *SoHo: Anderson and Archer's Essential Guide to Art and Life in Lower Manhattan* (New York: Simon and Schuster, 1970), p. 16.

23. Harbison, *Eccentric Spaces,* p. 53.

24. "Spaze insoliti: Dean & DeLuca," *Abitare,* March 1979.

25. K. G. Pontus Hulten, "The Machine As Seen at the End of the Mechanical Age" (New York: Museum of Modern Art, 1968), p. 3. Cf. Harold Rosenberg, "Past Machines, Future Art," in *The De-definition of Art* (New York: Collier, 1972).

26. Giedion, *Space, Time and Architecture,* pp. 130–35; see also James Bogardus, *Cast Iron Buildings: Their Construction and Advantages* (New York: T. B. Harrison and Co., 1858).

27. Greiff, *Lost America,* pp. 6, 11–12; Alan Gowans, "On Preservation," *Journal of the Society of Architectural Historians,* October 1965, pp. 25–26; Arthur Cotton Moore, Foreword, in Diane Maddox, *Historic Buildings of Washington, D.C.* (Pittsburgh: Ober Park Press, 1973).

28. Charles B. Hosmer, Jr., *The Presence of the Past* (New York: Putnam, 1965), pp. 24 ff.; Biddle, Foreword; Frampton, "Aura of the Past," pp. 47–48.

29. On the pre–World War II seeds of professionalism among historic preservationists in the federal government, see Charles B. Hosmer, Jr., *Preservation Comes of Age: From Williamsburg to the National Trust, 1926–1942,* 2 vols. (Charlottesville: University of Virginia Press, 1981).

30. Walter Muir Whitehill, "The Right of Cities to Be Beautiful," in *With Heritage So Rich: A Report of a Special Committee on Historic Preservation under the Auspices of the United States Conference of Mayors with a Grant from the Ford Foundation* (New York: Random House, 1966), p. 54.

31. Silver, *Lost New York,* Preface and Introduction.

32. See Ralph Andrew Luken, *Preservation versus Development: An Economic Analysis of the San Francisco Bay Wetlands* (New York: Praeger, 1976); and idem, *Here Today: The Historic Sites Project of the Junior League of San Francisco* (San Francisco: San Francisco Chronicle Press, 1968).

33. Eric Hodgins and Parker Lesley, "The Great International Art Market: Art — Great Art — Can Be the Most Lucrative Investment in the World," *Fortune,* December 1955, pp. 119 ff.; Ashton, *New York School;* Lee Seldes, *The Legacy of Mark Rothko* (New York: Holt, Rinehart and Winston, 1978), pp. 19–62.

34. Harold Rosenberg, "American Action Painters," in *The Tradition of the New* (New York: McGraw-Hill, 1965), pp. 25, 28–30, and idem, "Icon Maker: Barnett Newman" and "Rothko" in *The De-definition of Art;* cf. a "revisionist" interpretation of cold-war-era art in Peter Fuller, "American Painting since the Last War," in *Beyond the Crisis in Art* (London: Writers and Readers Publishing Cooperative, 1980), pp. 70–97; Tom Wolfe, *The Painted Word* (New York: Farrar, Straus and Giroux, 1975), p. 55.

35. Because of certain spatial rather than social values, the studio-house became a model for the standardized production of middle-class housing in the 1920s and 1930s and was especially important in the projects of architects like Le Corbusier (Reyner Banham, "Artists' Studio-Houses and the Modern Movement," *Architectural Review,* August 1956, p. 75; and idem, *Theory and Design in the First Machine Age,* 2d ed. [Cambridge, Mass.: M.I.T. Press, 1980], chap. 16).

4: ART IN THE ARMS OF POWER

1. See Dore Ashton, *The New York School* (New York: Viking, 1972); Lee Seldes, *The Legacy of Mark Rothko* (New York: Holt, Rinehart and Winston, 1978); or Tom Wolfe, *The Painted Word* (New York: Farrar, Straus and Giroux, 1975).

2. Calvin Tompkins, "The Art World: A Thousand Flowers," *New Yorker,* May 19, 1980, p. 136; Harold Rosenberg, "The Art Establishment," *Esquire,* January 1965, reprinted in *The Sociology of Art and Literature,* ed. Milton C. Albrecht et al. (New York: Praeger, 1970); see also Tompkins's profile of Leo Castelli, *New Yorker,* May 26, 1980.

3. For a concise discussion of the social background of American museums see Karl E. Meyer, *The Art Museum: Power, Money, Ethics,* A Twentieth Century Fund Report (New York: William Morrow, 1979).

4. On the history of artists and dealers in this period, see Harrison C. White and Cynthia A. White, *Canvases and Careers* (New York: Viking, 1965), or Raymonde Moulin, *Le Marché de la peinture en France* (Paris: Editions de Minuit, 1967).

5. See, for example, Meyer Shapiro, "The Introduction of Modern Art in America: The Armory Show," in *Modern Art, Nineteenth and Twentieth Centuries: Selected Papers* (New York: George Braziller, 1978).

6. Tompkins, profile of Castelli, p. 51. Tom Wolfe implies a somewhat different interpretation of the establishment of a museum like MOMA, "founded," as it was, "in John D. Rockefeller, Jr.'s living-room" (*Painted Word,* p. 38). Wolfe emphasizes the original commitment of the museum's patrician founders to modern art.

7. "[By 1960,] Lloyd had realized that as prices skyrocketed, the supply of Old Masters would soon be gone, many winding up in museums in America where tax laws made such donations advantageous to millionaires. Shrewdly, Lloyd foresaw that there was another fortune to be made in contemporary art. Using modern marketing techniques he could create a fierce demand for an artist's output — especially if the art was carefully doled out over a period of years and throughout the art capitals of the world" (Seldes, *Legacy of Mark Rothko,* p. 55). "Another recently emerged power is the artist's widow. . . . Commonly, the widow controls the entirety of her dead husband's unsold production; this enables her to affect prices by the rate at which she releases his work on the market, to assist or sabotage retrospective exhibitions, to grant or withhold documents or rights of reproduction needed by publishers and authors. . . . The result is that she is courted and her views heeded by dealers, collectors, curators, historians, publishers, to say nothing of lawyers and tax specialists" (Rosenberg, "The Art Establishment," pp. 393–94).

8. Ad Reinhardt, "Timeless in Asia," *Art News,* January 1960, p. 33.

9. Calvin Tompkins, *Off the Wall: Robert Rauschenberg and the Art World of our Time* (Garden City: Doubleday, 1980), pp. 133, 143–44; Tompkins, profile of Castelli; and Harold Rosenberg, "Young Masters, New Critics: Frank Stella," in *The De-definition of Art* (New York: Collier, 1972). MOMA's effort to collaborate with galleries is drawn from Marcia Bystryn's archival research in the correspondence of several New York galleries.

10. "The Museum World," *Arts Yearbook,* no. 9 (1967): 13–15.

11. Tompkins, profile of Castelli; and idem, "The Art Incarnate," *New Yorker,* May 5, 1980, pp. 114–18.

12. Rosenberg, "The Art Establishment," p. 394. Cf. the career of art dealer Sam Koontz outlined in Marcia Bystryn, "Art Galleries as Gatekeepers: The Case of the Abstract Expressionists," *Social Research* 45 (1978): 402–7.

13. See, for example, Sally O. Ridgeway, "When Object Becomes Idea" (Ph.D. diss., City University of new York, 1975), pp. 115 ff.

14. "De-aestheticization," in *De-definition of Art,* p. 38.

15. For more detail on SoHo galleries see Charles R. Simpson, *SoHo: The Artist in the City* (Chicago: University of Chicago Press, 1981).

16. "'It took me completely by surprise,' Janis said. 'Here we had been showing Pollock cheek-by-jowl with Léger, and de Kooning with Mondrian, and Klein with Klee, but when we took up the next generation our artists were furious. They didn't want to be associated with these people who became artists overnight'" (Tompkins, *Off the Wall,* p. 185).

17. "Screening process" and "directors" from the research of Marcia Bystryn.

18. This is a crucial point in explaining why "alternative space," including living lofts, becomes diffused as a commodity during the 1970s — a point missed, for example, in John Russell, "Art in Unexpected Places," *New York Times,* Feb. 24, 1980. Also see above, chap. 3, section entitled "The Middle Class in the Artist's Studio."

19. No one has really written about the metaphorical value of the artist's studio, but there is a little essay by French conceptual artist Daniel Buren, "The Function of the Studio," in *October* 10 (Fall 1979): 51–58; and the radicalized college classroom is depicted as "a studio space," with "a studio function" and a "studio-group" of students, in Ira Shor, *Critical Teaching and Everyday Life* (Boston: South End Press, 1980), p. 120. French essayist Pierre Sansot has written about the studio-apartment as a habitat that, not merely because of its small size but also because of some metaphorical value, permits both liberation and perfection, or both hedonistic pleasure and ascetic tidiness ("Les Bonheurs du studio," in *Poétique de la ville* [Paris: Editions Klincksieck, 1973], pp. 359–62).

20. Take, for example, avant-garde composer John Cage's sparsely furnished, floor-through studio on the Lower East Side in the 1950s. "*Harper's Bazaar* sent fashion models down there to be photographed, and uptown culturati manoeuvered for invitations to Cage's musical evenings" (Tompkins, *Off the Wall,* p. 100). Or for status-seekers in the 1960s, "a functioning relation to art or to artists . . . confers an advantage over the mere ambitious onlooker. Thus the art world swarms with fake collectors and entrepreneurs, people who visit studios and, on the pretext of intending to buy pictures or arrange deals, induce artists to pull out and display every scrap of their work, with no further result than to supply the visitors with material for insiders' talk" (Rosenberg, "The Art Establishment," p. 392).

21. Rosenberg, "On the De-definition of Art," in *De-definition of Art,* p. 13.

22. Tompkins, *Off the Wall,* pp. 74–75. See also ibid., chap. 15, "Towards Theater"; and Susan Sontag, "Happenings: An Art of Radical Juxtaposition" (1962), in *Against Interpretation* (New York: Farrar, Straus and Giroux, 1966).

23. Sontag, "Happenings," p. 268; issue devoted to the Fluxus Movement, *Lightworks,* 11–12 (1979): 26.

24. Andy Warhol and Pat Hackett, *POPism: The Warhol '60s* (New York: Harcourt Brace Jovanovich, 1980), pp. 132–33.

25. Clement Greenberg on Parsons' gallery, in Bystryn, "Art Galleries," p. 399; Gregory Battcock, "The Downtown Ten," *Arts Magazine,* April 1968.

26. *Lightworks,* 11–12 (1979): 29, 30.

27. James Gahagan, quoted in Gilbert Millstein, "Portrait of the Loft Generation," *New York Times Magazine,* Jan. 7, 1962. This fundamental change is the real basis of many of the art world phenomena that Tom Wolfe describes so graphically in *The Painted Word;* but Wolfe, who continues to depict the 1960s artists as "boho," completely misses the point.

28. See Rosenberg, "Frank Stella" and "Educating Artists," in *De-definition of Art;* Larry Rivers and Carol Brightman, *Drawings and Digressions* (New York: Clarkson N. Potter, 1980), p. 114.

29. Balzac, quoted in Arnold Hauser, *The Social History of Art,* 4 vols. (New York: Vintage, n.d.), vol. 4, p. 191.

30. Sontag, "One Culture and the New Sensibility," in *Against Interpretation,* p. 296.

31. This is the point of Rosenberg's title: the "de-definition" of art (see "Educating Artists," esp. p. 40, and "On the De-definition of Art," esp. pp. 12–13).

32. Ronald Berman, "Art vs. the Arts," *Commentary,* November 1979, p. 48.

33. Wolfe, *Painted Word,* pp. 96–97.

34. Joseph Bensman and Arthur S. Vidich, *The New American Society* (Chicago: Quadrangle, 1971), p. 125.

35. Interview with former store manager, Korvette's, Douglaston, Queens, July 1980.

36. *New York Times,* Sept. 4, 1977.

37. My interpretation of this development differs from the less "ideological" account in the authoritative book on the subject, Dick Netzer's *The Subsidized Muse: Public Support for the Arts in the United States* (New York: Cambridge University Press, 1978). See pp. 61 ff.: "The political history of the Arts Endowment [voted by Congress in 1965] follows the pattern of other new federal government activities. It had a long gestation period, during which repeated efforts to enact legislation failed. Rather suddenly, the political requisites for passage of a bill appeared: a friendly, if not aggressively promoting, White House; a number of very strong supporters in the Congress (in this case, Senators Pell and Javits and Congressman Brademas); and opponents who viewed the bill more as a poor idea than as a threat to their vital interests."

38. Peter Fuller, "Fine Art after Modernism," in *Beyond the Crisis in Art* (London: Writers and Readers Publishing Cooperative, 1980), p. 60.

39. On the proper choice of artists to represent America, see Frances K. Pohl, "An American in Venice: Ben Shahn and United States Foreign Policy at the 1954 Venice Biennale, or Portrait of the Artist as an American Liberal," *Art History* 4 (1981): 80–113. On the links between the Museum of Modern Art and the CIA, see Fuller, "American Painting since the Last War," in *Beyond the Crisis in Art,* pp. 78–82; and Eva Cockcroft, "Abstract Expressionism, Weapon of the Cold War," *Artforum* 12 (June 1974): 39–41.

40. Netzer, *Subsidized Muse;* Javits in *Congressional Record,* June 19, 1963, p. 11134.

41. Keynes, quoted in John B. Harris, *Government Patronage of the Arts in Great Britain* (Chicago: University of Chicago Press, 1970), and in Fuller, "Fine Art after Modernism," p. 60; and August Heckscher, "The Arts and the National Government," May 28, 1963, in *Congressional Record,* June 17, 1963, pp. 10939 ff. Cf. Arthur M. Schlesinger, Jr., on the similarities in art and the liberal state, in Serge Guilbaut, "The New Adventures of the Avant Garde in America," *October* 15 (Winter 1980): 76.

42. August Heckscher, *The Public Happiness* (New York: Atheneum, 1962), pp. 206–10, 223.

43. Personal interview, June 1980; *Public Happiness,* pp. 226–27.

44. *Public Happiness,* pp. 211–12.

45. Ibid., p. 222; Rockefeller and Dillon in *Business and the Arts: An Answer to Tomorrow,* ed. Arnold Gingrich (New York: Paul S. Eriksson, 1969); Alvin H. Reiss, "The Unlikely Alliance of Business and the Arts," *The American Way,* January 1973, p. 13.

46. Reinhardt, "Timeless in Asia," p. 33.

47. Tompkins, *Off the Wall,* p. 144, describes Alfred Barr's "custom in such cases" of inducing wealthy architect and MOMA trustee Philip Johnson "to buy [a work] for future donation to the museum." In this particular case, Barr convinces Johnson to buy one of Jasper Johns's flag paintings. Barr thought that the trustees would balk, so soon after the McCarthy period (in 1957), at buying a painting that seemed so arrantly to be . . . a flag.

48. "For the artist the new law [of 1969] was devastating. . . . The law did make speculation in art less attractive to private foundations by limiting the terms of their deductions for works of Art. But the individual wealthy non-creator who purchased the work might capitalize on it in many ways. . . . Find a rich friend . . . accountants advised their [artist] clients. Ask him to buy your painting, let it appreciate six months and then donate it to a museum. If the patron donated stocks or money equivalent to the direct value of the painting, everybody won. The donor got a better [deduction] than if he had given the painting outright and it looked as if the museum had sought the artist's work" (Seldes, *Legacy of Mark Rothko,* pp. 86 ff.).

49. *Congressional Record,* Apr. 4, 1963, p. 5815; Heckscher, "The Arts and the National Government."

50. *About Looking* (New York: Pantheon, 1980), p. 66.

5: FROM ARTS PRODUCTION TO HOUSING MARKET

1. Michael Winkleman, "The New Frontier: Housing for the Artist-Industrialist," *New York Affairs* 4, no. 4 (1978): 49; Dick Netzer, "The Arts: New York's Best Export Industry," ibid., 5, no. 2 (1978): 51.

2. The Tenth Street Studio withstood steadily rising property values until the 1950s. Then it was sold to real estate developers, who demolished it and put up a new apartment house. For its origins, see Mary S. Haverstock, "The Tenth Street Studio," *Art in America,* September 1966, p. 48.

3. Personal interviews on Fluxus and Greenwich Street, April–June 1980; on Westbeth see Willkie Farr and Gallagher, "Housing for Artists: The New York Experience" (Study prepared for Volunteer Lawyers for the Arts, New York, 1976), pp. 34–35. Eventually Westbeth was developed as artists' rental housing rather than a co-op, and the ensuing problems created or exacerbated certain tensions involving leases and entitlement to space in the building.

4. Unless otherwise noted, the personal material in this chapter comes from interviews conducted in New York in July and August 1980.

5. The City Hall-patrician connection contrasts with more distant relations between political officials and social elites in other cities, such as Philadelphia, where artists' access to loft buildings had a much rougher road (see Jim Stratton, *Pioneering in the Urban Wilderness* [New York: Urizen, 1977], p. 87).

6. *New York Times,* Mar. 19, 1973; also see *Wildflowers: Loft Jazz in New York* (Douglas Records, 1977).

6: DEMAND AND DEVELOPMENT IN THE LOFT MARKET

1. Reyner Banham, *Theory and Design in the First Machine Age,* 2d ed. (Cambridge, Mass.: M.I.T. Press, 1980), p. 216.

2. James K. Glassman, "Prisoners of Real Estate," *New Republic,* June 17, 1980.

3. Unless otherwise noted, material on investors and developers is drawn from personal interviews in New York from 1977 to 1980. On the sequence of investors in a neighborhood undergoing renovation cf. Howard J. Sumka, "Displacement in Revitalizing Neighborhoods: A Review and Research Strategy," Report written for the U.S. Department of Housing and Urban Development, Division of Community Conservation, Office of Policy Development and Research, Washington, D.C., 1978.

4. Information on the Brooklyn and Times Square conversions from *New York Times,* Aug. 8, 1980, and June 19, 1981.

5. My interviews with the developers were influenced by Christian Topalov's impressive study of real estate developers in Paris, *Les Promoteurs immobiliers: Contribution à l'analyse de la production capitaliste du logement en France* (Paris and The Hague: Mouton, 1974).

6. This is similar to Harvey Molotch's finding that local real estate investors "prepare," in some sense, a local market for the entry of the really powerful, large, national developers ("Capital and Neighborhood in the United States: Some Conceptual Links," *Urban Affairs Quarterly* 14 [1979]: 289–312).

7. New apartment construction figures from *New York Times,* June 8, 1980.

8. *New York Times,* Jan. 23, 1977, and Dec. 17, 1978.

9. All rent data from Peter Marcuse, "Rental Housing in the City of New York: Supply and Condition, 1975–1978" (Study prepared for the New York City Commission of Hous-

ing Preservation and Development, January 1979). Marcuse's data emphasize the housing plight of the poorest group of tenants more than that of the middle-class tenants.

10. On blow-out and monopoly rents in relation to inner-city housing see David Harvey, *Social Justice and the City* (Baltimore: Johns Hopkins University Press, 1973).

11. Building history taken from data collected by the Real Estate Board of New York and mortgage records, Department of Finance, New York City.

7: SPECULATION AND THE STATE

1. On the state's role in general, James O'Connor's *The Fiscal Crisis of the State* (New York: St. Martin's Press, 1973), still provides the best explanation; on local government, see Harvey Molotch, "The City as a Growth Machine: Toward a Political Economy of Place," *American Journal of Sociology* 82 (1976): 309–32.

2. For an analysis of the way this political system worked, see John Mollenkopf, "The Post-War Politics of Urban Development," *Politics and Society* 3 (1975): 247–96; and for national-level arrangements see David Gold, "The Rise and Decline of the Keynesian Coalition," *Kapitalistate* 6 (1977): 129–61.

3. Ada Louise Huxtable, "The Problems of Zoning," *New York Times,* July 13, 1980. See also Constance Perin, *Everything in Its Place: Social Order and Land Use in America* (Princeton: Princeton University Press, 1977), chap. 4; Richard F. Babcock and Fred P. Bosselman, *Exclusionary Zoning: Land Use Regulation and Housing in the 1970s* (New York: Praeger, 1973); Richard F. Babcock, *The Zoning Game* (Madison: University of Wisconsin Press, 1966); and Mark Gottdiener, *Planned Sprawl: Private and Public Interests in Suburbia* (Beverly Hills: Sage, 1977).

4. See, for example, Roger W. Schmenner, "The Manufacturing Location Decision," mimeographed (Cambridge, Mass.: Harvard University Business School, 1978).

5. Personal interviews, July and September 1980.

6. Zoning Committee, Community Board 2, Manhattan, September 1980; Anna Quindlen, "John Zuccotti: Out of Office, Still in Power," *New York Times,* Apr. 29, 1980. As the *New York Times* says, "Mr. Zuccotti remains a formidable behind-the-scenes figure in the world of the city's power elite."

7. Obituary, Abraham M. Lindenbaum, *New York Times,* July 5, 1980.

8. New York City, Board of Standards and Appeals, *Dockets,* 1969–79; Community Board 2, Manhattan, *Minutes,* 1969–79.

9. New York City Council, Int. No. 179, Feb. 10, 1978.

10. Peter Eilbott and William Kempey, "New York City's Tax Abatement and Exemption Program for Encouraging Housing Rehabilitation," *Public Policy* 26 (1978): 571–97.

11. George Sternlieb, Elizabeth Roistacher, and James W. Hughes, *Tax Subsidies and Housing Investment: A Fiscal Cost-Benefit Analysis* (New Brunswick: Center for Urban Policy Research, 1976).

12. City of New York, President of the Council, "J-51 Draft," February 1981.

13. Sternlieb, Roistacher, and Hughes, *Tax Subsidies and Housing Investment,* p. 60.

14. Eilbott and Kempey, "New York City's Tax Abatement," pp. 588–89.

15. Daniel R. Mandelker, Gary Feder, and Margaret P. Collins, *Reviving Cities with Tax Abatement* (New Brunswick: Center for Urban Policy Research, 1980), esp. pp. 47, 65.

16. See T. D. Allman, "The Urban Crisis Leaves Town," *Harper's Magazine,* December 1978, p. 54.

17. Susan S. Jacobs and Elizabeth A. Roistacher, "The Urban Impacts of HUD's Urban Development Action Grant Program, or Where's the Action Gone in Action Grants?" in *The Urban Impacts of Federal Policies,* ed. Norman J. Glickman (Baltimore: Johns Hopkins University Press, 1980), pp. 348–49, 356.

18. New York City Council, J-51 Hearings, Apr. 6, 1978.

19. Background on the Landmarks Conservancy from personal interviews, January 1978.

20. Figures on projects from *New York Times,* July 22, 1981; for a highly critical view of how the rich benefit from these provisions, see Robert L. Nessen, "Treasure Houses," *Harper's Magazine,* December 1978, pp. 16–20.

21. On the building, see Paul Goldberger, *The City Observed: New York* (New York: Random House, 1979), p. 84; on the Conservancy's involvement, *The New York Federal Archive Building: A Proposal for a Mixed Re-Use* (New York: Center for Advanced Research in Urban and Environmental Affairs, Graduate School of Architecture and Planning, Columbia University, 1976), p. 3. Additional material is from Community Board 2 and Ruth Wittenberg.

22. Mayor Abraham H. Beame to GSA, July 15, 1976.

23. The four Lipkis cases are *Lipkis* v. *Pikus,* decided in Civil Court, New York City, October 1978; the appeal of *Lipkis* v. *Pikus,* decided in New York State Supreme Court, March 1979; another appeal of *Lipkis* v. *Pikus,* decided by a five-judge panel in Appellate Division, New York State Supreme Court, November 1979; and *Lipkis* v. *Silleck,* decided in Civil Court, September 1979.

24. The Case of *155 Wooster Street Association* v. *Bengis* was decided on the landlord's appeal by the state supreme court in July 1979. *Mandel* v. *Pitkowsky* was decided on the landlord's appeal by a three-judge panel in the state supreme court in December 1979. *Captain Crow Management Ltd.* v. *Caligula Amusements Ltd.* was decided in Civil Court in May 1980.

25. Ross Wetzsteon, "A Sense of Loss in Dubrovnik," *Village Voice,* Sept. 3–9, 1980. On the emergence of tourism as a key new urban "industry," see D. R. Judd and M. Collins, "The Case of Tourism: Political Coalitions and Redevelopment in the Central Cities," in *The Changing Structure of the City,* ed. G. A. Tobin (Beverly Hills: Sage, 1979), pp. 201–32.

8: CAPITAL SHIFTS AND THE CULTURAL AVANT-GARDE IN URBAN AMERICA

1. The processes at work in the rise of loft living roughly parallel those that have been detailed in a small but growing literature on "gentrification" and "urban revitalization." However, that literature has failed, so far, to connect change in the users of residential space with change, on the one hand, in dominant urban forms or, on the other hand, in accumulation strategy (see, for example, the studies of particular cities in Shirley Bradway Laska and Daphne Spain, eds., *Back to the City: Issues in Neighborhood Renovation* [New York: Pergamon Press, 1980]). The critical literature that comprehends such processes of neighborhood change within a structural framework — most frequently, of cities in a world capitalist economy — suffers from a different kind of shortsightedness. In failing to locate the dynamism of urban revitalization in the use of real estate markets for an accumulation strategy that originates in the industrial sector, those critics are unable to relate the main phenomenon — the delocalization of industrial work — to the displacement of low-income residents from their homes. This conceptual failure unintentionally reproduces the substantive limitations of early, goodhearted, yet unsystematic attempts at radical urban social analysis. A notable exception is Roger Friedland's work, which finds that post–World War II urban renewal was formulated by local corporations in various cities as a response to problems of clearing land for downtown expansion ("Corporate Power and Urban Growth: The Case of Urban Renewal," *Politics and Society* 10 [1980]: 203–24). Except for

Friedland, critical discussion of urban revitalization focuses on the poor instead of the rich and on displacement rather than expansion. Nor do the discussants see the vital *cultural* connection between a particular use of urban space and general accumulation strategy — a methodological step that derives from recent historical studies of the nineteenth-century working class.

2. My interpretation of the use of the avant-garde contradicts Daniel Bell's illusion that the avant-garde has captured bourgeois society through a pervasive acceptance of modern art forms (see *The Cultural Contradictions of Capitalism* [New York: Basic Books, 1976], chaps. 1–3).

3. Eloise Spaeth, speaking in June 1951 to members of the American Federation of the Arts, in Frances K. Pohl, "An American in Venice: Ben Shahn and United States Foreign Policy at the 1954 Venice Biennale, or Portrait of the Artist as an American Liberal," *Art History* 4 (1981): 85.

4. The whole story of Lincoln Center, let alone its story from the viewpoint of real estate speculation, has not yet been told. For bits of information, however, see Peter Collier and David Horowitz, *The Rockefellers: An American Dynasty* (New York: New American Library, 1977), pp. 370–72; Robert A. Caro, *The Power Broker: Robert Moses and the Fall of New York* (New York: Vintage, 1975), pp. 1013–16; and Edgar B. Young, *Lincoln Center: The Building of an Institution* (New York: New York University Press, 1981).

5. It is a commonplace of critical scholarship that the social matrix of the industrial city separated "home" from "work." Here, however, both "home" and "work" are removed from any consideration as an "urban" problem, and yet, for the middle class, the city becomes all "home" and no "work." Nevertheless, for those members of the middle class who work in service-sector cottage industry, "home" now incorporates "work."

6. Previous analyses of the urban economy, at least those prior to the service-sector push of the 1970s, had emphasized the importance of small, aged, low-rent buildings for start-up businesses and the significance of clustering for small businesses (see Jane Jacobs, *The Death and Life of Great American Cities* [New York: Vintage, 1961]; and Edgar M. Hoover and Raymond Vernon, *Anatomy of a Metropolis* [Cambridge, Mass.: Harvard University Press, 1959]).

7. *New York Times,* Aug. 14, 1980.

8. Michael Winkleman, "The New Frontier: Housing for the Artist-Industrialist," *New York Affairs* 4, no. 4 (1978): 52–53.

9. Of the description of real estate developers' activity by "bourgeois" economists, he says, "The practitioners of real estate smile at these attempts [to call their calculations 'marginalism']. They themselves know that the hypothetical market is really only the perpetual creation of 'supply' by 'demand'" (*Les Promoteurs immobiliers: Contribution à l'analyse de la production capitaliste du logement en France* [Paris and The Hague: Mouton, 1974], p. 283).

10. Ralph Seligman, "Hoboken Rediscovered Yet Again," *New York Affairs* 5, no. 4 (1979): 30–31, emphasis added.

11. Winkleman, "New Frontier," p. 49. According to 1980 data from the U.S. Bureau of Labor Statistics and New York City's March 1981 report to the U.S. Treasury Department, New York still suffers from a net loss in the number of jobs, particularly in manufacturing but also in fields such as retail sales and construction, which the city administration contends gain from subsidies to real estate developers. Between 1977 and 1981 over twelve thousand jobs in the apparel and textile manufacturing industry were eliminated, while over seven thousand jobs were added in the banks (see the analysis by Wayne Barrett in the *Village Voice,* Mar. 11–17, 1981, and by Dave Lindorff in the *SoHo News,* Feb. 4, 1981).

12. An even better example is the city administration's decision, in 1980, to proclaim the Design Fair, a month of special events and exhibitions in honor of the interior design and

furnishings industry. But New York City has *no* productive activities in this sector. Production is decentralized, largely in the South. In New York, interior design and furnishings is *purely* a service-sector industry.

13. This is essentially the same conclusion that was reached by a team of researchers who recently looked at the various social, financial, and fiscal instruments that local governments devise to compensate for job loss in local industries by appealing for new investment from outside: see Robert Ross, Don M. Shakow, and Paul Susman, "Local Planners – Global Constraints," *Policy Sciences* 12 (1980): 1–25.

INDEX

The Johns Hopkins University Press

Loft Living: Culture and Capital in Urban Change

This book was composed in Times Roman text and Avant Garde display type by Capitol Communications. It was printed on S. D. Warren's 50-lb. Eggshell paper and bound in Kivar 5 by the Maple Press Company.